1.10

DARWIN'S FORGOTTEN DEFENDERS

The Encounter between Evangelical Theology and Evolutionary Thought

by David N. Livingstone

WILLIAM B. EERDMANS PUBLISHING COMPANY
GRAND RAPIDS, MICHIGAN
AND
SCOTTISH ACADEMIC PRESS
EDINBURGH, SCOTLAND

Copyright © 1987 by Wm. B. Eerdmans Publishing Co.
255 Jefferson Ave. S.E., Grand Rapids, Mich. 49503
This edition published 1987 jointly by
Eerdmans and Scottish Academic Press Ltd, Edinburgh
All rights reserved
Printed in the United States of America

Library of Congress Cataloging-in-Publication Data:

Livingstone, David N., 1953–
Darwin's forgotten defenders.

Includes bibliographical references and index.
1. Evolution—Religious aspects—Christianity—
History of doctrines—19th century. 2. Evolution—
Religious aspects—Christianity—History of doctrines—
20th century. 3. Evangelicalism—History—19th century.
4. Evangelicalism—History—20th century. 5. Princeton theology. I. Title.
BT712.L58 1987   231.7′65   87-13469

ISBN 0-8028-0260-5

Contents

For
Frances

PREFACE

The American historian Carl Becker once commented rather provocatively, "the facts of history do not exist for any historian till he creates them." In this book I have tried to re-create some of the facts of the evangelical encounter with Darwinian evolution. Inevitably I have been selective. Historians never have access to all the facts, and even those to which they do have access must be selected and interpreted in the light of the questions they are asking. My ambition has been to let the characters speak for themselves in the hope of preventing selection from degenerating into distortion.

Numerous friends have helped me in my journey of historical rediscovery. I am grateful to Harold Cunningham, Derek Thomas, and the late Alan Flavelle for enlightening conversations and for making the riches of their personal libraries available to me. John Grier kindly allowed me access to his late father's excellent collection of works by the Princeton theologians. Without the very considerable skills of Susan Ekin, assistant librarian at the Queen's University Science Library, and the editorial talents of Tim Straayer at Eerdmans, my work would have greatly suffered. David Hempton, George Marsden, Mark Noll, Ronald Numbers, and Roland Mushat Frye read the manuscript, and I am indebted to them all for their careful scrutiny and wise counsel. John Durant and Steven Pointer gladly allowed me to make use of their unpublished works. My greatest intellectual debt is to William Abraham, who first encouraged me to write the book and subsequently perused page after page with characteristic patience and perception.

Chapters 4 and 5 contain material originally published in the *Scottish Journal of Theology* and the *Evangelical Quarterly*, and I am grateful to the editors concerned for permission to reuse this material. I am also grateful to the Speer Library of Princeton Theological Seminary for allowing me access to B. B. Warfield's lecture notes on "Anthropology"; to the Yale University Library for permission to quote from James Dana's lecture "Relation of Evolution to Theism" in the Dana Family Papers collection; and to the Gray Herbarium Library of Harvard University for permission to quote from Dana's 1844 letter to Asa Gray.

Finally, to my wife Frances, a special note of appreciation for her constant encouragement, her balanced judgments, and her presentation of the *mot juste* on countless occasions. To all these I am indebted.

INTRODUCTION

A new wave of evolution-phobia is sweeping through Britain and America. "Creation science," championed by fundamentalist activists, has spread like wildfire, transforming an esoteric movement into a prevailing mood among many evangelical Christians. Combining political instinct and educational aggressiveness, the advocates of "scientific creationism" have put their stamp in no uncertain fashion on the cultural scene, particularly in the United States. Almost daily new books from propagandists pro and con find their way onto the shelves of the bookstores. Numerous articles on the subject appear in the glossy weeklies and a myriad Christian magazines. Even in the rarified atmosphere of the learned periodicals, a liberal page allowance has been granted to various assessments both scientific and sociological of the newly mobilized creationist forces.[1] What is especially interesting is that the creationists present their case as impeccably evangelical and thereby have created the impression that their agencies stand as guardians of Christian orthodoxy and doctrinal purity. Somehow there is the feeling that the cause they represent is just the latest, if the most dramatic, expression of a long tradition of evangelical antievolutionism.

The time is ripe to question the assumption that creationists bear the imprimatur of evangelical orthodoxy on the issue of evolution. The whole tradition of English-speaking evangelicalism since the middle of the nineteenth century needs to be reexamined to ascertain just what the response to the theory of evolution really has been. My claim is that while no evaluation has gone uncontested, there has been a remarkable assimilation of the evolutionary perspective by many evangelical scholars. Certainly at the popular level there have been many who have felt disturbed, but this has had as much to do with the irresponsible vulgarizing of the theory as anything else. It was less a cool, rational assessment of the theory's merits and liabilities than a kind of gut reaction to the parody "Darwinian Man, though well behaved, / At best is only a monkey shaved."

In considering the issue, I will focus on the leading representatives of evangelicalism in the areas of science and theology—not because they

---

1. In 1982 several articles on antievolutionism appeared in the *Proceedings of the Iowa Academy of Science*, and in 1983 the *Proceedings of the American Philosophical Society* ran two articles on the subject.

are ultimately more important than lay evangelicals but because they have on the whole offered more considered and articulate expressions of the tradition and have in particular offered more thoughtful evaluations of the Darwinian episode. If my case is sustained, and a considerable number of evangelical evolutionists are rediscovered, then the onus will be on the creationists to satisfy us that theirs is not a thoroughly modern movement cut off from the mainstream of the conservative Christian tradition. My argument may be seen as merely multiplying testimonials. So be it. I, for one, am convinced that the depth of evangelicalism's roots is not unrelated to the breadth of its appeal, and that the breadth of its appeal, in turn, determines the character of the tradition itself.

Furthermore, if I am correct, we ought also to revise the popular belief that science and religion are inevitably at odds. It is widely thought, of course, that there was such a warfare. But the findings I present challenge that assumption. If modern evangelical Christians have to think again about their own history, so too do those scientists who tell us that religious belief has always stood in the way of scientific advance. The inadequacy of such a triumphalist interpretation has already been exposed by numerous historians. Those interested in the rise of modern experimental science, for example, have uncovered important theological presuppositions central to the whole enterprise; others have spelled out in detail the rich conceptual interplay between natural theology and natural history; and James Moore's reassessment of Protestant reactions to Darwinism has substantially reshaped our understanding of the place of religion in Victorian scientific culture.[2] But the specific engagement of evangelical Christians with nineteenth-century evolutionism has yet to be explored. By filling this gap in the record I hope to show that the relation between science and Christianity in Darwin's century was far more complex than we are usually led to believe.

A major part of an enterprise such as this is to identify what were the central issues at stake. A key element therefore will be to set the story in its broader historical and intellectual context. To this end I propose first to sketch the involvement of evangelicals with the scientific project in the early decades of the nineteenth century, before Darwin published his theory. This will enable us initially to isolate more general issues (e.g., the question of the age of the earth) from later specifically Darwinian issues

---

2. See, for instance, Eugene M. Klaaren, *Religious Origins of Modern Science: Belief in Creation in Seventeenth-Century Thought* (Grand Rapids: Eerdmans, 1977); Clarence Glacken, *Traces on the Rhodian Shore: Nature and Culture in Western Thought from Ancient Times to the End of the Eighteenth Century* (Berkeley and Los Angeles: University of California Press, 1967); James R. Moore, *The Post-Darwinian Controversies: A Study of the Protestant Struggle to Come to Terms with Darwin in Great Britain and America, 1870-1900* (Cambridge: Cambridge University Press, 1979). See also Colin A. Russell, *Cross-Currents: Interactions between Science and Faith* (Grand Rapids: Eerdmans, 1985).

and to determine how those with conservative theological commitments coped with the challenge. It will also serve to bring to light the philosophical context within which scientists practiced their profession and reveal just how important theology was in the explanations they advanced.

Darwin's own theory, of course, is more often dismissed than discussed, and more often discussed than discerned. For one thing, he did not invent the concept of evolution. That idea has a very long history in the Western tradition, stretching back at least to the time of the Greeks. In the years immediately preceding the publication of the *Origin of Species*, the term "evolution" was widely used to describe the embryological development of the fetus, the astronomical history of the solar system, and the historical development of society. What is more, Darwin himself did not use the word until the sixth edition of his book, and even then seems to have used it with some hesitation. So Darwin certainly did not create evolution. What he did was to put forward an explanation of a mechanism by which evolutionary change could take place—namely, natural selection. This quite obviously means that those who resisted natural selection did not necessarily reject evolution. Indeed, as we shall see, a whole school of evolutionary biology emerged to challenge Darwinian orthodoxy toward the end of the century. We shall examine this position in due course and bring to light those objections to Darwinism that led many in Britain and America to identify with what was called Neo-Lamarckism. Many Christians, we will discover, were happy to align themselves with this version of evolution. This interlude will in itself take us a long way down the road to understanding the precise nature of the Darwinian challenge. I also intend to supplement this account with some reflections on what I take to be the metaphorical character of the theory of natural selection. For when we stop to ask whether "Nature" can select, we can begin to make sense of the perennial tendency to elevate evolutionary theories into an all-embracing view of the world.

This ground-clearing exercise prepares the way for a look at the immediate and subsequent responses of evangelical scientists to Darwin's ideas. The focus here will be largely on the United States simply because this is where the creationist campaign began and has had its greatest impact. We quickly find something quite surprising. Darwin's cause in America was championed by the thoroughgoing Congregationalist evangelical Asa Gray, who set himself the task of making sure that Darwin would have "fair play" in the New World. Let us be clear right away that this cannot be dismissed as capitulation to the social pressure of academic peers. To the contrary, Gray had to take on one of the most influential naturalists in America at the time to maintain his viewpoint—none other than Louis Agassiz, a Harvard colleague who vitriolically scorned Darwin's theory. But Gray was not alone. Many of his countrymen, associates in science and brothers in religion, took the same stand. And indeed even those who ultimately remained unimpressed with if not hostile to Darwin were quite prepared to admit that evolution had occurred. It is surely not without significance that Christian botanists, geologists, and biologists— that is to say, those best placed to see with clarity the substance of what Darwin had proposed—believed the evidence supported an evolutionary natural history.

What then of the theologians? Here I intend to concentrate largely, but not exclusively, on the Princeton school, because its faculty were in many ways the classical theological architects of modern conservative evangelicalism. At this point, perhaps more than anywhere else, we must allow the characters to speak for themselves, for the terrain is full of surprises. Even Warfield, the exponent of a particularly stringent view of biblical inerrancy, was an open supporter of the evolutionary perspective. This is a crucial case, because many creationist propagandists explicitly base their own doctrine of scriptural authority on the Warfieldian model. The extent to which they neglect to inform us of Warfield's own views about evolutionary biology, therefore, reflects the degree of their inconsistency at the very least. Other actors figure in the drama, of course, and the ways in which they conceptualized the Darwin problem will be just as instructive.

Some observations on the early promoters of creation science— their organizational maneuvers, their scientific credentials, and their denominational affiliations will finally serve to answer the question of how they are to be related to the great figures of nineteenth-century evangelical religion. We will not fail to notice, moreover, that evolutionists were represented in the pages of the twelve-volume fundamentalist manifesto *The Fundamentals*, published between 1910 and 1915. This in itself points to a radical disjunction between an earlier pluralistic fundamentalism and its later, more caustic counterpart.

It is not my purpose in this book to judge Darwin at the bar of science. From the perspective of a mere historian of the debate, I cannot say whether the Darwinian theory has now been so falsified as to require a new paradigm. Nor can I review the state of play in a dozen disciplines from genetics to geology in which evolution is a crucial issue. My aim is rather to describe a tradition of evangelical scholarship devoted to the evolution question. I hope to show that a substantial number of the most distinguished representatives of evangelical orthodoxy found the theological resources to absorb the latest scientific findings. As a consequence I cannot agree with Henry Ford that "history is bunk." History surely has its own lessons to teach; indeed, in this case I think we will uncover an evangelical tradition too long awaiting rediscovery.

CHAPTER 1

IN PERSPECTIVE

Every schoolboy knows that when Soapy Sam Wilberforce, the Bishop of Oxford, had his wings clipped by Thomas Henry Huxley in their debate over Darwin and the ape, it was just the latest in a series of defeats that Christianity had sustained at the hands of science. Warfare had long raged, but this most recent skirmish confirmed that science had found its greatest champions in Master Darwin and "Bulldog" Huxley. A certain Dr. John William Draper was on the platform that day in 1860 at the infamous Oxford meeting of the British Association for the Advancement of Science, that august body affectionately known as the British Ass. To prevent there being any doubt as to the relevant *dramatis personae* of this two-thousand-year melodrama, Draper published his *History of the Conflict between Religion and Science* in 1874. Draper's conflict metaphor proved to be captivating, and it provoked a whole spate of similar military reveries, perhaps most conspicuously Andrew Dickson White's *History of the Warfare of Science with Theology in Christendom* (1896) and James Y. Simpson's *Landmarks in the Struggle between Science and Religion* (1925).[1]

It is not so important that these all-too-common schoolboy assurances are based on misinformation and half-baked history. We will return later to Wilberforce and Huxley to find out what really happened. For the time being it will suffice to take note of the fact that the idea of a death-struggle between science and religion has captured the popular

---

1. The warfare model is discussed in full in Colin A. Russell's essay "Some Approaches to the History of Science," in *The "Conflict Thesis" and Cosmology*, Units 1-3 of *Science and Belief: From Copernicus to Darwin* (Milton Keynes: Open University Press, 1974); and James R. Moore, *The Post-Darwinian Controversies: A Study of the Protestant Struggle to Come to Terms with Darwin in Great Britain and America, 1870-1900* (Cambridge: Cambridge University Press, 1979).

mind. The psychological impact is broadly felt—even among those who have never heard of Wilberforce or Huxley, not to mention Draper, White, or Simpson. Many people have come to assume that what they think is true of science and religion generally is surely true ten times over of evolutionary science and evangelical religion. The spectacle of latter-day reprises of the Scopes "monkey trial" has done little to dispel the image. Most people assume that if there were any evangelical evolutionists, they were either intellectually deviant or historically aberrant.

Hitherto ignorance has played as significant a part as propaganda in perpetuating this mirage. The fact is, however, that the historical conflict between science and Christianity is historical only in the sense that it is the creation of historians. I do not mean to say, of course, that there have never been confrontations between the ecclesiastical heirarchy and the advocates of science. My point is that the conflict model is a particularly crude tool for reconstructing the historical relationship between science and faith. This is made clear, for instance, when we ask questions about the reasons for the emergence of modern experimental science.

Why, it may be asked, was science as we think of it today first practiced in sixteenth-century Europe and seventeenth-century England? Some scholars maintain that it was linked to the economic transformation of society resulting from the growing strength of its manufacturing class; some hold that it arose in response to the needs of a maritime nation for practical navigational aids; some talk of a Protestant "ethic" or "ethos" wedded to the needs of a nascent capitalism; others point to the more purely theological revolution of the Reformation. Yet divergent though these accounts may be, it is generally agreed that the growth of the scientific enterprise was closely bound up with the spirit of Puritanism.

Certainly the Puritans had no exclusive corner on science even if a disproportionate number of them were involved with scientific pursuits. Nor did they display any coherent ecclesiastical or political ideology. And yet for some an emphasis on the doctrine of the "priesthood of all believers" induced an antiauthoritarian stance in matters of church polity that spilled over to the scientific sphere and led to a rejection of the scholarly authority of the Ancients when it conflicted with actual scientific experience. Furthermore, in both theological and scientific spheres, the Puritans published their views in the vernacular, the language of the people, rather than in Latin, the language of the scholar; they encouraged a greater respect for workers in practical sciences such as chemistry, surveying, and navigation; and they helped liberate science from ecclesiastical and other forms of censorship by affirming that God has revealed himself not only in the book of Scripture but also in the book of nature.[2]

---

2. On this, for various perspectives, see R. Hooykaas's *Religion and the Rise of*

The interconnections between Puritanism and science are of course subtle and complex, but we can be sure that the military metaphor does little to advance our understanding in this case. Indeed, even John Draper was forced to concede that science was the twin sister of the Reformation; they were born together, he confessed, and they belong together.[3]

But what of the evolution episode? Surely here there is an undeniable antagonism. Was the Wilberforce-Huxley altercation not just the public expression of deep-seated antipathies? In order to answer this question, I think it is important first to reflect on the relationship between science and theology in the early Victorian period, before the advent of the Darwinian revolution, particularly with an eye to the role played by those of an evangelical persuasion.

NATURAL THEOLOGY AND NATURAL SCIENCE

During the first half of the nineteenth century, scientific research was transacted within a framework derived from natural theology.[4] The best way to explain what I mean by *natural* theology in this context is to contrast it with *revealed* theology, by which is meant the body of doctrines derived from God's revelation particularly in the pages of Scripture. By contrast, natural theology concerns the knowledge of God that is said to be available from contemplation of the natural world. One of the most characteristic strategies of the natural theologians was to argue that certain truths about the Creator can be deduced from evidences of his design in nature. Natural design, they argued, points to a God who is purposeful, bountiful, and beneficent.

This idea has a long history in the Western tradition, stretching back at least to the Apostle Paul, who in his epistle to the Romans affirms that God's eternal power and glory are manifest in his creation. Yet it was in the late seventeenth and eighteenth centuries that the natural theology tradition achieved its greatest intellectual florescence. Then it numbered among its most scholarly advocates such eminent scientific practitioners

---

Modern Science (Edinburgh: Scottish University Press, 1972); *The Intellectual Revolution of the Seventeenth Century*, ed. Charles Webster (London: Routledge & Kegan Paul, 1972); Christopher Hill's *Intellectual Origins of the English Revolution* (Oxford: Oxford University Press, 1965); Michael Hunter's *Science and Society in Restoration England* (Cambridge: Cambridge University Press, 1981); John Dillenberger's *Protestant Thought and Natural Science: A Historical Interpretation* (London: Collins, 1961); and Richard Westfall's *Science and Religion in Seventeenth-Century England* (New Haven: Yale University Press, 1958).

3. Draper, *History of the Conflict between Religion and Science* (London: Henry S. King, 1875).

4. On this, see John Hedley Brooke's "Natural Theology in Britain from Boyle to Paley," in *New Interactions between Theology and Natural Science*, Units 9-10 of *Science and Belief: From Copernicus to Darwin*.

as John Ray, Thomas Burnet, and Robert Boyle. In popular terms, however, it reached its zenith in the immensely influential writings of William Paley. In *Natural Theology*, first published in 1802, Paley put forward his famous clock analogy, which ran something like this. Suppose that while enjoying a moment's rest during an afternoon stroll down a country lane, you glance down and discover a watch lying in your path. Would it not be entirely reasonable to assume that the instrument had been designed for a specific purpose, since all its parts fit together in very precise ways for particular functions? A watch clearly implies a watchmaker. And so it is, Paley argued, with nature. Do not all the adaptations of different animals that suit their particular needs and fit them perfectly to their environments imply a Grand Designer whose purposes are evident in his creation? And if so, surely natural science is engaged in expounding nothing less than the very mind of the Creator. As Paley put it in typically rhetorical fashion,

> Can it be doubted, whether the *wings of birds* bear a relation to air, and the *fins of fish* to water? They are instruments of motion, severally suited to the properties of the medium in which the motion is to be performed: which properties are different. Was not this difference contemplated, when the instruments were differently constituted?[5]

Paley's perspective was widely accepted by early nineteenth-century natural scientists, and his line of argument in this quotation is typical of their general approach. By focusing on the perfect adaptation of organisms to environments, they first of all cemented the organic and inorganic worlds together in a single explanatory system. Because God had created each species in and for its own geographical province, there was a direct correspondence between the characteristics of the animals and their surrounding environments. Second, they devoted themselves to enumerating examples of these wonderful adaptations to nature. Often imaginatively and always extensively, they spelled out in the minutest detail how particular organs perfectly suited particular regions. They perceived the history of life and the history of the earth to be welded together, and it became their aim to show how the different forms of life successively revealed in the fossil record had been perfectly fitted to changing environmental conditions. The vitality of this whole tradition of natural history is nowhere better reflected than in the Bridgewater Treatises, a series commissioned by the will of the eighth Earl of Bridgewater, the Reverend Francis Henry Egerton, who directed that each of the treatises was to be presented by a scientific author to demonstrate the "Power, Wisdom and Goodness of God, as Manifested in the Creation."

---

5. Paley, *The Works of William Paley* (London: T. Nelson & Sons, 1853), p. 498.

This version of the design argument did not, however, enjoy an uncontested consensus within either the theological or scientific communities. On the theological side, criticism came from many quarters. Evangelical, Catholic, High Anglican, and Liberal Anglican representatives all voiced their fears, sensing that while natural theology had considerable moral worth and intellectual value, it could in the end reveal very little about the ultimate purposes of God. Still, whatever their misgivings, few critics expressed outright opposition; far more common were those who made it clear that their support was qualified. There were also reservations expressed on the scientific side. It was not easy to see how the presence of many nasty things in nature—noxious insects, natural disasters, and painful diseases, for example—squared with the idea of the beneficent design of an all-powerful Creator. And what were natural theologians to make of the many cases in which there is no especially close relationship between organism and environment, in which the same structures would seem to be perfectly suited to many different environmental conditions?

Because of objections such as these, an alternative version of the design argument gained prominence during the 1840s. This alternative is usually traced to the work of the great British anatomist Richard Owen, although it was to some extent prefigured in Peter Mark Roget's Bridgewater Treatise of 1834. I will pause here to elucidate Owen's version briefly, because this particular reconstitution of the natural theology tradition is crucial for my account of evangelical responses to Darwin.

HOMOLOGOUS ORGANS, from Francis Hitching's *The Neck of the Giraffe; or, Where Darwin Went Wrong* (Pan Books, 1982)

Instead of locating design in the useful adaptation of organs to function, Owen identified divine purpose in the general patterns or plans he detected in nature. For example, in Paley's scheme one would scarcely expect to find a similar structure among many different animal types designed for moving along the ground, through the air, or in the water. The environments are different, and so, you might think, would be the structures. Not so. The forelimbs of a man, horse, bat, mole, and dugong, in fact, have a strikingly similar structure. Time and time again, in widely divergent environments and among many different animals, the same archetypal pattern presents itself. This suggested to Owen and others a Creator working more according to a transcendental plan than, in piece-meal fashion, accommodating each creature to its own environment. Thus the corresponding parallels in animal structure ("homologous relations" as they were called) provided an alternative method for many naturalists to retain their commitment to a religious view of the world and, at the same time, fidelity to the scientific enterprise.[6] So whereas Paley's was a *utilitarian* construal of design emphasizing the ways in which particular organic features are perfectly fitted to environment, Owen's was a much more *idealist* formulation in the sense of presupposing transcendental or archetypal plans.

Throughout the first half of the nineteenth century, natural theology was a diverse enterprise serving many purposes—sometimes scientific, sometimes apologetic, sometimes social. It encouraged some to engage in more widespread empirical investigation to trace the unifying divine pattern running through the course of nature. In the hands of others it became an apologetic tool to engage infidels and challenge their presuppositions. On occasions it served as a mediating device between scientists and their opponents. Presenting an immensely powerful Creator whose design had persisted during unnumbered ages enabled some geologists to liberate their research from overly narrow biblical exegesis. And it had also a social value: it enabled the "gentlemen of science" at the newly formed British Association for the Advancement of Science to transcend sectarian and denominational loyalties.[7]

---

6. Useful discussions of Paley's and Owen's approaches can be found in Peter J. Bowler's "Darwinism and the Argument from Design: Suggestions for a Reevaluation," *Journal of the History of Biology* 10 (1977): 29-43; and Dov Ospovat's "Perfect Adaptation and Teleological Explanation: Approaches to the Problem of the History of Life in the Mid-Nineteenth Century," *Studies in the History of Biology* 2 (1978): 33-56.

7. Some of these functions are discussed in Muriel Blaisdell's "Natural Theology and Nature's Disguises," *Journal of the History of Biology* 15 (1982): 163-89; John Hedley Brooke's "The Natural Theology of the Geologists: Some Theological Strata," in *Images of the Earth: Essays in the History of the Environmental Sciences*, ed. L. J. Jordanova and Roy S. Porter (Chalfont St. Giles: British Society for the History of Science, 1979), pp. 39-64; and Jack Morrell and Arnold Thackray's *Gentlemen of*

Whatever the complexities and ambiguities in the natural theology tradition, it is clear that the argument from design, in one form or another, pervaded scientific explanation during the early Victorian period. This means that the idea of opposing Christian doctrine could not have been further from the minds of most of those engaged in the great debates of the era. Rather, as Robert M. Young has made plain,[8] the motivation of many of the major scientific theorists was not to place nature, man, and God in opposition to one another but rather to reconcile them. This cannot be dismissed as a mere ideological ploy to preserve religious respectability and social standing, for most naturalists were happy to have their pursuits serve the complementary and, as they themselves acknowledged, higher ends of theology.[9]

Natural theology, then, provided much of the style and idiom of scientific discourse in the period. And if the relations between science and theology in the decades before Darwin were not always cordial, they were certainly far from hostile. Surely nothing better illustrates this than the participation of evangelicals in Victorian scientific culture both in Britain and America. So it is vital that we turn now to this theme. Here I want both to emphasize that evangelicals were deeply involved with the science of their day and, more important, to reflect on their engagement with its scientific theories.

PRE-DARWINIAN BRITAIN

An obvious place to begin is with the contributions of the great Scottish divine the Rev. Dr. Thomas Chalmers. Chalmers was first exposed to some of the formative intellectual influences of his life during his student days at St. Andrews University in the 1790s. Here the utopian radicalism of the political theorists appealed to his sense of social justice; and although this enthusiasm later diminished in the shadow of the excesses of the French Revolution, it nevertheless continued to fuel his challenge to the churches, while he was a reforming minister in Glasgow, to come to terms with the evils of urban poverty. It was at St. Andrews too that Chalmers first tasted the intellectual delights of mathematics. Later in Edinburgh he further cultivated this interest by studying under the

Science: Early Years of the British Association for the Advancement of Science (Oxford: Clarendon Press, 1981).

8. Young, "The Impact of Darwin on Conventional Thought," in The Victorian Crisis of Faith, ed. A. Symondson (London: S.P.C.K., 1970), pp. 13-35; and "Natural Theology, Victorian Periodicals and the Fragmentation of a Common Context," in Darwin to Einstein: Historical Studies on Science and Belief, ed. Colin Chant and John Fauvel (Harlow: Longman, 1980), pp. 69-107.

9. On this, see Alvar Ellegård, Darwin and the General Reader: The Reception of Darwin's Theory of Evolution in the British Periodical Press, 1859-1872 (Göteborg: Acta Universitatis Gothenburgensis, 1958).

eminent geologist-mathematician Playfair. His devotion to theology also came later through the reading of Jonathan Edwards, who fired his imagination with an overwhelming sense of the sovereignty of God expressed in his providential government of the world. Subsequently Chalmers was to surface as the most spectacular visitor to the London preaching circuit before he assumed the Edinburgh Chair of Divinity in 1827. Indeed, his power and passion as a preacher had already been proved at the Tron Church in Glasgow, where, it is said, his sermons on Thursday afternoons brought local businesses to a standstill.

With such intellectual and oratorical gifts, Chalmers inevitably emerged as the champion of the evangelical movement in the Church of Scotland, in which role he led the way in the 1843 Disruption of the established Presbyterian Church to form the new Free Church of Scotland. In addition to his involvement in ecclesiastical politics and his teaching and pastoral duties in the University, Chalmers found time to contribute the first Bridgewater Treatise, *On the Power, Wisdom and Goodness of God as Manifested in the Adaptation of External Nature to the Moral and Intellectual Constitution of Man* (1833)—a work he supplemented some three years later with his *Natural Theology*. As their titles suggest, these works were firmly cast in the Paleyan mold. To be sure, Chalmers was never wholeheartedly committed to natural theology as *theology*. Indeed, he appended a whole section to his Bridgewater Treatise on the defects of natural theology. He insisted that it could never be more than a precursor to Christianity; in apologetic terms, it could do little more than remove arguments against belief in God. In other words, he maintained that while natural theology could help undercut the bases of unbelief, it was powerless to create positive faith. But, as I have already suggested, there were many whose commitment to the natural theology perspective was tentative and yet who, at least for certain purposes, happily aligned themselves with it. So it was in Chalmer's case: he held that the most convincing argument in nature for the existence of God, which was to be found in the universality of conscience, could pose important questions even if it gave no answers.

Yet, while believing that natural theology could not provide the ultimate answer to the human dilemma without the help of special revelation, Chalmers nonetheless remained convinced that divine design permeated the structure of the universe and that science could help elucidate the nature of God's presence in creation. By this tactic Chalmers at a stroke disarmed those religionists who felt the whole scientific undertaking to be useless and unworthy. At this level, at the very least, Chalmers's natural theology was scientifically liberating. But it also had apologetic value. On the one hand it could be used to affirm the internal coherence of a Christian view of the world and, on the other, to eliminate those misunderstandings of the creation that could be construed as reasons for religious unbelief. He was adopting the latter strategy when, for example, he set out to demonstrate that even if the universe was as vast as the astronomers claimed, that in itself did nothing to destroy confidence in the rationality of belief in God's control of the universe.

The case I am making here is minimal. I am simply arguing that for the practice of science, Chalmers found a fitting framework in natural theology, whatever its theological limitations. He urged that science in both its theoretical structure and its vocational rationale should be grounded in natural theology's argument from design. The symbolic significance of this encounter with science by a prominent evangelical can scarcely be overestimated whatever the conservatism of Chalmers's scientific convictions. And yet it needs to be remembered that Chalmers had no objection to interpolating lengthy stretches of geological time into the Bible at the beginning of creation, provided the Genesis narrative was not subjected to a trendy allegorizing hermeneutic.[10]

Hugh Miller was another striking amateur Victorian scientist and evangelical Scotsman. A stonemason from the highland village of Cromarty on the Moray Firth, he was, next to Chalmers, the leading figure in the Disruption of the Church of Scotland. Self-made man, wide-ranging essayist, occasional poet, and crusading evangelical editor, Miller was a brilliant geologist and paleontologist and among the most engaging popularizers of science in mid-nineteenth-century Britain.[11] For literary style he was commended by Dickens and Ruskin; in science he was highly rated by Huxley, Lyell, Agassiz, Murchison, Owen, and Darwin; as a moralist he was admired by Thomas Carlyle. As George Rosie has shown, Miller was a romantic Scottish nationalist who thoroughly approved of the union with England, a highly skilled laborer who penned sentimental verse, a fierce Presbyterian stalwart who favored Catholic emancipation, a devout evangelical who defended secular education. Perhaps the case of Hugh Miller, more than anyone else in the era, served to smash those categories of interpretation by which historical complexity is so often reduced to stereotyped heroes and villains.

By the late 1840s Miller was one of Edinburgh's most colorful literati, his reputation resting in part on his editorial care of *The Witness*, the main organ of the evangelical wing in Scottish church life. In the autumn of the periodical's first year, 1840, Miller presented its readers with a

---

10. In my discussion of Chalmers I have drawn on the following sources: Charles Coulston Gillispie, *Genesis and Geology: A Study of the Relations of Scientific Thought, Natural Theology, and Social Opinion in Great Britain, 1790-1850* (New York: Harper & Row, 1959); Walter Cannon, "The Problem of Miracles in the 1830's," *Victorian Studies* 4 (1961): 5-32; David Cairns, "Thomas Chalmers's Astronomical Discourses: A Study in Natural Theology," *Scottish Journal of Theology* 9 (1956): 410-21; and Daniel F. Rice, "Natural Theology and the Scottish Philosophy in the Thought of Thomas Chalmers," *Scottish Journal of Theology* 24 (1971): 23-46.

11. Biographical details on Miller are available in George Rosie's *Hugh Miller: Outrage and Order* (Edinburgh: Mainstream Pubishing, 1981).

HUGH MILLER, from Thomas Brown's *Annals of the Disruption, with Extracts from the Narratives of Ministers Who Left the Scottish Establishment in 1843* (MacNiven & Wallace, 1884)

charming seven-part series of weekly articles entitled "The Old Red Sandstone," containing reminiscences of his youthful foragings in the sandstone quarries of the Highlands. The essays proved to be so popular that the following year Miller expanded them into a full-length book and dedicated it to the distinguished geologist Sir Roderick Murchison. *The*

Old Red Sandstone immediately established his scientific reputation, and the fact that it went through some twenty-six editions attests to its having been a classic of Victorian popular science. The book was the fruit of Miller's long labors as a quarryman. Amateur paleontology though it was, it was anything but dilettantish. During those ten years he had painstakingly amassed a tantalizing collection of fossil fragments that had led him into uncharted intellectual territory. It was an area of research that lacked both basic nomenclature and scientific explanation.

Poring over the scattered fragments of creatures long since departed, Miller sought to knit the pieces together into a coherent pattern. The result was the first elucidation of the organic history of the old Scottish Devonian sandstone strata. In many ways Miller's discoveries were on the frontiers of geological knowledge. This was acknowledged at the time by the celebrated Swiss naturalist Louis Agassiz, who paid Miller the tribute of naming one of the fossils after him—*Pterichthys Milleri*, Miller's winged fish. Compliments flooded in from such savants as Murchison and Buckland in England and Silliman in the United States. *The Old Red Sandstone* was a genuine contribution to Victorian geology.

Miller's book shows the infiltration of certain elements in idealist natural history into his thinking. That is to say, Miller felt he could see clear traces of an ideal plan in nature. This was true in the pattern of individual growth, for instance. Like many others, he saw a close parallel between the embryological development of the fetus and the entire history of the species to which it belongs. This, of course, attested to the plan of God:

> The individual fish, just as it begins to exist, presents the identical appearances which were exhibited by the order when the order began to exist. Is there nothing wonderful in analogies such as these,—analogies that point through the embryos of the present time to the womb of Nature, big with its multitudinous forms of being? Are they charged with no such nice evidences as a Butler would delight to contemplate, regarding that unique *style* of Deity, if I may so express myself, which runs through all His works, whether we consider Him as God of Nature or Author of Revelation? In this style of type and symbol did He reveal himself of old to his chosen people: in this style of allegory and parable did He again address himself to them when He sojourned among them on earth.[12]

More than this, however, Miller's discoveries impressed him with a profound sense of history, of the earth stretching back eons into the mists of primeval time. Besides, such reflections soon brought him face to face with the hottest topic in contemporary scientific philosophy—the pos-

---

12. Miller, *The Old Red Sandstone; or, New Walks in an Old Field* (1841; rpt., Edinburgh: William P. Nimmo, 1877), p. 246.

sibility of an evolutionary history of life. On this issue, Miller was uncompromising. He had no more time for the evolutionary speculations of a Lamarck or a Chambers than had Darwin himself. In this, of course, he perpetuated mainstream pre-Darwinian scientific orthodoxy. But this opposition must not be allowed to obscure the ease and energy with which Miller accommodated contemporary theological assumptions about the age of the earth to the findings of science. Thus in his polemical tract *Footprints of the Creator*, written in 1849 as a rebuttal to Chambers's crude but spirited revamping of Lamarckianism, Miller asserted that belief in the great antiquity of the globe was the result of hard-nosed empirical investigation by geologists, not prior predisposition. As a result, the "old, and, as it has been proven, erroneous reading of the Mosaic account" had quite rightly given way before the results of geology. Miller also made it plain that in the interests of truth this position had also been adopted by such ministers of the orthodox churches as Sumner, Sedgwick, Buckland, Coneybeare, Pye Smith, Chalmers, Duncan, and Fleming.[13] Clearly Miller held that the antiquity of the earth and evolutionary hypotheses were two quite separate issues.

For this work Miller received the applause of Richard Owen, who felt that in it he had found some of his own favorite ideas beautifully expounded. Not surprisingly, when Miller came to address the Edinburgh meeting of the British Association in 1849, he devoted his final remarks to extolling the profundity of Owen's work on comparative anatomy. And as if to provide the ultimate imprimatur on Miller's idealist inclinations, Louis Agassiz prefaced the 1850 reprint of *Footprints* with a thirty-seven-page sketch of its author. All this is not to say that Miller abandoned the older teleological argument in favor of the newer homological version. His suggestion that the successive organic forms reflected progressive improvement in the geographical "dwelling-place" puts that beyond dispute. Rather it shows Miller's transitional stance between the two versions of natural theology.

His predilection for seeing God's design in the general plan of the universe marked just one of the ways by which Miller differed from the thinking of his close friend and ecclesiastical mentor Thomas Chalmers; there was another important departure. Chalmers would brook no tampering with a literalistic reading of Genesis, but Miller was prepared to strike a rather more radical path. He simply could not agree with Chalmers's forcing the whole gamut of geological time in at the beginning of the biblical text. Rather, he wanted to interpret the Genesis days in a metaphorical fashion. *The Testimony of the Rocks* (1856), Miller's crowning effort, contains a method of harmonizing the record of Genesis and the record of geology pointedly different from the efforts of such earlier

---

13. Miller, *Footprints of the Creator; or, The Asterolepis of Stromness* (Edinburgh: W. P. Nimmo, Hay & Mitchell, 1849), p. 255.

reconcilers as Chalmers and Pye Smith. His approach here, as ever, was neither sloppy in scholarship nor triumphalist in spirit. Comparing himself to the Christian geographer who practiced his subject in a day when a round earth was dismissed as unscriptural and to the Christian astronomer working at a time when the notion of a heliocentric universe was heresy, Miller said that his only reply as a Christian geologist to the learned opposition of any theologians was frankly to question the validity of their handling of Scripture. Ecclesiastical authority could not outweigh scientific experience.

The core of Miller's harmonizing scheme lay in his understanding of the nature of biblical language. The first chapter of Genesis, he said, employed the language of "optical appearances"—that is, it was anthropomorphic. The account of the making of the sun and moon, for example, was not a description of the absolute initial creation of these heavenly bodies; it was rather the record of their first appearance to a hypothetical observer on the earth's surface. And from this principle Miller argued that Scripture was intended neither to provide a scientific account of creation nor to teach the principles of science. His simple conclusion was that each day of the creation narrative represented vast periods of geological time—the day-age theory of the earth as it later came to be known.

Miller's case is certainly an interesting one, not only for the breadth of his acclaim as a natural scientist but also for his response, as a leading Scottish evangelical, to the major geological theories of his day. This is not to say that he stood alone on this issue, however. His contemporary John Fleming, professor of natural history at King's College, Aberdeen, took a very similar stand.[14] Fleming had served the Church of Scotland as a pastoral minister for over a quarter of a century before exchanging the clerical robe for the academic gown in 1834. As an academic he remained deeply involved in the affairs of his mother church, siding with Chalmers and the evangelicals during the upheavals of 1843, joining the nascent Free Church, and moving to the chair of Natural Science in Edinburgh's New College. But it was when Fleming was still in ministerial harness that he made perhaps his most significant contribution to geology, in a paper that appeared in the 1826 *Edinburgh Philosophical Journal* under the rather imposing title "The Geological Deluge, as Interpreted by Baron Cuvier and Professor Buckland, Inconsistent with the Testimony of Moses and the Phenomena of Nature."

If it was the harmonization of the paleontological record with scriptural chronology that detained Hugh Miller, it was the philosophical underpinnings of scientific geology that engaged the Rev. Fleming. The

---

14. There is a useful analysis of Fleming's geology in Davis A. Young's essay "Nineteenth Century Christian Geologists and the Doctrine of Scripture," *Christian Scholar's Review* 11 (1982): 212-28.

catastrophist school of geology—a major tenet of which was that the Mosaic deluge had substantially determined the geomorphology of the earth—was then in its heyday under the coregency of Cuvier in France and Buckland in England. Cuvier and Buckland did accept a long earth history (a point that clearly distinguishes their position from the flood geology of modern-day creationists), but they were convinced that the surface geography of the globe had resulted from the catastrophic up-heavals of a universal flood some four thousand years ago. Fleming's response to their argument is interesting in a number of respects.

First, Fleming's critique is so uniformitarian that it has been characterized as anticipating in outline the major theses of Charles Lyell's celebrated three-volume *Principles of Geology*.[15] Fleming questioned the validity of the geological evidence for the Cuvier-Buckland model, arguing that the characteristics of ancient gorges and valleys are just what would be expected from the long-term action of the same forces that currently sculpt stream channels. Fleming could not see how canyons would be formed under flood conditions; prolonged fluvial action was a far better explanation than any colossal inundation. Moreover, he dismissed as philosophically gratuitous the supposition that forces of a different order had operated in the past on the grounds that it opened the door to untrammelled speculation.

Second, somewhat ironically, it was the Mosaic testimony itself that had pushed Fleming toward his uniformitarian viewpoint. Quite simply, he suggested, for all their talk of the biblical flood, the catastrophists did not take the biblical witness seriously enough. According to Cuvier and Buckland, every species was destroyed by the flood, whereas the biblical narrative records the preservation of a pair of each. Moreover, if the flood had been as violent as they supposed, the ark would have been so much tossed about that it would not have landed as close to its point of departure as the Bible reports. And if the flood were so vigorous as to excavate deep valleys that changed the whole face of antediluvian geography, Moses would not have recognized the subsequent landscape. Finally, there was the little problem of the olive leaf, which implied the survival of at least some soil and vegetation.

Yet if Fleming felt his reading of geology was sustained by his reading of Genesis, it certainly was anything but the substitution of one scriptural geology for another. He castigated those who assumed "that the first principles of geology were revealed to Moses, and communicated in the Book of Genesis."[16] In fact, he contended that the absence of a

---

15. Gillispie, *Genesis and Geology*, p. 123.
16. Fleming, "The Geological Deluge, as Interpreted by Baron Cuvier and Professor Buckland, Inconsistent with the Testimony of Moses and the Phenomena of Nature," *Edinburgh Philosophical Journal* 14 (1826): 205.

genuine geological history in the pages of Scripture had led to the cosmogonic fantasies of Burnet, Woodward, and the like. But this is not to say that he believed his principles to imply any radical divorce of science from theology; he was too committed to natural theology for that. Indeed, his *Philosophy of Zoology* (1822) found its apologia in a contemplation of the wisdom of God's plan in nature.

The harmonizing strategies of Hugh Miller and John Fleming, I suggest, were far from untypical among evangelicals involved in early nineteenth-century geology in Britain. If Miller's reinterpretations seem rather *déjà vu* in the light of Fleming's proposals, Fleming's career in turn might almost be seen as that of a Playfair *redivivus*. For John Playfair too had tramped the ministerial round in the parishes of the Church of Scotland before retiring to an Edinburgh professorship from which he issued his magisterial defense of James Hutton's geology in a work entitled *Illustrations of the Huttonian Theory of the Earth* (1802). With his geology grounded just as firmly in natural theology as that of his Edinburgh successors, Playfair rejected any suggestion that scientific questions could be resolved by resorting to the Scriptures. He also embraced Hutton's thoroughgoing uniformitarianism and confirmed that the earth was vastly older than the timescale allotted by the good Archbishop Ussher. Some sense of Playfair's philosophy may be gauged from the following extracts.

> The geologist sadly mistakes, both the object of his science and the limits of his understanding, who thinks it his business to explain the means employed by INFINITE WISDOM for establishing the laws, which now govern the world.
>
> The authority of the Sacred Books seems to be but little interested in what regards the mere antiquity of the earth itself; nor does it appear that their language is to be understood literally concerning the *age* of that body, any more than concerning its *figure* and *motion*. The theory of Dr. Hutton stands here precisely on the same footing with the system of COPERNICUS; for there is no reason to suppose, that it was the purpose of revelation to furnish a standard of geological, any more than of astronomical science. It is admitted, on all hands, that the Scriptures are not intended to resolve physical questions, or to explain matters in no way related to the morality of human actions; and if, in consequence of this principle, a considerable latitude of interpretation were not allowed, we should continue at this moment to believe, that the earth is flat; that the sun moves round the earth; and that the circumference of a circle is no more than three times its diameter.[17]

---

17. Playfair, *Illustrations of the Huttonian Theory of the Earth* (Edinburgh: Cadell & Davies, 1802), pp. 121, 126.

To recite supporting testimony from further British sources would be repetitive to no good end. Suffice to say that in the contributions of William Buckland, William Coneybeare, and to some extent Adam Sedgwick—all conservative Anglican clergymen, all pioneers of English geology, and all catastrophists in the Cuvier school—similar conceptual alignments are readily apparent. Just as Buckland found mineral resources so very conveniently related to stratigraphical structure, and Sedgwick followed the path from geology to natural religion, so Coneybeare observed in Scripture only such scientific facts as directly impinged on human history. Instead of dwelling on figures such as these, however, I want to devote the rest of this chapter to the situation in North America, where evangelicals were no less involved with the scientific practice of their day.

THE AMERICAN SCENE

Chief among the New World devotees of Chalmers and Miller was Edward Hitchcock. Professionally respected, ecclesiastically Congregationalist, and temperamentally hypocondriac, Hitchcock championed the cause of the geologist-theologian in the United States for nearly half a century. The story begins in 1814, the year he came of age. It was also the year his health broke down. While convalescing, he fell from a chilly Unitarianism into the warmth of evangelical grace. The plain old-fashioned doctrines of the Puritans, as he described it, had led him back to the orthodox Congregationalism of his father, and within two years, while holding the principalship of Deerfield Academy, he embarked on a course of study for the ministry of the church. Before he took up his first pastoral duties in Conway, Massachusetts, however, Hitchcock went down to Yale to put the finishing touches on his ministerial training. While there he came under the spell of Benjamin Silliman, who enflamed his passion for geology every bit as much as for theology. When he settled into his manse in the Pioneer Valley, Hitchcock continued to inventory the geology and mineralogy of the Connecticut River. Silliman kept him in touch with theoretical developments in Europe.

From the outset Hitchcock felt a special obligation to articulate his twin faith in science and religion and, quite understandably, found the tradition of British natural theology the most appropriate vehicle of communication. His *Utility of Natural History*, which appeared in 1823, contains geological demonstrations of the existence and attributes of God conceived in terms of the conventional catastrophist framework that supported the Noachian deluge by reference to "diluvium"—deposits now attributed to glacial action. Like his European masters, Hitchcock relieved any apparent tension between geological time and Genesis time by suggesting either that the "days" could be taken figuratively or that a

EDWARD HITCHCOCK, from George P. Merrill's *The First One Hundred Years of American Geology* (Yale University Press, 1924; copyright © 1952, Mrs. G. P. Merrill)

gap could be interpolated between the first two verses of the Bible. Taken straight from Buckland, these hermeneutic maneuvers shaped Hitchcock's early "Christian geology," and it is no surprise to find him enthusiastically reviewing Buckland's *Reliquiae Diluvianae* for the readers of the *Christian Spectator* and the *American Journal of Science and Arts*.

For four years Hitchcock shepherded the Congregational flock in Conway. Then in 1825 he was offered the professorship of chemistry and natural history at the newly formed Amherst College, and thus he abandoned the church pulpit for the lecture-hall platform. Resorting temporarily to Yale to prepare himself under Silliman's tuition, Hitchcock then began a lifelong association with Amherst. There he taught geology and natural theology in the main and carved out for himself a distinguished reputation in the history of American geology. The first geological survey of Massachusetts, for example, was completed under his direction in the early 1830s; in 1840 he became the first chairman of the Association of American Geologists and later headed the State Survey of Vermont; and, immensely prolific, he still found time to write more than twenty books and more than seven times that many academic papers, tracts, and pamphlets.

A more detailed perusal of Hitchcock's curriculum vitae need not detain us here. Before leaving him, however, we would do well to note two related themes in his geology. First, there is his catastrophist understanding of geohistory. Exegeting catastrophist geology requires some little care and, while I want to defer for the moment a general consideration of that matter, it is true that Hitchcock's reflections on the topic serve to introduce it rather nicely. Let me just assert firmly at this point that, contrary to the beliefs of some, it is not the case that catastrophists of this period were obscurantist fundamentalists whereas Lyellian uniformitarians were enlightened scientists. When Hitchcock defended a modified catastrophism, he was promoting a solidly *scientific* judgment. He confirmed that catastrophists did not postulate the former existence of geological forces different *in kind* from those currently in operation. Rather they supposed, to use Hitchcock's own words, "these causes to have acted with far greater intensity formerly than at present."[18] If Hitchcock felt he could use this methodological principle for religious reasons—say, for example, to bolster the idea of a biblical flood—that was a quite separate matter logically. Indeed, such a construal of geology's fundamental methodological axiom (i.e., that geological processes may not have always operated at their present rate or intensity) has subsequently been vindicated. Lyell's systemic uniformitarianism has required tempering to preserve it as a viable working principle. So any suggestion that catastrophists were necessarily yielding up their science to their

---

18. Hitchcock, *Report of the Geology, Mineralogy, Botany and Zoology of Massachusetts* (Amherst: J. S. & C. Adams, 1833), p. 517.

religion in the advocacy of their own position simply will not do. What makes the matter even more intriguing is that it was actually this viewpoint that undergirded Hitchcock's progressivist scheme for geological history. In his *Elementary Geology* of 1840 he affirmed, "It appears that every successive general change, that has taken place on the earth's surface has been an improvement on its condition. Animals and plants of a higher organization have been multiplied with every change, until at last the earth was prepared for the existing races."[19]

In one other respect Hitchcock's career is instructive. No less insulated from cultural influences than anyone else, he made no virtue of consistency or inflexibility. The shifting focal point of his natural theology provides a pointed illustration, and his clash with Moses Stuart a useful place to start. Stuart, professor of sacred literature at Andover, was perhaps the most influential Congregationalist of his generation. In the 1836 issue of the *Biblical Repository* he attempted to undercut Hitchcock's position by grounding scriptural hermeneutics in philology rather than geology. He hoped that this would cut science loose from its biblical moorings and thereby relieve biblical exegesis of scientific anxieties, but Hitchcock would have none of it.

The apparatus of Hitchcock's natural theology committed him to the view that science must be related to Scripture in detail. He believed that detailed corroboration between the book of nature and the book of Scripture was both possible and desirable. A symbolic understanding of the days of Genesis provided the tool by which such an equivalence could be achieved. By the time the second edition of Hitchcock's magnum opus, *The Religion of Geology*, appeared in 1859, however, the conceptual landscape had significantly altered. He had written the first edition (1851) in the flush of enthusiasm over the first American editions of Hugh Miller's work with its day-age theory, but by 1859 Hitchcock had rid himself of what Stanley M. Guralnick calls "the burden of exact correspondences."[20] "If we can only be satisfied with general principles," he wrote, ". . . without attempting to find something in Scriptures corresponding to all the details of science, or something in nature corresponding to every particular in revelation, we shall find harmony and mutual corroboration where an unwise and unauthorized attempt to extend the parallelism to details might leave us in doubt and perplexity."[21] Indeed, natural theology, Hitchcock had already confirmed, could no longer be practiced in the Paley mode. *The Religion of Geology* constituted his attempt to bring

---

19. Hitchcock, *Elementary Geology* (Amherst: J. S. & C. Adams, 1840), pp. 156-57.

20. Guralnick, "Geology and Religion before Darwin: The Case of Edward Hitchcock, Theologian and Geologist (1793-1864)," *Isis* 63 (1972): 541.

21. Hitchcock, *The Religion of Geology*, 2d ed. (Boston: Phillips, Samson, 1859), p. 526.

that perspective up to date. Now he urged that the grand aim of science was by no means to elaborate direct biblical correlations but was rather to discover the laws of nature—laws which themselves led the mind to their heavenly Author. For Hitchcock, the divine lawgiver had replaced the divine watchmaker.[22]

As with his British counterparts, Hitchcock's passion for reconciling Genesis and geology cannot be lampooned as bizarre or eccentric. His fundamental assumptions were shared by a great many scientists in his day even if they were expressed with less frequency or style. Benjamin Silliman, Hitchcock's teacher and lifelong friend, exemplifies this perhaps more than anyone else.[23] As occasional in publication as his student was prolific, his influence on American geology was nonetheless seminal. When President Dwight of Yale decided to appoint him to the chair of chemistry and natural history in 1802, it may have cut short a brilliant legal career before it had begun, but it established natural science in the American university curriculum.

In order to learn the tools of his trade, Silliman resorted first to Philadelphia, then to London, and finally to Edinburgh. As he later reflected, Edinburgh was at that stage the stronghold of British geology. In the years following his return to Yale, Silliman began to exert a dominating influence on American science not so much through original research as through his power as a teacher, his educational statesmanship at Yale, and his inauguration and coordinating editorship of the *American Journal of Science*, which was for many years known simply as *Silliman's Journal* and which remains a major geological periodical to this day. A whole generation of American chemists, geologists, and mineralogists passed through his hands at Yale, and beyond this professional sphere his public lectures from New Orleans to Boston did much to stimulate scientific interest throughout the country. His successive lecture series during the 1830s and '40s at the Lowell Institute in Boston culminated in audiences of two thousand cramming into the lyceum to hear him extol the wonder of God's creation and the virtues of useful science—and allay any

---

22. For this discussion I have drawn on Guralnick's "Geology and Religion before Darwin," and Philip J. Lawrence's "Edward Hitchcock: The Christian Geologist," *Proceedings of the American Philosophical Society* 116 (1972): 21-34.

23. The standard biography of Silliman is John F. Fulton and Elizabeth H. Thomson's *Benjamin Silliman, 1779-1864: Pathfinder in American Science* (New York: Henry Schuman, 1949). Valuable material can also be found in John C. Greene's article on Silliman in vol. 12 of the *Dictionary of Scientific Biography* (New York: Scribner's, 1975), pp. 432-34; Margaret Rossiter's "Benjamin Silliman and the Lowell Institute: The Popularization of Science in Nineteenth-Century America," *New England Quarterly* 44 (1971): 602-26; George P. Merrill's *The First One Hundred Years of American Geology* (New Haven: Yale University Press, 1924); and Charles Schuchert's "A Century of Geology—The Progress of Historical Geology in North America," *American Journal of Science* 46 (1918): 45-103.

BENJAMIN SILLIMAN, from George P. Merrill's *The First One Hundred Years of American Geology* (Yale University Press, 1924; copyright © 1952, Mrs. G. P. Merrill)

religious fears about the new science by harmonizing Genesis and geology.

Silliman shared Hitchcock's concern to correlate the findings of geology and Mosaic revelation. He outlined his own reconciliation in an appendix to the second American edition of Bakewell's *Introduction to Geology* (1833), which, like its predecessor, had been issued under his editorial scrutiny. He made it clear that the authority of the Pentateuch could not be arbitrated at the bar of science and that no living geologist based any system of earth history on biblical sources. Yet he still insisted both that the physical laws of earth deformation were just as much the work of the Creator as the material on which they acted and that it was far from inappropriate to seek mutual corroborations between sacred page and fossil record. His own reconciliation was presented in tabular form, linking the creatorial statements of Genesis with their geological correspondences; the whole was bolstered by supporting citations from such sources as Cuvier, Humboldt, Jameson, and Mantell.

Another guest at the Lowell Institute in the 1840s was the Swiss geographer Arnold Guyot. The extent to which popular science had gripped the imagination of Boston lecture-goers can perhaps be gauged by the fact that he delivered his nightly addresses in his native French. Subsequently Guyot was to occupy the chair of Physical Geography and Geology at Princeton—a professorship specially created for him. While there, he lectured the Princeton seminarians for six years on "The Connection of Revealed Religion and Physical and Ethnological Science" and went as a delegate of the Presbyterian Church of America to the Geneva convention of the Evangelical Alliance in 1861.

Guyot however had first come to America under rather nasty circumstances. The Neuchâtel Academy in Switzerland, where he was a professor of history and physical geography, had been suppressed by the revolutionary council of Geneva in 1848. Jobless, Guyot had half-heartedly but desperately followed his old friend Louis Agassiz to the New World. It was a big change. The Guyot family roots were deeply embedded in the soil of the Neuchâtel region; Guyot himself had studied at the local university before going to Germany to complete his education. There, in Karlsruhe, he fell in with Louis Agassiz and Karl Schimper, both proponents of natural history in the great German idealist tradition, and he absorbed the newest ideas in botany, embryology, and zoology. And then, too, it was in Neuchâtel that the preaching of the Rev. Samuel Petit-Pierre had so galvanized his faith that he determined to forsake science for theology. He began serious preparation for the ministry of the church in Berlin. The Berlin of the time was intellectually dazzling, and Guyot soon found scientific diversion not only in Humboldt and Hegel but also from Steffens in psychology and the philosophy of nature, Mitscherlich in chemistry, Hofman in geology, and Dove in physics and meteorology. But it was Karl Ritter who made the profoundest impression. He, more than any other, so integrated evangelical faith and geographical thought that the creation came to life as a grand organism animated by the will of an all-wise Divine Intelligence. Guyot found this near beatific vision so overwhelming that he dedicated himself to furthering the Ritterian philosophy. Guyot, however, took care not to divorce sublime contemplation from mundane spadework. Prompted by Agassiz, he spent some weeks during the summer of 1838 in the Alps making a series of fundamental observations on moraines, the differential flows of glaciers, and the banded nature of ice, all with a view to testing Agassiz's glacial theory. The results were communicated orally, and it was with a mixture of pleasure and chagrin that he later saw his conclusions confirmed by Agassiz and Forbes—they were the ones who received the accolade of scholarly acclaim.

Guyot had been teaching at Neuchâtel some nine years when political events intervened to truncate his Swiss career. Reluctantly he took Agassiz's advice and crossed the Atlantic. But the calamity proved to be a blessing in disguise. Within a few months his Lowell lectures on "Comparative Physical Geography" were arranged, delivered to a large and appreciative audience, and published under the title *The Earth and Man*. Fashioned after Ritter's cosmology and conceived on a grand scale, the work was presented as a geographical testimony to the harmonies of nature and history that everywhere expressed the foresight and control of a beneficent Providence. It was full of organic metaphors. Emphasizing the interplay of continental physiography and the path of human history, Guyot's *Earth and Man* revolved around the idea of development in earth history, organic growth, and social progress alike. It was a radical departure from conventional geography. It was, by its very nature, a frontal attack on traditional textbooks with their physiographic inventories and commercial catalogues. By contrast, it offered an ecological approach, grounded in organic analogy and sensitive to the interdependent relationships in nature. Guyot believed that this vision could be sustained only by natural theology in the idealist vein. As he testified, "All is order, all is harmony in the universe, because the whole universe is a thought of God; and it appears as a combination of organisms, each of which is only an integral part of one still more sublime. God alone contains them all, without making a part of any."[24]

We shall return to Guyot presently when we assess post-Darwinian evangelical science. But before moving on it is worth reemphasizing how conceptually rich Guyot's natural theology proved to be, whatever its obvious drawbacks. In the interwar years when the celebrated geo-

---

24. Guyot, *The Earth and Man: Lectures on Comparative Physical Geography in Its Relation to the History of Mankind* (1849; rpt., New York: Scribner's, 1897), p. 82.

morphologist W. M. Davis issued his reflections on the American geographical tradition, he underscored Guyot's originality when he said that *The Earth and Man* "was pervaded by a spirit of rational correlation, and may therefore be regarded as having given us the first great impulse toward the cultivation of geography as a serious and independent science."[25] As I have tried to show, this ecological geography was the outgrowth of Guyot's reading of the design argument and can scarcely be dismissed as an unfortunate theological appendage.[26]

As the organic metaphor proved to be Guyot's inspiration, the machine metaphor best expressed the evangelical faith of his contemporary Matthew Fontaine Maury. This is perhaps not so surprising given their diverse backgrounds and education. Guyot had grown to intellectual maturity in the grace of Teutonic high culture, whereas Maury was brought up in the backlands of rural Tennessee, where he dreamed of following in his brother's footsteps as a naval officer.[27] It was with great delight that, as a midshipman, he was assigned to the new forty-four-gun frigate the *Brandywine* in 1825, when he was nineteen years old. His naval education to that point had been at best paltry, however, and the conditions for training on the job deplorable; nor did this change when he was transferred to the *Vincennes* on its round-the-world voyage. Still, the lack of facilities for formal training did not deter him; he set to work to master the navigational volumes in the ship's library.

His first scholarly ventures in the early 1830s arose directly from his needs as a navigator. As acting sailing master of the sloop of war *Falmouth*, Maury searched for reliable information on winds and currents—a search that proved so frustrating that he decided to keep his own detailed records of the navigation of Cape Horn. The results were subsequently published in the July 1834 issue of the *American Journal of Science and Arts* ("Silliman's Journal"). Encouraged by this, he pressed on with preparations for a *Treatise on Navigation*, which was published in 1836. The book was highly praised and soon became a standard text in the field. But in the same year that it appeared, disaster struck. A stagecoach accident in Somerset, Ohio, left him with a dislocated knee joint, a fractured femur, and an uncertain naval future.

---

25. Davis, "The Progress of Geography in the United States," *Annals of the Association of American Geographers* 14 (1924): 165.

26. Biographical sketches of Guyot are available in James D. Dana's "Biographical Memoir of Arnold Guyot," *Biographical Memoirs: National Academy of Sciences* 2 (1886): 309-47; and in Albert V. Carozzi's article on Guyot in vol. 5 of the *Dictionary of Scientific Biography* (New York: Scribner's, 1971), pp. 599-60.

27. In addition to Frances Leigh Williams's biography *Matthew Fontaine Maury: Scientist of the Sea* (New Brunswick, N.J.: Rutgers University Press, 1963), source material on Maury can be found in John R. Meyer's essay "The Life and Philosophy of Matthew Fontaine Maury, Pathfinder of the Sea," *Creation Research Society Quarterly* 19 (1982): 91-100; and in Preston E. James, *All Possible Worlds: A History of Geographical Ideas* (Indianapolis: Bobbs-Merrill, 1972), pp. 196-201.

Fortunately there were both immediate and long-term compensations. Not only did convalescence give him time to push for naval reform in the pages of the *Richmond Whig*, particularly on the question of the need for a naval academy, but the misfortune also resulted in his appointment as superintendent of the Navy Depot of Charts and Instruments. A distinguished career in science was now well underway—a career that would culminate in his receiving many international scholarly honors, including an LL.D. from Cambridge and honorary memberships in numerous scientific societies. When Maury was nominated to head the new U.S. Naval Observatory, he found himself in an ideal position to issue a series of pioneering reports of astronomical and oceanographic observations. Yet while these communications were the outcome of painstaking data collection and enumeration, they were not merely computational records. Maury sought to synthesize his material into a coherent system, one of the best-known features of which was his general model of atmospheric circulation depicting the equatorial doldrum belt, the trade winds, the mid-latitude and polar calms, and the Westerlies.[28] Despite its flaws, this scheme was almost universally accepted and taught in schools.

Given Maury's daily dealing with astromonical and marine notation, it is quite understandable that his natural theology should be construed in mechanistic terms; after all, he did subsequently hold the chair of physics at the Virginia Military Institute from 1862 until his death in 1873. His *Physical Geography of the Sea* (1855) perhaps best exemplifies this. It was, as Alexander von Humboldt confessed, a trailblazing work establishing a whole new field of scholarship. At the same time it was solidly founded on the Paleyan view of the world. Maury's interpretation of the land-water proportions of the globe; his idea of balancing compensations in the inorganic and organic realms alike; his mechanistic model of energy transfers between earth, sea, and air; and his understanding of atmospheric and marine circulation systems were all presented in terms of natural law guided by Providence. The following extract is typical of his thinking.

> The sea, therefore, we infer, has its offices and duties to perform; so may we infer, have its currents, and so, too, its inhabitants; consequently, he who undertakes to study its phenomena, must cease to regard it as a waste of waters. He must look upon it as a part of the exquisite machinery by which the harmonies of nature are preserved, and then he will begin to perceive the developments of order and evidences of design which make it a most beautiful and interesting subject for contemplation.
>
> To one who has never studied the mechanism of a watch, its main-spring or the balance-wheel is a mere piece of met-

---

28. Maury, "On the General Circulation of the Atmosphere," *Proceedings of the American Association for the Advancement of Science* 3 (1850): 126-47.

al. . . . Take it to pieces, and show him each part separately; he will recognize neither design, nor adaptation, nor relation between them; but put them together, set them to work, point out the offices of each spring, wheel, and cog, explain their movements, and then show him the result; now he perceives that it is all *one* design. . . . So, too, when one looks out upon the face of this beautiful world, he may admire the lovely scene, but his admiration can never grow into admiration unless he will take the trouble to look behind and study, in some of its details at least, the exquisite system of machinery by which such beautiful results are accomplished. To him who does this, the sea, with its physical geography, becomes as the main spring of a watch.[29]

Despite such metaphysical reflections, it was the thoroughly empirical tenor of Maury's work that most impressed his contemporaries. William Leighton Jordan, for example, castigated oceanographic work that was determined solely by theory, comparing it unfavorably with the "true science" of Maury. "It is a degradation of the term 'scientific' to apply it to such theorizing," Jordan insisted. "How much more really scientific—how much nobler is the spirit of the true 'Physical Geographer' who completely subordinates theory to fact. This is the spirit which breathes through Maury's writings, and enables the reader to turn over the pages with a refreshing confidence that he need fear no delusion."[30] Jordan's praise may be overly eulogistic, but it shows nevertheless that evangelical commitments were far from incompatible with scholarly detachment.

Matthew Maury's science was in many ways typical of scientific practice in Victorian Britain and Jacksonian America. The fascination with measurement, inventory, social utility, and indeed natural theology dominated scientific work in the era of what Susan Faye Cannon has called "Humboldtian science" in honor of its greatest advocate.[31] Here I have restricted myself to a sample of British and American scientists whose theological commitments were staunchly conservative and whose scholarly concerns were fairly closely related to the questions subsequently raised by the Darwinian revolution.[32] The careers of many other savants in the period call for similar exegesis; obvious candidates would include, say, Michael Faraday in physics, Humphrey Davy in chemistry,

---

29. Maury, *The Physical Geography of the Sea* (New York: Harper & Brothers, 1855), pp. 53-54.

30. Jordan, *The Ocean: Its Tides and Currents and Their Causes* (London: Longmans, 1873), p. 267.

31. See Cannon, *Science in Culture: The Early Victorian Period* (New York: Dawson & Science History Publications, 1978), pp. 73-110.

32. The way in which American theologians were able to accommodate the earlier "naturalistic" nebular hypothesis is charted by Ronald L. Numbers in *Creation by Natural Law: Laplace's Nebular Hypothesis in American Thought* (Seattle: University of Washington Press, 1977), especially pp. 77ff.

the Edinburgh physicist David Brewster, artist and telegrapher Samuel Morse, and physicist Joseph Henry of Princeton. Rather than detail their contributions and outlooks, however, I think this is an appropriate point to stop and review the dimensions of pre-Darwinian evangelical science.

REVIEW

My claims are modest.

First, I want to underscore the fact that evangelicals eagerly participated in early nineteenth-century science. This is not to say that evangelicals were dominant in the scientific culture but rather that they were adequately represented, that their contributions were far from inconspicuous, and that those who would assume a warfare between science and religion can do so only by suppressing their presence.

Second, and in keeping with the more general patterns of thought, evangelicals conducted their science within the natural theology frame of reference. Again, this does not imply uniformity. Some retained a long-standing allegiance to the Paley school, others felt Owen's morphology introduced a much-needed liberalization of that perspective, and still others wavered between the two. There were those who adhered closely to the strictures of a Mosaic cosmology and those who were satisfied with a more metaphorical understanding of the Pentateuchal narrative. Still, all were convinced that the creation bore the unmistakable stamp of its Creator, whether expressed in the general laws of nature or in the detailed adaptations of creatures to their environment.

Third, there was no evangelical consensus on the philosophy of geology. If some found catastrophism both scientifically and theologically appropriate, others insisted on the need for a modified version, and others still (especially the Scottish Calvinists) were far more attracted to Huttonian uniformitarianism. There was certainly no simple Christian-catastrophist correlation.

Finally, evangelicals in science had remarkably little difficulty in adjusting their theology to the idea of a lengthy earth history, and numerous harmonizing schemes were confidently, if not always consistently, advanced. This, once again, is not to say that there were no misfits. Philip Henry Gosse's portrayal of a God building fossils into the geological strata to give the impression of age is only a more dramatic instance. But by and large, Christian geologists had both encountered and accommodated the issue of the age of the earth long before the appearance of Darwin's theory. Whatever Darwin challenged, it certainly was not this. Nor does it seem to me that Darwinism created a crisis concerning the doctrine of Scripture. The transformation of species was presumably no greater an obstacle to evangelical exegesis of Genesis than an archaic earth. To elucidate just what it was that so many found menacing in Darwin will be our next concern.

CHAPTER 2

REFLECTIONS ON A REVOLUTION

Charles Darwin was born with a silver spoon in his mouth.[1] Quite appropriately for the author of a treatise on "the preservation of favored races in the struggle for life," his own ancestral pedigree was impeccable, even sparkling. When Charles's first cries shattered the winter air of Shrewsbury in February 1809, they signaled his arrival in a family representing the very best of rural England's intellectual aristocracy. His grandfather Erasmus Darwin was in every way a man of large proportions—in bodily size, poetic imagination, social vigor, scientific energy, and zest for life. His father, a medical practitioner, was well known and even better connected. His mother, Susannah Wedgwood, was the daughter of Josiah Wedgwood, the famous potter. To people such as these, breathing the clear air of cultural refinement, the young Charles must have seemed an academic aberration. His seven years at Dr. Butler's boarding school brought only a public rebuke from the headmaster that he was a wastrel, dissipating his energies on shooting, dogs, and rat catching. Nor did things improve very much when he went up to Edinburgh in 1825 to study medicine. There he was overcome with an acute attack of boredom in his lectures on pharmacy, chemistry, and anatomy, and the repulsion he endured while attending surgical operations in this preanaesthetic age merely strengthened his resolve to forsake the medical field. His father was pained, but the writing was on the wall: this son was not going to follow in father's footsteps. Holy Orders seemed the last

---

1. I have relied on the following sources for biographical details about Darwin: Peter Brent, *Charles Darwin* (London: Heinemann, 1981); Jonathan Howard, *Darwin* (Oxford: Oxford University Press, 1982); Wilma George, *Darwin* (London: Fontana, 1982); and *Charles Darwin, 1809-1882: A Centennial Commemorative*, ed. Roger G. Chapman and Cleveland T. Duval (Wellington, New Zealand: Nova Pacifica, 1982). There are also a number of useful pieces in the special Darwin issue of the *Biological Journal of the Linnean Society* 17 (1982).

resort, so Darwin was dispatched to Christ's College, Cambridge, to prepare for entering the Church of England as a clergyman. He proved to be no more keen on ordination than he had been on operations, however, and having just scraped through his examinations, he returned home.

CHARLES DARWIN, from a watercolor by George Richmond. Reprinted with permission of Down House and the Royal College of Surgeons of England

But if Darwin found formal education in all these establishments less than captivating, it certainly did not mean that he learned nothing while attending them. In fact he had acquired, albeit in a rather desultory form, a pretty good working knowledge of the chief object of his affections—nature. Profoundly in love with the natural world, Darwin had been an inveterate collector of everything from plants to pebbles ever since his schooldays. And when he arrived in Edinburgh, these pursuits were further encouraged by Robert Grant, a Lamarckian zoologist who introduced him to the local natural history society. Robert Jameson was another stimulus, accompanying Darwin on geological excursions to the Firth of Forth to collect marine specimens. But it was in Cambridge that he encountered some of the most influential intellectual currents. First, there were the books: Paley's *Evidences of Christianity*, Sir John Herschel's *Preliminary Discourse on the Study of Natural Philosophy*, and particularly Alexander von Humboldt's *Personal Narrative of Travels to the Equinoctial Regions of the New Continent*. Each in its own way opened up new vistas to the young student and kindled in him a yearning to see the world firsthand. Then there were his friendships. The professor of botany John Henslow took the lapsed medical student under his wing, entertained him at his own table, fired him with a passion for the world of nature, and gave him renewed confidence in himself. Along with the geologist Adam Sedgwick, Henslow sensed in the voluntary but devoted pupil a rare talent and a potential brilliance that would eventually shake the very foundations of their own system of natural history.

It is not too surprising, then, that it was the action of Henslow that now rescued Darwin from the doldrums when he got back home to "The Mount" in September 1831. With little to look forward to beyond the legalized bloodshed of the autumn shoot, the invitation to join the Admiralty survey ship HMS *Beagle* must have seemed just what it was—the opportunity of a lifetime. In fact it was Henslow who had proposed Darwin for the post of naturalist on the survey voyage to the coasts of Patagonia, Tierra del Fuego, Chile, and Peru.[2] The very names must have conjured up an aura of the exotic to a young untraveled English gentleman. Father, however, was not pleased. It was, after all, an unpaid job with no prospects. But Uncle Jos Wedgwood intervened to plead his young nephew's case, and on 27 December 1831 one of the most significant expeditions in the history of science weighed anchor in the port of Plymouth.

The *Beagle*'s five-year circumnavigation of the globe, as Darwin later confessed, was by far the most important event in his life and

---

2. Even though Darwin was proposed by Henslow for the post of ship's naturalist, he did not actually officially occupy that position. Robert McKormick, the ship's surgeon, was the official naturalist. Darwin apparently traveled on the *Beagle* as a companion to Captain Fitzroy.

determined his whole future career. It was his real training ground in science, and if he found nothing to alleviate the constant misery of sea-sickness, it was more than compensated for by the invigoration of spectacular new geological, botanical, zoological, and anthropological forms. Whether trawling from the ship, scrambling about beaches, cutting through dense jungle undergrowth, or struggling up volcanic mountain slopes, Darwin busied himself with indefatigable curiosity mapping, collecting, and classifying. As much as anything else, the voyage confirmed in Darwin's mind the superiority of Lyell's work on geology over all rivals; his *Principles of Geology* was Darwin's constant companion. Later his own brilliant theory of the origin and distribution of coral reefs earned him the respect of England's master geologist. So when Darwin returned to the mellow colors of a West Country autumn in 1836 with an armful of notebooks, specimens by the box load, and memories to last a lifetime, he stood on the verge of a respected if conventional scientific career. More than twenty years had to elapse before the storm was to break.

For the twenty-nine-year-old Darwin, 1839 must have seemed a high point. It was during that year that he married his cousin Emma Wedgwood, was elected to a fellowship of the Royal Society, and saw the

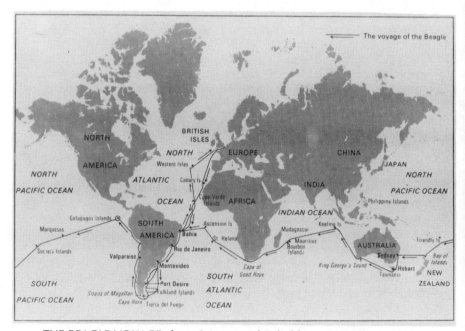

THE BEAGLE VOYAGE, from *Science and Belief from Copernicus to Darwin*, Block 5, Unit 13, p. 61. Copyright © 1974, The Open University Press.

publication of his first day-by-day natural history descriptions of the *Beagle* voyage. By now, he had been living in London for a couple of years and had immersed himself in every kind of scientific pursuit, from presenting learned papers before the Geological and Zoological Societies to fraternizing with the scientific luminaries of his day. His involvement with Christianity, long tepid, chilled further as his grand theory began to take shape during these years. He fleshed out his creative insights in a series of sketches and essays in the early 1840s, and although he never intended them for publication, they were later to confirm his scholarly priority on the theory of natural selection. All this feverish activity eventually began to give way to lassitude, however. His robust health already beginning to fail, in 1842 with wife and two children Darwin left London for the quiet isolation of Down House in Kent. Insomnia, fatigue, and intestinal discomfort (the cause of which has never been ascertained) were to trouble Darwin for the remaining forty years of his life in the village of Downe, where he restricted himself to a regimen of four hour's work a day, garden strolls, occasional pony rides, and periods of relaxation with a novel.

Over the next dozen years or so Darwin continued to tinker with his revolutionary hypothesis, giving only Joseph Hooker the privilege of perusing the crucial 1844 essay. During this period, he turned to a completely new line of research—the classification of an understudied group of marine crustacea, barnacles. The results were published between 1851 and 1854, and were immediately hailed as the definitive treatment of the subject. Meanwhile, his secret theory continued to ripen, and, by 1854, urged on by close personal friends, he finally felt ready to go public. He set to work on a treatise of gargantuan proportions. Then in 1858 there came a bolt from the blue. From the wilds of Borneo a letter arrived from a young man called Wallace, and with it a short essay that encapsulated the very kernel of Darwin's whole theory! Darwin was deeply shaken. But he was a gentleman, and, bound by the strictest codes of Victorian morality, he refused to take advantage of the absent young naturalist. Lyell and Hooker gave timely advice urging him to allow some of the 1844 essay and an extract from an 1857 letter to Asa Gray to accompany the reading of Wallace's paper at the Linnean Society. Darwin consented, the joint thesis was communicated, and . . . the learned audience went home without so much as a whimper.

Spurred into action, Darwin redoubled his efforts. He now set out to write an "abstract," as he called it, of the mammoth work he had had in mind. It turned out to be a 700-page book published under the famous title *On the Origin of Species by Means of Natural Selection; or, The Preservation of Favoured Races in the Struggle for Life.* It appeared 24 November 1859. The reaction was neither as instant nor as sensational as we are usually led to believe. Certainly there were debates, and some indeed were characterized by acrid polemics (when it came to a fight, "Bulldog"

Huxley stood to the fore while Darwin kept a low profile down in Kent). But overall the reception was sedate, and the whole event was upstaged by the publication of the controversial *Essays and Reviews* in 1860, setting the agenda for much of the new liberal theology.

The Huxley-Wilberforce encounter, however, has achieved such legendary status that it is worth our consideration here, if only to expose its excesses. The story goes something like this. Matters came to a head in 1860 at the Oxford meeting of the British Association for the Advancement of Science. Darwin was ill and could not attend. But even in the absence of the great man himself the lines were already clearly drawn, and the Oxford air was filled with rumors that a clerical assault was to be mounted at Section D's Saturday session. Sure enough, when the time came, Samuel Wilberforce, the Bishop of Oxford, force-fed by Owen and crammed to the teeth with Owenesque anatomy, waxed lyrical in his

Left, SAMUEL WILBERFORCE; *right*, THOMAS HENRY HUXLEY: cartoons by "Ape" in *Vanity Fair*, 24 July 1869 and 28 January 1871, respectively (The Queen's University of Belfast Library)

damnation of the monkey theory and threw his extravagant gauntlet at Huxley's feet—"If anyone were to be willing to trace his descent through an ape as his *grandfather*, would he be willing to trace his descent similarly on the side of his *grandmother?*" Wilberforce's reserves of wit and sarcasm, however, were no match for Huxley's impassive brilliance. He gravely approached the lecturn and in a few short sharp strokes exposed as utterly vacuous the good Bishop's "science":

> I asserted—and I repeat—that a man has no reason to be ashamed of having an ape for a grandfather. If there were an ancestor whom I should feel shame in recalling it would rather be a man—a man of restless and versatile intellect—who, not content with an equivocal success in his own sphere of activity, plunges into scientific questions with which he has no real acquaintance, only to obscure them by an aimless rhetoric, and distract the attention of his hearers from the real point at issue by eloquent digressions and skilled appeals to religious prejudice.

With crisp clarity Huxley summarized Darwin's theory, gave a thumbnail sketch of salient evidence, and sat down with neither flourish nor ceremony. The Bishop, Irvine colorfully tells us,

> had suffered a sudden and involuntary martyrdom, perishing in the diverted avalanches of his own blunt ridicule. . . . At length Joseph Hooker rose and botanized briefly on the grave of the Bishop's scientific reputation. Wilberforce did not reply. The meeting adjourned. Huxley was complimented, even by the clergy, with a frankness and fairness that surprised him.[3]

What actually happened is far more difficult to determine than this little tale suggests. For one thing, no written record was kept and the received story was patched together from the reminiscences of various people over thirty years later. For another, it was Hooker, contemporaries agreed, who most fully answered the arguments of Wilberforce. Certainly the Bishop was eloquent and funny, and it was his rhetoric that most rubbed Huxley the wrong way. But his scientific criticisms, as even Darwin admitted, were fair. So why has the legend grown up? One suggestion is that while Wilberforce was perfectly entitled to have an opinion about science in his own time, the later drive toward "scientific" science (or, if you like, professional science) meant that outsiders were less welcome in the sacred halls of science. And this in turn fostered a re-creation of the debate favoring Huxley as representative of true free scientific spirit at its

---

3. Irvine, *Apes, Angels and Victorians: A Joint Biography of Darwin and Huxley* (London: Weidenfeld & Nicolson, 1956), p. 6.

best.[4] Curiously enough, the important thing is not what actually happened but rather the fact that this particular record of the encounter has become part of the history of the "conflict" between evolution and religion. That there was some sort of confrontation can scarcely be doubted. But it seems likely that any high drama there might have been was centered far more than anything else on the determination of some to exorcise the British Association of its amateurish, unprofessional image.

If this little stage play set the scene for Darwin's public hearing in Britain, his reception in the United States was far more carefully orchestrated, though no less tense. This time the forum was the Boston Society of Natural History, and the protagonists were William Barton Rogers (who would later become the first president of MIT) and Louis Agassiz (Harvard's Swiss professor at the Lawrence Scientific School). It was almost the exact antithesis of what the Oxford confrontation was supposed to have been: here the contestants were of comparable scientific stature, the pace was more leisurely, and the arguments and counterarguments were carefully weighed. The clash, at the same time, was well worth seeing, as students later recalled. Agassiz was romantic, eloquent, passionate; Rogers, cool, rational, and controlled. Still, as the meetings wore on, Rogers more and more placed the stamp of his authority on the debate. Turning Agassiz's progressivist paleontology against him and pressing him to explain his terms precisely, Rogers outflanked every move Agassiz made and finally clinched the argument with a detailed interpretation of the New York fossil-bearing strata. Of course Rogers did not prove the validity of Darwin's theory, but he did succeed in establishing the point that the value of Darwin's views should be settled by scrutiny rather than authority, by science rather than dogma.[5]

Meanwhile back at Down House, Darwin continued to polish his prize theory and over the years slipped out one new edition after another. At the same time he pushed on toward a more and more comprehensive evolutionary philosophy including an evolutionary interpretation of humankind—physically, mentally, and morally. Two books on this subject and one on variation under domestication further developed ideas he had only glancingly referred to in *The Origin of Species*. Soon they too were complemented by several book-length treatments of botanical themes. And finally a volume on the role of earthworms in the formation of

---

4. On this, see J. R. Lucas, "Wilberforce and Huxley: A Legendary Encounter," *The Historical Journal* 22 (1979): 313-30; Owen Chadwick, *The Victorian Church* (London: Adam & Charles Black, 1970); and Sheridan Gilley, "The Huxley-Wilberforce Debate: A Reconsideration," in *Religion and Humanism*, ed. Keith Robbins (Oxford: Basil Blackwell, 1981), pp. 325-40.

5. For a good summary of the Rogers-Agassiz debate, see Edward J. Pfeifer, "United States," in *The Comparative Reception of Darwinism*, ed. Thomas F. Glick (Austin: University of Texas Press, 1972), pp. 168-206.

vegetable mold brought to fruition an interest he had sustained for over forty years.

For Darwin now each year that passed was comfortably like the one before. Of course more and more international honors were lavished upon him—honorary degrees, society memberships, and so on. He had moved, as Brent says, beyond controversy and into adulation. Still, there were a few changes. As the cascade of books might suggest, Darwin had become more and more absorbed in his research. And this, as he himself confessed, dulled his appreciation of some of the finer things in life, such as art, music, and literature. Yet if his taste for these things had become shallow, he nevertheless retained a passionate love of nature. As his son Francis recalled, his father's love of flowers was "a kind of gratitude to the flower itself, and a personal love for its delicate form and colour."[6] How well this depicts the figure of the aging Darwin: gentle, retiring, tirelessly inquisitive, stooping down with searching eyes to ask some profound question of a common weed or worm.

Darwin died at home 19 April 1882, surrounded by family and friends. If in life he had challenged the very fabric of Victorian society's self-perception, in death he received the ultimate stamp of establishment approval—burial in Westminster Abbey. Sir John Lubbock in particular had worked hard to achieve this, and the great national dailies were warm in their appreciation. It would have been a national reproach, the *Standard* printed, to have denied him a place among the illustrious dead who had made the country famous. So, with political, educational, and scientific dignitaries looking on, the abbey choir sang the specially composed farewell anthem to Charles Darwin, "Happy Is the Man Who Finds Wisdom and Getteth Understanding."

DARWIN'S THEORY: WHAT IT WAS . . .

It was his time on board the *Beagle* that first led Darwin to question much that he had been taught and even more that he had assumed. But of all his queries, none had more far-reaching consequences than his growing doubt that all the various species of plants and animals had remained unchanged since the creation of the world. These suspicions mounted as his travels brought him face to face with more and more puzzling patterns in the geographical distribution of species.[7] First, in neighboring regions of South America Darwin noticed that one species was replaced by a different but closely similar species. On the pampas, for instance, he had seen specimens of the South American ostrich, and when the voyage

---

6. See Robert E. Fitch, "Charles Darwin: Science and the Saintly Sentiments," *Columbia University Forum*, Spring 1959, pp. 7-11.

7. In preparing this material, I have drawn especially on Gavin De Beer's article on Darwin in vol. 3 of the *Dictionary of Scientific Biography* (New York: Scribner's, 1971), pp. 565-77.

reached the shores of Patagonia farther south, he encountered a smaller but otherwise very similar version. Now why, he wondered, were these two species structurally so similar, yet different not only from each other but also from their African counterparts? Second, Darwin found that there was a close resemblance between various species on oceanic islands and their adjacent continents. In the Cape Verde Islands, African-like species were present, whereas in the Galápagos archipelago they were more South American in character—and this despite the very similar physical geography of the two island groups. Third, within the Galápagos Islands themselves, where Darwin had expected to find identical species, he was surprised to learn that the finches, for example, differed both in structure and in behavior from one island to the next: some ate insects, others seeds, and their bills reflected their different dietary habits.

How, Darwin pondered, was he to make sense of this quite stunning complexity of organic forms? Had every single species been specially created by divine fiat, and if so, why should a creator bother to multiply so many species with different characteristics to perform almost identical functions? Or was it all quite artibrary and meaningless? Or was there some other alternative that could enable a coherent pattern to be discerned? Gradually Darwin came to see that the problem would become much less intractable if the received wisdom about the permanence of species turned out to be wrong. If species in fact could change and diverge, by whatever means, then many modern variations could be traced to a single common ancestor. And as for the Galápagos finches, he surmised that each species might have been modified for different ends— different purposes that fitted or adapted them to their respective modes of life.

Darwin knew he had hit on something big. So in 1837, after he got home, he opened his famous notebook on the transmutation of species. The power of the idea more and more gripped him. It could resolve so many problems in natural history. For one thing, the structural similarities, which Owen was so fond of pointing out, between the bones of a human arm, the foreleg of a dog, the wing of a bat, and so on could make a lot of sense if the species were related by descent from common ancestors. Then again, light might be thrown on the embryological parallels between lizards, chicks, and rabbits—all so similar in embryo, so different in adulthood. It was clear to Darwin that the evolution of species could help to make sense of a multitude of tantalizing analogies in the structures of widely divergent animals. Despite this, however, he never claimed to have demonstrated empirically one species changing into another. His method was thoroughly deductive in the best Newtonian fashion;[8] he simply argued that if evolution had occurred, it would account

---

8. On this, see Michael Ghiselin, *The Triumph of the Darwinian Method* (Berkeley and Los Angeles: University of California Press, 1969).

for many hitherto unexplained facts in nature. Indeed, there remained one central problem still to be cracked: how did the modification of species actually occur? What was the mechanism of evolutionary change?

Two quite separate events provided Darwin with the clue he needed. The first came, strangely enough, from his love of pigeons. It was plain as a pikestaff to everyone in the pigeon business that a careful breeder could produce an almost infinite variety of pigeon forms. Darwin sensed something quite vital here and, determined to track it down, he sustained over many years a staggeringly comprehensive correspondence with pigeon fanciers all over the north of England, extracting from them remorselessly but courteously the information he needed. Then, when he was still measuring the anatomical proportions of newly hatched pigeons, he came across something else—Thomas Malthus's *Essay on the Principle of Population*, which had been published forty years previously in 1798.

Writing in the aftermath of the French Revolution, Malthus had pointed out a universal tendency of human beings to multiply exponentially, exerting an increasing pressure on the available environmental resources until scarcity produced the horrors of poverty, disease, starvation, and war. This was, he maintained, a law of nature: populations inevitably increase until restrained by the limits of food supply. Malthus, it should be remembered, was an Anglican clergyman, and his scheme was put forward in the context of natural theology. But Darwin nonetheless found in it the missing link he sought. Applying the law to plants and animals (which, unlike human beings, are incapable of increasing their resources), Darwin realized that they must die if they multiply beyond the capacity of the food supply available to sustain them. Here was the basis of natural selection—the idea of a struggle for existence. It was a notoriously simple notion; Huxley later murmured, "How extremely stupid not to have thought of that."

Whatever its simplicity in Huxley's eyes, Darwin's theory continues to be widely misunderstood and misapplied. The difficulty certainly cannot lie in any logical complexity, for as Stephen Jay Gould has shown, it can be reduced to two clipped factual propositions and an inevitable conclusion:

1. Organisms vary, and these variations are inherited (at least in part) by their offspring.
2. Organisms produce more offspring than can possibly survive.
3. On average, offspring that vary most strongly in directions favored by the environment will survive and propagate. Favourable variation will therefore accumulate in populations by natural selection.[9]

---

9. Gould, *Ever since Darwin: Reflections in Natural History* (Harmondsworth: Penguin, 1980), p. 11.

The thoroughly hypothetico-deductive character of the theory, I must point out, is not merely the product of Gould's propositional format. It was in fact the way Darwin himself conceptualized his theory. And since there is at least one fragment of the *Origin* that neatly captures the essence of Darwin's vision and that remained virtually unaltered throughout the six editions of the book, it is worth quoting directly from the creator of the theory himself:

> If under changing conditions of life organic beings present individual differences in almost every part of their structure, and this cannot be disputed; if there be, owing to their geometrical rate of increase, a severe struggle for life at some age, season, or year, and this certainly cannot be disputed; then, considering the infinite complexity of the relations of all organic beings to each other and to their conditions of life, causing an infinite diversity in structure, constitution, and habits, to be advantageous to them, it would be a most extraordinary fact if no variations had ever occurred useful to each being's own welfare, in the same manner as so many variations have occurred useful to man. But if variations useful to any organic being ever do occur, assuredly individuals thus characterised will have the best chance of being preserved in the struggle for life; and from the strong principle of inheritance, these will tend to produce offspring similarly characterised. This principle of preservation, or the survival of the fittest, I have called Natural Selection. . . . Thus the small differences distinguishing varieties of the same species, steadily tend to increase, till they equal the greater differences between species of the same genus, or even of distinct genera.[10]

This then was natural selection. But simple as it was, it carried with it a number of revolutionary implications. For one thing, it was a thoroughly nonprogressivist model of change. The whole theory assumed that the variations in animals were quite random (or at least obeyed laws as yet unknown to scientists), and this meant that the theory did not presume any sense of evolutionary history moving in any inevitable direction. Second, Darwin thought of animal groups as populations rather than types or species. He looked on the emergence of a new species merely as a by-product of the process of a particular population becoming more adapted to a particular environment. In other words, natural selection was a theory of population change or, if you like, a model for explaining the differential reproductive success of animal groups. Third, the variations that Darwin envisioned were relatively small. He never spoke of whole new species suddenly appearing; indeed, such an event would pose

---

10. Darwin, *The Origin of Species by Means of Natural Selection; or, The Preservation of Favoured Races in the Struggle for Life*, 6th ed. (London: John Murray, 1872), pp. 159-61.

a problem for the theory, since it would obviate the need for natural selection to preserve, generation after generation, beneficial adaptations.

. . . AND WHAT IT WAS NOT

If this is what natural selection involved, I think it is just as important to make it clear what it was not. For Darwin's theory continues to be widely misconstrued. Two of these misconceptions can be dispelled quite rapidly; a third will require rather more careful scrutiny.

The first misunderstanding grew out of the phrase "the survival of the fittest"—which, as it turns out, was not Darwin's own formulation at

CHARLES DARWIN, *Vanity Fair*, 30 September 1871 (The Queen's University of Belfast Library)

all. It had been coined by the social theorist Herbert Spencer, who had been writing about aspects of social evolution (e.g., in his *Social Statics* of 1851) long before Darwin made available his carefully elaborated theory. When Darwin used the phrase "survival of the fittest" he only referred to the survival of the fitter—that is, the survival of those individuals or species more likely to leave offspring. He was not speaking of any sort of perfect adaptation to the natural milieu but merely of relatively superior or inferior fittedness to the prevailing conditions. Almost as if to guard himself against this sort of misunderstanding, Darwin made it a point never to designate the structure of organs as "higher" or "lower." In light of this, it is perhaps unfortunate that in later life he was persuaded to adopt Spencer's dictum, for it left his theory open to the charge of tautology—that is, that the survival of the fittest amounts to no more than the survival of whatever survives. Such an argument, of course, entirely ignores the fundamental point of Darwinism that forms better adapted to their ecological niches leave more offspring than competitors.

A closely related phrase requiring clarification is "the struggle for existence." As used by Darwin and his modern-day successors, the idea of struggle does not primarily imply the savagery implicit in Tennyson's well-known phrase "Nature red in tooth and claw." Again, it simply refers to the fact that some members of a population will be better adapted to the environment than competitors—better adapted in terms of leaving more descendants. Thus, Darwin's "struggle for existence" is less a literal than a metaphorical struggle. As he himself wrote in the *Origin*, "I should premise that I use the term Struggle for Existence in a large and metaphorical sense including dependence of one being on another, and including (which is more important) not only the life of the individual, but success in leaving progeny."[11]

Certainly many of Darwin's followers were far less restrained in their use of the metaphor of struggle. Some, for example, used it in reference to society, in an attempt to justify the cutthroat ethics of late nineteenth-century capitalism. They asserted that the social equivalent of the biological struggle was laissez-faire economics—the free play of market forces. Not that Darwin never flirted with certain "Social Darwinian" ideas, but, as he outlined it in the *Origin*, he meant natural selection to be a theory of relative reproductive success. The well-known case of what is commonly called the Midlands' Moth, in which environmental changes accompanying the Industrial Revolution favored the survival and reproduction of a mutant variety of the insect (it was better able to elude predators because its darker wings provided it with better camouflage on soot-darkened tree bark), would seem to be precisely the sort of process Darwin had in mind.

---

11. Darwin, *The Origin of Species*, p. 78. Tennyson's phrase, incidentally, dates from a decade prior to the publication of *The Origin*.

The third misconception is rather more delicate, but much more important. It concerns the relationship between Darwinian biology and uniformitarian geology. Since it is often thought that uniformitarianism is vitally linked to the theory of evolution, it is important to settle the issue once and for all.[12] Let us be clear from the outset that the idea that evolution is uniformitarianism applied to biology is simply wrong. Certain versions of catastrophism were, in fact, far more compatible with the theory of evolution than uniformitarianism. The very fact that Charles Lyell, the leading architect of geological uniformitarianism, was a long-standing opponent of Darwin's idea of species transmutation should immediately put us on the alert. To begin to unpack the various issues involved here, I want to first look at just what uniformitarianism meant and then how it was related to evolution theory.

The origin of uniformitarianism is conventionally traced to the writings of James Hutton. When Hutton affirmed that the earth's surface showed "no vestige of a beginning,—no prospect of an end," he was suggesting two ideas: first, that all the past geological changes on the globe had been brought about by the slow agency of forces still in operation, and second, that the earth exhibited a continuous repetition of geological cycles—elevation and denudation following each other in endless succession. In Hutton's work, however, these ideas were not expressed in a completely rigorous or consistent fashion; for example, he was a catastrophist of sorts and also believed in certain gradual modifications of the earth's surface. So it was left to Charles Lyell to present the most systematic expression of uniformitarianism in his 1830 *Principles of Geology*. Its subtitle neatly encapsulates the thesis: "An Attempt to Explain the Former Changes of the Earth's Surface by Reference to Causes Now in Operation." Lyell believed that the course of nature had been uniform from the earliest ages and that the same sorts of causes now in action had produced former changes in the earth's surface. Pondering Lyell's systematization of the principle "the present is the key to the past," it becomes clear that there are two logically quite separate ideas associated with uniformitarianism that need to be scrutinized.

---

12. The following sources are indispensable to understanding uniformitarianism: R. Hooykaas, "The Parallel between the History of the Earth and the History of the Animal World," *Archives Internationales d'Histoire des Sciences* 10 (1957): 1-18; Walter F. Cannon, "The Uniformitarian-Catastrophist Debate," *Isis* 51 (1960): 38-55; R. Hooykaas, *Natural Law and Divine Miracle* (Leiden: E. J. Brill, 1959); Stephen Jay Gould, "Is Uniformitarianism Necessary?" *American Journal of Science* 263 (1965): 223-28; R. Hooykaas, "Geological Uniformitarianism and Evolution," *Archives Internationales d'Histoire des Sciences* 19 (1966): 3-19; George Gaylord Simpson, "Uniformitarianism: An Inquiry into Principle, Theory, and Method in Geohistory and Biohistory," in *Philosophy of Geohistory*, ed. Claude C. Albritton (Stroudbury, Pa.: Dowden, Hutchinson & Ross, 1975), pp. 256-309.

The first is what is sometimes called "methodological uniformitarianism" or "actualism." This is the proposition that natural laws do not change and that those now operating are sufficient to explain the geological history of the planet. By itself there was nothing in this formula antagonistic to catastrophist geology; in fact, many catastrophists adopted it as a principle of proper scientific procedure. For example, the fact that the earth is cooling down in accordance with unchanging natural laws does nothing to rule out the possibility of sudden convulsions, cataclysms, or even changes in the intensity of geological forces—in other words, catastrophes. Or again, the constant erosive pressure of a river in its bed may quite suddenly result in its bursting through its banks and flooding a surrounding plain. A whole series of catastrophes in geology could well be the result of uniformitarian forces. At this point, then, there was no necessary contradiction between uniformitarianism and catastrophism. This particular position was adopted by such figures as Elie de Beaumont, von Buch, Frapolli, and Coneybeare.

The second theme in the Hutton-Lyell formula is what can be called "substantive uniformitarianism"—the belief that during the history of the earth, the intensities and rates of natural processes and the material conditions have remained uniform. In a letter to Murchison in 1829, for example, Lyell insisted that causes "never acted with different degrees of energy from that which they now exert."[13] In essence, therefore, this version of uniformitarianism is not a method for research but a system of geological history. It is, moreover, an ahistorical model, or, as later terminology has it, a dynamic steady state theory. As a proposed description of past geological processes, it has not stood the test of new data. Geologists have long acknowledged that there is good evidence to believe that geological forces have not always operated in the same way or at their present rate or intensity.

The ultimate inadequacy of substantive uniformitarianism, however, must not deflect us from the main point in question: What were the implications of uniformitarianism for evolution theory? Lyell deemed Darwin's hypothesis wholly unsupported by geological evidence. The reason is not difficult to see. Lyell maintained that there was a direct parallel between the history of the earth and the history of life on earth. So he held that if the former remained ultimately unchanged, by definition the latter must have also. Accordingly, when Huxley said that "consistent uniformitarianism postulates evolution as much in the organic as in the inorganic world," this could be the case only if uniformitarianism was *in*consistent. Actually, the catastrophism propounded by the geologist Coneybeare was far more compatible with evolution. His was a historicist

---

13. Lyell, *Life, Letters and Journals of Sir Charles Lyell, Bart.*, vol. 2 (London: John Murray, 1881), p. 234.

model postulating a time scale of almost any length short of infinity and, more important, unidirectional trends in earth history. If then the earth had undergone "successive development," and biological history mirrored geological history, a progression of organic forms is just precisely what one would expect to find in natural history. So it is no surprise that catastrophist geologists were of the opinion that the marks of each great revolution in the history of the earth were to be found in successive batches of new fossils in the paleontological record. Nor will it now come as a surprise that while Darwin had learned his method of studying nature from Lyell's uniformitarianism, when he came to cite geological evidence for his theory it was the progressivist paleontologists of the catastrophist school (Buckland, Sedgwick, Miller, Agassiz, de Beaumont) to whom he turned.

These reflections help, I think, to challenge two quite different sorts of assumptions about the nature of geological uniformitarianism. First, it surely demonstrates that those who sought (and still seek) to demolish the evolutionary edifice by invalidating uniformitarianism and reinstating catastrophism were tilting at windmills. On the one hand, substantive uniformitarianism and biological evolution never were easy bedfellows. On the other hand, the progressivist temper of nineteenth-century catastrophism made it far more susceptible to evolutionary interpretations. At the same time, the genuinely scientific motivation of much catastrophist geology shows how shallow have been those histories identifying its supporters with religious prejudice or scientific conservatism. Neither in principle nor in practice was there any direct correlation between Christian geologists and catastrophist geology. If there were those who found in it reinforcement for their ideas of a biblical flood, it does not of necessity mean that they read the history of the earth through Mosaic spectacles. And of course the way in which geological and biological theory interfaced during the period was vastly more complex than many pro- and anti-evolution propagandists would lead us to believe.

I do not want to pursue this particular question further here. I believe it important instead to try to ascertain what it was in the structure of Darwin's theory that challenged contemporary theological conceptions. In my view, the doctrine of Scripture was not the crucial issue. Certainly some lost sleep over this question, but as I have already shown, conservatives had already developed strategies for accommodating their understanding of the Genesis narrative to the long-earth assumptions of geology. The assault came instead on the philosophical front. It sprang from Darwin's challenge to the Victorian understanding of the character of the universe and of "man's place in the natural order." These, I feel sure, arose from the rather specific way that Darwin conceptualized his theory. So we will now turn to the logical character of Darwin's theory as a prelude to identifying the main theological challenge that it posed.

DARWIN'S MERE METAPHOR

Darwin's theory of natural selection was a grand biological metaphor. In order to understand the metaphorical character of the scheme fully, however, I want to digress temporarily to look at the nature of scientific understanding in general and scientific model-building in particular.

One of the chief tools that scientists use in research is the theoretical model. In their endeavor to come to grips with some aspect of reality hitherto unexplained, researchers look around for some broadly similar process that they do understand, and then try to interpret the problem under investigation in the light of this information. They construct a sort of picture to represent what they understand to be the nature of the processes at work, and then, following the normal procedures of scientific analysis, they test the model against the real world to determine how successful it is. Basically they use, we could say, an analogy or a metaphor. And this metaphor becomes a kind of screen or lens through which the subject is viewed; some aspects are ignored while others are emphasized or organized in specific ways.[14] A good example of this is the model of the atom as a miniature orbital system: the subatomic particles, it is conjectured, behave *as if* they are a tiny orbital system. Now, it is because of this comparative process underlying scientific thinking, that some philosophers of science have argued that science is erected on metaphors—on systematically developed metaphors. They claim that the use of metaphors is inevitable and therefore quite fundamental to the scientific enterprise; it is not a question of whether or not to use metaphors but rather whether the metaphor in question has explanatory value.

Clearly scientists do resort to metaphorical thinking in their creation of theoretical models, and clearly good metaphors do have very rich explanatory power. But they also have some drawbacks. Perhaps the greatest danger is that scientists can forget that their models are only *representations* of reality, not reality itself. Take the metaphor "the human being is a machine," for instance. Doubtless there are many ways in which human beings behave like very sophisticated machines; their brains, some tell us, work in many respects like a computer; the nervous system can be studied in cybernetic terms; their genetic makeup is often depicted in the language of engineering technology. But it must not be

---

14. For a philosophical introduction to the use of metaphor in science, see Max Black's *Models and Metaphors: Studies in Language and Philosophy* (Ithaca, N.Y.: Cornell University Press, 1962); Mary B. Hesse's *Models and Analogies in Science* (Notre Dame, Ind.: University of Notre Dame Press, 1966); and W. H. Leatherdale's *The Role of Analogy, Model and Metaphor in Science* (Amsterdam: North Holland Publishing Company, 1973).

forgotten that these are only pictures, and that people are not merely machines. This point is brought out well by C. M. Turbayne when he notes that the use of a metaphor involves the pretence that something is the case when, literally speaking, it is not—a pretence that is not infrequently dropped either by those who have developed the metaphor or their followers:

> There is a difference between using a metaphor and taking it literally, between using a model and mistaking it for the thing modelled. The one is to make believe that something is the case; the other is to believe that it is. The one is to use a disguise or a mask for illustrative or explanatory purposes; the other is to mistake the mask for the face. . . . After the disguise or mask has been worn for a considerable time it tends to blend with the face, and it becomes extremely difficult to "see through" it. . . . It is not necessarily a confusion to treat items belonging to one sort in the idioms appropriate to another. . . . On the other hand it is a confusion to present the items of one sort in the idioms of another—without awareness. . . . It is to mistake, for example, the theory for the fact, the procedure for the process, the myth for history, the model for the thing, and the metaphor for the face of literal truth.[15]

When we turn to Darwin's theory, it is not at all surprising to find both the strengths and weaknesses of metaphorical thinking close at hand. A moment's reflection on Robert Young's pertinent question "Does Nature select?" suggests that there is a metaphor hiding somewhere in the idea of natural selection.[16] The basic strategy Darwin adopted for unraveling the species question was, as I have said, to show that species are ephemeral rather than permanent. As we have seen, his lifelong study of pigeon breeding convinced him that new variations could easily be produced under the control of the breeder. Here was his metaphor. Darwin looked at nature *as if* it were a breeder; in other words, he developed an analogy between the breeder's selective activity and natural selection. The metaphor certainly provided a very potent model for interpreting population change, and so long as Darwin could remember that he was comparing an *artificial* process with a *natural* one (thereby risking reading an anthropomorphic element into a natural phenomenon), it had great explanatory power. Clearly there was a tension in the metaphor—as indeed there always is in scientific models. But Darwin was alert to it and sought to forestall criticism with the following:

---

15. Turbayne, *The Myth of Metaphor* (New Haven: Yale University Press, 1970), pp. 3-4.
16. See Young, "Darwin's Metaphor: Does Nature Select?" *The Monist* 55 (1971): 442-503.

It has been said that I speak of natural selection as an active power or Deity; but who objects to an author speaking of the attraction of gravity as ruling the movements of the planets? Every one knows what is meant and is implied by such metaphorical expressions; and they are almost necessary for brevity. So again it is difficult to avoid personifying the word Nature; but I mean by Nature, only the aggregate action and product of many natural laws, and by laws the sequence of events as ascertained by us. With a little familiarity such superficial objections will be forgotten.[17]

But despite this disclaimer, Darwin himself soon began to slip away from the metaphorical basis of the model, absolutizing the analogy. It soon becomes clear that Darwin simply transferred the behavior of Paley's God to Nature and its laws. Writing to his American confidant Asa Gray, for example, he affirmed that "I think it can be shown that there is such an unerring power at work in *Natural Selection* (the title of my book), which selects exclusively for the good of each organic being."[18] On many occasions, the *Origin* displays rank anthropomorphism, as the following extracts indicate.

> We have seen that man by selection can certainly produce great results, and can adapt organic beings to his own uses through the accumulation of slight but useful variations given to him by the hand of Nature. But Natural Selection, as we shall hereafter see, is a power incessantly ready for action, and is as immeasurably superior to man's feeble efforts, as the works of Nature are to those of Art.[19]

> It may be said that natural selection is daily and hourly scrutinising, throughout the world, every variation, even the slightest; rejecting that which is bad, preserving and adding up all that is good; silently and insensibly working, whenever and wherever opportunity offers, at the improvement of each organic being in relation to its organic and inorganic conditions of life.[20]

---

17. Darwin, *"The Origin of Species" by Charles Darwin: A Variorum Text*, ed. Morse Peckham (Philadelphia: University of Pennsylvania Press, 1959), p. 165. See also the discussion in James A. Secord's essay "Nature's Fancy: Charles Darwin and the Breeding of Pigeons," *Isis* 72 (1981): 163-86.

18. Darwin, in *The Life and Letters of Charles Darwin*, vol. 2, ed. Francis Darwin (London: John Murray, 1887), p. 125.

19. *The Origin* (Peckham edition), p. 145.

20. *The Origin* (Peckham edition), pp. 168-69. This is the rendering of the first edition; it is significant that in the second edition he modified it to read, "It may metaphorically be said that natural selection. . . ."

THE THEOLOGICAL THREAT

We have now seen that if Darwin's metaphor was both rich and arresting, it also incorporated some conflicting ideas. Plainly Darwin had turned Paley on his head. All the highly specialized and coordinated adaptations that Paley itemized as indicative of design were explained by Darwin in a plain, causal, naturalistic way. Natural selection offered a thoroughly nonteleological means of explaining natural history, a means of explaining organic evolution that needed no recourse to the idea of design or designer. Indeed, there were those who saw natural theology and natural selection as the two great competing philosophies of biological explanation. Patrick Geddes, in his article on biology in *Chambers's Encyclopaedia*, for example, noted the "substitution of Darwin for Paley" and confirmed that "the place vacated by theological and metaphysical explanation has simply been occupied by that suggested to Darwin and Wallace by Malthus in terms of the struggle for existence."[21]

Not surprisingly, *this* is what many Christians found so objectionable in Darwinism: it subverted design. But, as we shall see when we consider the reaction of evangelical scientists and theologians, it became a very common strategy among Christians to reconstruc natural theology and natural selection in such a way as to be able to invoke an evolutionary teleology—a strategy far more typical than outright rejection of the entire theory of evolution.

In any event, we should keep in mind the point that Darwin clearly shared many of the underlying insights of natural theology. He repeatedly noted that there were few books he admired more than Paley's *Natural Theology*. It was simply the nature of Darwin's metaphor that led him almost inevitably to fall back into vocabulary that was thoroughly anthropomorphic, purposive, teleological—and it was this element in his depiction of Nature (with a capital "N") that enabled evolution to be so readily elevated to mythological status. In fact, some evolutionists have come to regard natural selection as a fully creative agency comparable to poetic, musical, or indeed divine creativity.

Although we do not need to subject these latter claims to critical scrutiny at this point, it is nevertheless clear that Darwin did not destroy either the sense of design in the world or the argument from design. Certainly he undermined the idea of God as a divine Watchmaker, and at least for a time this created something of a fuss, for Paley had by then become one of the chief cornerstones in the evangelical conception of the created order. But there were other ways than Paley's—notably Owen's idealist alternative—that were better suited to cope with the encounter. And so the design argument came to be more commonly expressed in

---

21. Geddes, in vol. 2 of *Chambers's Encyclopaedia* (London and Edinburgh: W. & R. Chambers, 1925), p. 164.

holistic than utilitarian forms, in organic rather than mechanistic terms. God was portrayed as guiding the whole evolutionary process rather than as creating each adaptation, as having made the world in such a way as to "make it make itself," and as following a transcendent archetypal plan. It is interesting to find those with such different metaphysical convictions as T. H. Huxley and Asa Gray confirming this. Huxley stated that "the theological equivalent of the scientific conception of order is Providence," while Gray confessed to de Candolle that his congratulation to Darwin for his "striking contributions to teleology" contained "a vein of petite malice, from my knowing that he rejects the idea of design, while all the while he is bringing out the neatest illustrations of it."[22]

Darwin's challenge to the Paleyan idea of design engendered some theological anxiety among Christians, but his suggestion that human beings and apes must have had a common ancestor aroused more popular controversy. Many believed that this assertion dislodged mankind from the privileged position of being created in the very image of God. At least initially there were many who feared that human dignity would be degraded if it were conceded that the human race had come from apes rather than from the hand of God. The "monkey-to-man" theory was parodied left, right, and center. The cartoonists portrayed Darwin himself with flowing beard or monkey tail. When the dust finally settled, however, evangelical Christians had formulated a variety of tactics for coping with even this assault. Some accepted an evolutionary account of animal development but ruled out human evolution. Others probed the biblical data and decided that the idea of the image of God did not refer to the human bodily form, which meant that there need be no problem with accepting an evolutionary history for the human body. The accepted duality of body and soul provided some with a useful anthropological vehicle for integrating theological and biological conceptions of humanity. Still others argued for the possibility of the existence of human beings before Adam—"Pre-adamites" as they were called—and suggested that the biblical data might only deal with Hebrew ancestry. There was no consensus but rather a variety of proposals put forward by individuals of impeccable theological orthodoxy as judged by the standards of their own time. All in all there was something of a realization that being descended from anthropoid forebears was no less dignified than being made from the dirt of the ground.

We should also note that the issue of historical continuity between

---

22. See Loren Eiseley, *Darwin's Century* (New York: Anchor Books, 1961); and Roger Chapman, "Charles Darwin: The Scientist and His Science," in *Charles Darwin, 1809-1882*, pp. 101-30. The conceptual resonances between natural theology and natural selection are scrutinized by John Hedley Brooke in "The Relations between Darwin's Science and His Religion," in *Darwinism and Divinity*, ed. John Durant (Oxford: Blackwell, 1985), pp. 40-75.

CHARLES DARWIN, as seen by a cartoonist of the time, from *Hornet*, 22 March 1871. Reprinted with permission of Guildhall Library, City of London

human beings and animals was not solely a problem for evangelical Christians. Many others balked at linking the history of Victorian gentlemen with that of apes and ants. A. R. Wallace, for instance, insisted that when human beings emerged, natural selection ceased to operate on them and was overtaken by intellectual selection—a radical disjunction in the process. Huxley asserted that human ethics consisted in society working against the natural evolutionary process, not mirroring it. Later emergent evolutionists were to insist that the advent of human beings initiated a quite different order of evolutionary development.

My point, once again, is not to assess the validity of any of these competing options but merely to show that in the debate over evolution, evangelicals were more concerned with the issues of design in the world and human biological history than with such matters as the age of the earth or the nature of scriptural inspiration. Moreover, these problems were easily resolved by many evangelical scientists and theologians in the period as a variety of harmonizing models became available.

All this is not to deny that there were genuine crises of faith in the Victorian era. But these, as a number of historians of science have shown us, were part of a larger debate concerning the nature and structure of society that affected Christians as much as anyone else.[23] In the half century from 1830 to 1880, the whole fabric of the Victorian creed underwent dramatic transformations. Having gone through an economic cycle of overproduction, recession, unemployment, and urban starvation, many began to have serious doubts about the viability of the Victorian social structure. Revolution was in the air. Doctrines championed by established religious dignitaries who upheld the status quo were subjected to the radical critiques of self-taught working-class intellectuals. Radical politics and irreligion tended to go hand in hand. One expression of this shift to a new rationale for social practice was the struggle for cultural power between the votaries of the ecclesiastical establishment and the priests of the new science. Many shifted from dependence on the church to dependence on science as an institution to legitimize social values. And yet this transfer contained profound continuities as well. Both regarded nature as bound by eternal laws and both sought solutions, whether soteriological or material, to the manifest evils in the world.

The Darwinian episode, then, was only one element in an ongoing *cultural* conflict during the middle decades of the nineteenth century—a "conflict" centered less on the minutiae of Darwin's theory than on the role science was to play in the future of human society. In this particular debate the lines of demarcation were often blurred both because many Christians regarded their engagement with the scientific enterprise as part of their "spiritual calling" and also because there were many scientific objections to Darwinism that led to the proposal of alternative evolutionary schemes. In light of this, I want to devote the final pages of this chapter to a reconsideration of the reception of the *Origin* by Darwin's scholarly critics.

---

23. See the excellent discussion by James R. Moore, "1859 and All That: Remaking the Story of Evolution-and-Religion," in *Charles Darwin, 1809-1882*, pp. 167-94.

SCIENTIFIC RESPONSES AND ALTERNATIVES

It would be quite wrong to imagine that the only objection to Darwin's theory when it was first published came from religious quarters. From the standpoint of the science of the day, there were in fact a number of major problems with Darwinian evolution.[24] One of the earliest criticisms was put forward by Fleeming Jenkin, a Scottish mathematician and engineer, in a paper published in the *North British Review* in 1867. He focused on the question of inheritance. In the era before Mendelian genetics, heredity was conventionally regarded as entailing the blending of the characteristics of both parents in their offspring. The idea was that the paternal and maternal elements were fused together in an offspring to produce features midway between the two. Given this theory, Jenkin showed that if one parent possessed a feature that particularly fitted it to its environment, it would eventually be lost within a very few generations by being swamped by or blended into the surrounding population. Hence, he concluded, individual variations could never contribute to the emergence of a new species. Darwin felt the force of this criticism and openly admitted it. In response, he reemphasized the importance of geographical isolation in the formation of new species, and over time he moved progressively further toward adopting the Lamarckian view (which we will presently discuss). A satisfactory resolution of this problem had to await the coming of the Mendelian model, however.

Jenkin was involved with another telling criticism of Darwinism, this time in association with William Thomson, Lord Kelvin. On the basis of their physical computations estimating the age of the earth (using among other things measurements of terrestrial heat loss), they argued that the amount of geological time needed for the operation of the natural selection mechanism simply was not available. Darwin keenly felt the power of this assault and confessed that it was probably one of the gravest criticisms as yet advanced against his theory. Huxley sensed these hostile currents too, and rather lamely urged that if the geological clock was wrong, all naturalists had to do was modify their notion of the rapidity of change. The answer, of course, was not as simple as that. Thomson's physics remained a hindrance for the nearly fifty years that it continued to provide the chronology of British geology.

Another problem was pressed by the English anatomist and zoologist St. George Mivart. In his *Genesis of Species* (1871), Mivart, a Catholic, agreed that evolution of organic forms had taken place, that the human body had evolved from lower species, and that natural selection did operate during the process, but he rejected the contention that natural

---

24. Criticisms of Darwin's position are discussed in full by Peter J. Vorzimmer in *Charles Darwin: The Years of Controversy* (London: University of London Press, 1972).

selection could in itself provide a complete explanation of evolutionary history. He pointed to many cases in which he said natural selection had not played any role at all. Others echoed this view, saying that even if natural selection could explain the survival of a feature once it had arisen, it was nonetheless powerless to account for the origin of the feature in the first instance. They also wondered about the evolution of apparently useless features. If, as Darwin taught, natural selection worked on a strict principle of utility, how could organs with no apparent value have developed and survived? Mivart spoke of an internal progressive force, directly guided by God, that served as the main agent in producing new variations. Others were more inclined to propose that changes in organic form resulted from a conscious response on the part of creatures to their environmental stimuli.

Darwin was also embarrassed by gaps in the fossil record, which seemed to call his essentially gradualist theory into question. He frankly admitted the lack of intermediate fossil forms to date, but hoped that future work would clarify the problem. He also had difficulty explaining the degeneration or atrophy of organs, particularly where their reduction was almost complete. All of these problems pushed him toward his eventual reluctant espousal of Lamarckism.

Besides these, there were other scientific difficulties with Darwin's theory, though we need pursue the matter no further here. My reason for citing the few I have is not to criticize Darwin's formula but rather to how that there were genuinely scholarly hesitations about the *Origin* when it was initially introduced. It is naive to assume that all opposition to it was either prejudicial or obscurantist. I also want to emphasize that opposition to Darwinian natural selection was not equivalent to a rejection of evolution. Many of Darwin's most thoughtful opponents actually did embrace some version of evolutionary theory.[25] And we should keep in mind the fact that Darwin was often the first to admit the validity of his critics' points. He fairly reviewed their misgivings in the successive editions of his book and, like every other scientist, struggled with the problem of structuring his theory in the most coherent way possible. In the end, as I have said, he turned to a Lamarckian version of evolutionary theory. And since this interpretation enjoyed a widespread resurgence particularly in the United States, I want briefly to summarize the viewpoint.

Jean Baptiste de Lamarck had put forward his own theory of evolution in the year Darwin was born, but his *Philosophie Zoologique* of 1809 and his later works, which contained revolutionary transformist doctrines, were wholeheartedly repudiated by the authoritative Georges Cuvier and fell into disrepute. Even Chambers's 1844 *Vestiges of the Natu-*

---

25. On this, see Peter J. Bowler, *The Eclipse of Darwinism: Anti-Darwinian Evolution Theories in the Decades around 1900* (Baltimore: The Johns Hopkins University Press, 1983).

ral History of Creation, designed to publicize the Lamarckian perspective
for English-speaking audiences, did little more than add fuel to the fires
of opposition to his mentor. Lamarck's time had not yet come. Nevertheless, his writings contained two elements that would later achieve
renewed prominence. The first was the idea that an innate life force
impelled evolutionary history ever onward and upward, causing a progressive increase in organic complexity. There was a plainly idealist,
antimaterialist strain in the theory in that it assumed an ideal chain of
being linking the simplest organisms to the most complex, and emphasized the centrality of a transcendent force in the process. Second,
Lamarck suggested that by the exercise of will, organisms could consciously and directly adapt themselves to their surroundings and pass the
modification on to offspring. This doctrine came to be known as "the
inheritance of acquired characteristics."

Lamarck's vision was preserved in the work of dedicated disciples
like Geoffroy St. Hilaire, but it received new life in the United States,
where variations of it were promoted under the label "Neo-
Lamarckism." Proponents did not reject Darwinian natural selection *in
toto*; they merely supplemented it with a Lamarckian veneer. The result
was a distinctive American Neo-Lamarckian school of biology fashioned
under the influence of Hyatt (of the Boston Society of Natural History),
Packard (professor of zoology and geology at Brown), and Cope (a paleontologist working in Pennsylvania). A number of factors had impelled
them in the direction of Lamarck. For one thing, his theory gave a dynamic impulse to the ideal chain of being—something lacking in the theory
promoted by their Harvard mentor Louis Agassiz, to whose views we will
presently turn. Lamarckism allowed them to retain much of what
Agassiz had taught and yet adopt evolution. Lamarckism also seemed to
answer more than satisfactorily many of the very worst obstacles Darwin
faced. Since it involved a direct, conscious response to the environment, it
allowed for a far more rapid evolutionary tempo and hence a smaller
amount of geological time in which to accommodate organic evolution. It
also resolved the problem of how variations actually arise. And since it
suggested that organic responses to environmental stimuli can occur
among many members of a population at the same time, it answered the
objections about swamping raised by pre-Mendelian genetics. Lamarckism could also explain the retrogression and loss of organs more easily: it
simply attributed atrophy to disuse. On many fronts then, it seemed a
superior theory. The only difficulty was that no one was able to point to a
single undisputed case of the inheritance of an acquired character.

Biological Lamarckism, of course, has not stood the test of time. But
it is important here not just because it was widespread in the English-
speaking world (largely through the efforts of Herbert Spencer) but also
because it served to reduce tensions between religion and evolution. It
was obviously more easily reconciled than orthodox Darwinism with

providential interpretations, inasmuch as the idea of an intrinsic life force impelling evolution along a foreordained path is plainly teleological. So the metaphysics of the Lamarckians became almost as conspicuous as their science and, as we shall see, provided at least some Christians with an evolutionary theory that could actively sustain their theological convictions.

Lamarckian evolution also had social ramifications that made it rather appealing to many. "Social Darwinism" was often enough used to "scientifically" justify unrestrained economic competition and policies of noninvolvement, while its Lamarckian counterpart was more often used in arguments promoting direct intervention in the affairs of society.[26] The Lamarckians felt that a laissez-faire approach to social issues was tantamount to a denial of human creativity and the very principle of evolutionary development. Convinced that they could change the future course of social evolution, they supported policies for improving social conditions. They threw their weight behind programs for educational reform, for example, in the hope that its value would accumulate in the society generation by generation. They also lent their support to various environmental movements in the belief that these too would improve the long-term condition of humanity. And some advocates felt that Darwin's talk of struggle and competition had obscured the evolutionary significance of group solidarity and cooperation both in the organic and social spheres. Of course there were conflicts and confusions. They often could not decide, for example, whether in these cases inheritance was physical (through biological processes) or cultural (through social institutions).

Here again, I think it needs to be said, the complexity of the ways in which the study of society could be "biologized" reveals how shallow so many assaults on the social application of evolution have been. There was no direct relationship between evolutionary biology and nasty social practices. On one controversial topic after another—race, poverty, industrial competition, eugenics, heritable disease, criminality, insanity—evolutionists took widely differing stands. And, as I will presently show, evangelicals had as many scientific things to say about these issues as anyone else.

REFLECTIONS ON A REVOLUTION

It is now time to pause and reassess the significance of the Darwinian impact. The salient points are readily apparent. Charles Darwin proposed a bold new theory called "natural selection" for explaining how

---

26. For more on this, see Greta Jones's *Social Darwinism in English Thought: The Interaction between Biological and Social Theory* (Sussex: Harvester Press, 1980); and R. C. Bannister, *Social Darwinism: Science and Myth in Anglo-American Social Thought* (Philadelphia: Temple University Press, 1979).

evolutionary change might take place. With it he was able to marshall an impressive array of empirical data into a coherent framework of interpretation. In the marketplace of ideas he had thrown down a real challenge. But a challenge is not a conflict, and a conflict is not a conquest. On the scientific front many subjected Darwin's challenge to painstaking critical scrutiny. Some readily aligned themselves with Darwin. Others had scholarly reservations about his proposals and constructed several alternative evolutionary schemes. In the religious world, Darwin's assault on the traditional understanding of design and on the special status of human beings caused some headaches, but when the initial fuss died down and the theory was assessed more calmly, it soon became clear that there were many ways of pouring oil on troubled water.

Several key points emerge, then, as we reflect on the impact of the Darwinian revolution. The "conflict" between science and religion was more a matter of the subsequent reinterpretation of the events than it was the actual experience of very many participants. Dissent over Darwinism was not the same as disquiet about evolution. The complexities of the period forbid simple stereotypes of heroes and villains. And finally, whatever the genuine drawbacks in Darwin's new theory, most came to feel that some sort of evolutionary perspective made sense. So let us now turn to those evangelical Christians working in science at the time to find out how they responded to the challenges of the so-called evolution revolution.

CHAPTER 3

SERVANTS OF SCIENCE AND SCRIPTURE

For the American scientific community the fat was in the fire even before Darwin's book first appeared. The joint Darwin-Wallace communication to the Linnean Society of London may scarcely have caused a stir among the British gentlemen of science, but three thousand miles away at the American Academy of Arts and Sciences, the currents were deeply felt as Asa Gray and Louis Agassiz first opened the accounts in a confrontation that was to last for more than a decade. The conceptual alignments of these early debates are particularly instructive. They are almost the exact antithesis of what anyone nourished on creationist literature would be led to expect, and for this reason alone the Agassiz-Gray encounter seems a logical place to begin.

AGASSIZ AND GRAY: THE DYNAMICS OF A DEBATE

Swiss by birth, German by aspiration, and American by adoption, Louis Agassiz became a legend in his own lifetime.[1] He was born in Switzerland in 1807 and grew up in an intellectual tradition boasting the names of Zwingli, Rousseau, and Pestalozzi. But like many other young intellectuals of his generation, Agassiz felt drawn to the great German centers of learning. So in the late 1820s he left home for the University of Heidelberg. There he fell in with Alexander Braun and Karl Schimper, who initiated him into the scientific aspects of Goethe's nature philosophy. The vitality represented in this speculative movement deeply impressed the young Agassiz and left him with a lifelong admiration for the

---

1. The authoritative biography of Agassiz is Edward Lurie's *Louis Agassiz: A Life in Science* (Chicago: University of Chicago Press, 1960). See also Bert James Lowenberg's essay "The Reaction of American Scientists to Darwinism," *American Historical Review* 38 (1932-33): 687-701.

brilliance of the German tradition. This idealist philosophy had a special influence on him particularly as it impinged on his academic specialty—paleontology.

Agassiz's study of fossil remains convinced him that there was a direct link between the structure of animals that had lived in the past and those still alive. This induced in him a profound, almost mystic sense of the unity of the natural world. There seemed to be an ideal plan knitting the entire system of nature into a coherent whole. These views were reinforced when, during the summer of 1827, Agassiz took up the writings of Lorenz Oken and learned of his arguments that a common structural plan underlay all animal features and that each individual creature aspired to the fulfillment of its own ideal type.

The influence of this tradition on Agassiz was both deep and lasting. All his life he insisted that ancient and modern species were "permanent representations of a divine idea" and bore no genetic relationship to each other. The chain of being, in other words, was linked by common structures, not by common descent. Agassiz, the son of a Protestant divine, found it easy to infuse German idealism with religious sentiments. The Absolute Being, as he styled it, was present in all nature. Natural history, therefore, was simply the study of the way in which individual life forms approximated the pattern stamped upon them by the Creator. His religion was certainly not evangelical but rather a synthetic blend of theism and romantic idealism. Not surprisingly, he later found the Unitarianism of Harvard most congenial. It allowed him all the latitude he needed in scientific inquiry and provided a comfortable system of beliefs in which to nourish his pluralistic philosophy.

Agassiz's natural history, however, was not purely metaphysical. In 1827 he enrolled with Alexander Braun in the newly founded University of Munich. Here, working with Döllinger, he learned the scientist's craft. Patient, painstaking, detailed empirical study was the stuff that science was made of. His later association with Georges Cuvier further drove the lesson home. Their influence soon made him impatient with the excesses of the speculative natural history he had embraced in Heidelberg. But he was eventually able to tie these two diverse traditions—idealist and empiricist—together in such a way as to create his own distinctive school of natural history. It was to influence a whole generation of American naturalists. Exactitude and precision, theory and speculation all played their parts in Agassiz's science.

Between 1835 and 1845 Agassiz carried out his most original scientific research while a professor at Neuchâtel Academy. His studies on the glacial formations in Switzerland and then in Central Europe and England convinced him that there had once been a continental Ice Age. It was a brilliant theory and provided the key to understanding many of the geographical patterns of plant and animal life. But for Agassiz the theory had cosmic implications. The glacial period, he believed, was a spectacular demonstration of divine power in causing catastrophes. It further substantiated his belief in the fixity of species, for an ice age provided a permanent physical barrier between the species of the past and those of the present. Meanwhile Agassiz's scientific reputation continued to flourish. He gathered around him at Neuchâtel an enthusiastic group of young researchers including Arnold Guyot. Then in 1846 Agassiz crossed the Atlantic to lecture at the Lowell Institute. Here and elsewhere in the United States his lectures were a resounding success. America was as enthusiastic about Agassiz as he was about it. To the Americans, Agassiz represented the brilliant heights of European culture; he had captured their imaginations and soon enjoyed something of the public renown that Humboldt had received in Europe. To Agassiz, America represented the future with all its limitless possibilities. When he was offered a Harvard professorship in 1848, he therefore decided to make his home in the New World.

Both philosophically and scientifically, Agassiz was quite unprepared for Darwin's thunderbolt in 1859. The idea of the transmutation of species was totally contrary to his tenacious belief in the fixity of species. Nor was his doctrine of archetypal plans any more compatible with Darwin's theory, though several of his students reinterpreted it in evolutionary terms. It was, then, almost inevitable that Agassiz would become the leading opponent of Darwin not just in America but in the world. And he did not hesitate to use the weight of his public position to try to suppress the theory of evolution. However, many of those who had been his most devoted supporters ten years earlier felt that their hero was now less able. Public performance, administrative endeavor, and the sheer donkey work involved in building up the Museum of Comparative Zoology had kept him from genuine research. Further, some now suspected that his intransigence sprang more from a closed mind than from scholarly considerations.

Since Agassiz is often lauded as a sort of precursor of "creation science," it is worth pausing briefly to mention just how special his doctrine of special creation really was. Quite simply, he believed that every race of mankind had been specifically created by God for particular geographical zones. This view was so distasteful to Charles Lyell that he confessed that Agassiz had driven him far into the Darwin camp. "For when he attributed the origin of every race of man to an independent starting point, or act of creation," Lyell confessed, ". . . I could not help thinking that Lamarck must be right."[2] For Agassiz himself, this doctrine had direct ideological implications. On the one hand, it could be used as a scientific defense for the institution of slavery. On the other, Agassiz used

---

2. Lyell, in *Life, Letters and Journals of Sir Charles Lyell, Bart.*, vol. 2, ed. K. M. Lyell (London: John Murray, 1881), p. 331.

it to oppose interracial marriage vigorously. Miscegenation, he said, was as offensive a sin against nature as incest was against civilized society.[3] This deep visceral revulsion against the black race in particular dated from the time of his first visit to the United States, when he wrote to his wife expressing his profound distaste for personal contacts with blacks even in restaurants. He pursued the theme, moreover, in the pages of the *Christian Examiner*, the leading Boston Unitarian journal, which reflected the liberal theology of Harvard and the religious culture of New England. There he argued for at least a dozen separate creations and made it clear that he could not accept a literal interpretation of the biblical record.

I do not say these things to defame Agassiz's character. Scientific racism was all too common in the America of his day. But his statements do throw into significant relief the creationist claim that the theory of evolution bred a racist spirit. In fact creationism could, and often did, foster racist sentiments. And as we shall see, Christians were often divided on the question of the physical unity of the human race and of the relative status of the different human types.

By 1858 one American naturalist had decided to take on the challenge of Agassiz. The setting was the American Academy of Arts and Sciences. The issue was the question of the transmutation of species. The assailant was the Harvard professor of botany Asa Gray. By the late 1850s Gray was the leading American botanist, enjoying a worldwide reputation, particularly in the field of botanical taxonomy.[4] He had begun his professional life as a medical doctor, and his early experience in that position with Dr. James Hadley had quickened his interests both in science and religion. During the period of his apprenticeship in Bridgewater, New York, he built up a collection of plants and made his first contacts with John Torrey, then America's top botanist. By the winter of 1831, Gray had had enough of medicine; early the following year he abandoned his practice.

For the next five years Gray held a number of part-time teaching posts and library positions. At the same time he vigorously pursued his botanical interests with Torrey, eventually collaborating with him in writing *Flora of North America*. Torrey's influence was profound. His firm Presbyterian faith deeply impressed Gray, and early in 1835 the young botanist turned in faith to the God who, as he put it, "is both able and willing to save all who come unto him." These words serve to indicate Gray's dissatisfaction with harshly predestinarian versions of the Re-

---

3. See Stephen Jay Gould, "Flaws in a Victorian Veil," *New Scientist*, 31 August 1978, pp. 632-33.
4. The standard work on Gray is A. Hunter Dupree's *Asa Gray* (Cambridge: Harvard University Press, 1959).

ASA GRAY. Reprinted with permission of the Herbarium Library, Royal Botanic Gardens, Kew

formed tradition, an aspect of his conversion experience that dominated his theological outlook from the start. He was attracted to a modified doctrinal Calvinism burnished with the reinterpretative impulses of New School Presbyterianism, though his convictions were thoroughly evangelical. He often stated that the Nicene Creed encapsulated the heart of his faith.

Gray's faith served to further his interest in science. Calvin's doctrine of the Christian calling merely confirmed his determination to devote himself to science. To study nature, he felt, was to probe the designs of God. As with Torrey, Gray's evangelical piety and scientific standards went hand in hand; he soon began to reflect the spiritual as well as the botanical interests and qualities of the older man. And he became busy on all fronts. In his botanical work with Torrey, he helped to accomplish the shift from the older Linnean system of classification to the natural system of Alphonse de Candolle. On the religious side, he spent busy Sundays teaching a class of black boys and deeply involving himself in the affairs of the church.

Over the next few years Gray took part in a number of projects: he was a member of the scientific corps of the United States Exploring Expedition, he spent a year traveling in Europe, and he continued his research with Torrey. Then in 1842 he was appointed to the Fisher professorship of natural history at Harvard. At the time Harvard was a stronghold of American Unitarianism, but Gray never hesitated to indicate his preference for evangelicalism. On his first Sunday he traveled out of Cambridge and into Boston to join with the Congregationalists at Park Street Church. His reputation as an orthodox Christian soon spread, and Edward Hitchcock writing to him in 1846 was pleased to tell him of the "very delightful season of special religious interest in our college."[5]

Gray's Christian orthodoxy had direct implications for his science. It made him suspicious of the German idealism he had flirted with in his earlier days. And it also made him a devotee of William Paley and the Bridgewater Treatises. In the extent to which he maintained a thoroughly empiricist approach to science and eschewed nature mysticism in the best Reformed fashion, Gray had far more in common with representatives of the British empirical tradition than with those in New England being swept by religious currents into Transcendentalism. Indeed, it was his uncompromising "scientific" approach to the study of nature that brought him to the attention of Charles Darwin. At this stage in the early 1850s, Gray was quite opposed to the idea of the transformation of species, as he had been since the first appearance of Chambers's *Vestiges* in 1844. But the fact that Darwin and Gray were both empiricists was a far stronger link between them than the belief in the constancy of species that Gray shared with Agassiz. So Darwin admitted Gray into a close circle of confidants and in 1857 discussed the theory of natural selection with him.

As Gray pursued his own research on American and Japanese botany, he came to see that Darwin's ideas about transmutation could help him explain the distribution of plant species. The genera of plants in

---

5. Hitchcock, in a letter to Asa Gray dated 23 March 1846 (Archive, Gray Herbarium Library, Harvard University).

North America and Eastern Asia, he came to believe, should no longer be regarded as separate creations but as the descendants of a common flora that glaciation had pushed southward. He announced his findings at the January 1859 meeting of the American Academy. It provided the occasion for a full-scale debate with Louis Agassiz, a debate that symbolized the confrontation between two entirely different systems of natural history, the idealist and the empirical. More than anything else, it was a watershed in the history of scientific method.

When Darwin's *Origin of Species* appeared toward the end of the same year, Gray set himself the task of making sure that Darwin would get a fair hearing in the New World. He certainly had his misgivings about elements in the book, but the doctrine of Scripture was not one. He had, after all, long accepted Lyell's geology and had accommodated his understanding of Genesis accordingly. Not that this accommodation involved any harmonization. He had already told his brother George that since the Bible was simply not a scientific textbook, there was no need for "reconciliation." But Gray also saw some positive moral value in the theory. From evangelicalism he had learned the moral worth of every member of the human race, and he did not hesitate to go against the opinions of his peers in expressing his distaste for slavery. Now from evolution he learned, in a sly stab at Agassiz, that "the very first step backwards makes the Negro and the Hottentot our blood-relations;—not that reason or Scripture objects to that though pride may."

On one major point of Darwin's theory, however, Gray demurred. It was on the question of design in the world. In keeping with his longstanding approval of Paleyan natural theology, Gray knew what he must do. He needed to rid Darwinism of its apparent materialism by showing that natural selection did not exclude design. In fact, he went beyond this to claim that Darwin's book actually elaborated evidences of purpose in one case after another. He saw it as a splendid, if unintended, contribution to natural theology.

Gray made these points in by far the most competent reviews of the *Origin* to appear in the United States. And he was not slow to point out that the Darwinian jigsaw had a vital piece missing. Natural selection, he said, could certainly determine which variations should survive, but "really, we no more know the reason why the progeny occasionally deviates from the parent than we do why it usually resembles it." Moreover, Gray confessed to his readers that he could not see the results of adaptation as the product of blind chance. The secret elixir that Darwin needed to give coherence to his theory was the action of the Creator. Gray repeated these arguments twice in Silliman's *Journal* for 1860, faced Agassiz and Bowen with them in public debate, and published a three-part essay in the *Atlantic Monthly* showing the compatibility of Paley and Darwin. Darwin himself was very pleased with the latter pieces and arranged at his own expense a separate printing of Gray's "Free Examination of Darwin's Treatise on the Origin of Species, and of American Reviewers." Across the top in Gothic script was printed the motto "Natural Selection Not Inconsistent With Natural Theology."

Eventually Darwin was to reject this harmonizing strategy because he came to believe that the design argument had received a fatal body blow from natural selection. There are, I think, good reasons for agreeing with Darwin as far as Paley's utilitarian version is concerned. In any event, Gray continued to defend design in the specifically Paleyan guise, and his efforts ultimately failed to carry the day. But the argument could be reformulated in ways that made it less open to Darwin's apparently fatal onslaught. Darwin himself insisted to Gray that he had never intended to write atheistically, but he did confess that he was less able than Gray to see evidence of design and beneficence on all sides. On the contrary, he was profoundly disturbed by the troubling amount of misery in the world. He could perhaps accept that the general laws of nature were designed, but to see every characteristic from the shape of his nose to his useless tonsils as specifically planned was just too much. Gray held fast to Paley's argument nonetheless, urging that Divine Wisdom could foresee the results of each development and thereby guide the natural selective processes. As I have said, Christians were soon to abandon this version in favor of a more holistic design located in the regularity of natural law, but Gray's stance as an evangelical shows both his fidelity to empirical science and his sense of where the pressure point between Christianity and Darwinism really was.

As Gray resisted the implicit reductionism of Darwin, so he opposed Spencer's inflation of evolutionary biology into a cosmic worldview. To strengthen his critique, Gray joined forces with the Harvard pragmatist philosopher Chauncey Wright. Wright was not a Christian himself, but he made a point of insisting that Darwin's hypothesis had no direct bearing whatsoever on religious, philosophical, or social matters. Together Gray and Wright opposed the fashionable synthesis of Darwin and Spencer and promoted a strictly scientific Darwinism. They felt a real need for underscoring the distinction between evolutionary biology and what they saw as the speculative morass of social evolutionism. They sensed the mythological power of Darwin's metaphor and were determined to oppose it.

In the post–Civil War period, Gray occasionally pushed out the odd anonymous article on Darwinism. Sometimes he chided the religious opponents of Darwin; sometimes he attacked the agnosticism of Huxley. But anonymous as the articles were, a young Congregationalist pastor in Andover, George Frederick Wright, thought he could sense a coherent message behind the scattered fragments. When he discovered that Gray was the author, he was delighted. And so began an allegiance that was to last until Gray's death in 1888.

AN EVANGELICAL ALLIANCE

George Frederick Wright was the product of enlightened Puritanism in its Congregationalist mold. Doctrinally evangelical, socially radical, and educationally progressive, Wright came to stand for the distinguished and intellectually sophisticated tradition of New England Calvinism.[6] Like four of the five other members of his family, Fred Wright attended Oberlin College in the late 1850s, when it was under the leadership of Charles G. Finney. The Oberlin emphases on personal faith, regeneration, humanitarianism, and abolitionism were distilled in Wright's own thinking, and he passionately devoted himself to these causes. When he graduated from the College in 1859, he immediately entered Oberlin's Theological Seminary to prepare for the ministry. His first charge on graduating took him and his young bride to Vermont in the early 1860s. While there he read the works of Darwin and Lyell, and under their influence he prepared his first scholarly article. It was a categorical defense of the inductive method of reasoning and set the style for his own future research. Meanwhile he spent his spare time geologizing about the foot of the Green Mountains and got interested in a subject that was to dominate much of his later work—glaciation.

In 1871 Wright accepted a call from the First Christian Church in Andover. During his first years there he pondered what bearing his work on glacial geology might have on such questions as the antiquity of the human race and the authority of the Bible. That his conclusions were staunchly evangelical will emerge as we pursue the details of his career. He had been in Andover only three years when he read Asa Gray's anonymous review of Hodge's *What Is Darwinism?* He was now deeply interested in the Darwinian controversies and soon found that the unnamed author had become his guide in matters of science and natural theology. When the two men eventually met, Wright encouraged Gray to gather the series together into a single publication. As he complained in a letter to Gray in June 1875, "the infidel class of Darwinian expositors have had the ear of the public entirely too much, and have needlessly added to the alarm of orthodox people."

Gray was a bit reluctant to embark on the job of updating articles,

---

6. See William James Morison, "George Frederick Wright: In Defense of Darwinism and Fundamentalism, 1838-1921," Ph.D. diss., Vanderbilt University, 1971. There is also a thorough review of Wright's contributions in James R. Moore's *The Post-Darwinian Controversies: A Study of the Protestant Struggle to Come to Terms with Darwin in Great Britain and America, 1870-1900* (Cambridge: Cambridge University Press, 1979), pp. 280-98. See also Michael McGiffert, "Christian Darwinism: The Partnership of Asa Gray and George Frederick Wright, 1874-1881," Ph.D. diss., Yale University, 1958. Ronald L. Numbers provides a new interpretation in his essay "From Christian Darwinist to Fundamentalist: The Strange Career of George Frederick Wright," forthcoming.

some of which were now fifteen years old. But Wright pressed him, and he hesitantly agreed to go to work. Gray wanted to make sure that the collection would be seen to display Christian theism and not some vague Spencerian Unknowable, so he introduced himself to his readers as "one who is scientifically, and in his own fashion, a Darwinian, philosophically a convinced theist, and religiously an acceptor of the 'creed commonly called the Nicene.'"[7] And just in case this would not do the trick, he turned to Wright for help in writing the last chapter, the only new essay in the volume. His aim, he told Wright, was simple. He intended to develop "a right *evolutionary teleology*" and present the argument for design from the exquisite adaptations so evident in evolutionary history. Wright was delighted to be asked, and he contributed suggestions concerning the wording of the chapter, entitled "Evolutionary Teleology." The resulting book, which appeared in 1876 under the title *Darwiniana*, received a chorus of praise in the religious press, particularly those publications under Congregational influence.

Over the next few years Gray and Wright continued to cooperate on various schemes. During the winter of 1879 they conferred regarding the preparation of Gray's forthcoming Yale lectures on natural science and religion. Wright meanwhile was establishing quite a reputation of his own. In matters theological his patent orthodoxy in the midst of controversies at Andover attracted the attention of Edwards Amasa Park, who, on retiring, urged Wright to take up the cudgels against Andover's departure from its evangelical heritage. And to guarantee the continued orthodox stance of the journal *Bibliotheca Sacra*, Park consigned his editorship to Wright in 1883—a position Wright was to hold for nearly forty years.

Wright, in fact, had already been a regular contributor to the journal. In the years from 1875 to 1880 he had addressed his largely clerical audience in a series of five articles on themes ranging from the nature of scientific proof to the analogies between Calvinism and Darwinism. Later, in 1882, he pulled these pieces together, added a couple of new essays, and published the lot in a book entitled *Studies in Science and Religion*. A number of themes ran like high-voltage current through the series. First, Wright continually insisted that while God is the final or ultimate cause of life, Darwin had supplied a pretty good explanation of the secondary causes. And Wright was ever enthusiastic about secondary causes. Like Gray, his whole background had made him suspicious of speculative philosophy. The solidly historical character of the Christian faith made it more closely allied to modern science than to "the glittering generalities of transcendentalism."[8] The implications were plain. Simply

---

7. Gray, quoted by Dupree in *Asa Gray*, p. 366.
8. Wright, *Studies in Science and Religion* (Andover, Mass.: W. F. Draper, 1882), p. vi.

to say "God created the world" in answer to scientific questioning was to undermine the whole scientific enterprise, to cut off the very possibility of scrutiny before it had begun. And, even worse, Wright pointed out that such an approach would undermine the rational foundations not just of science but of the very proofs on which divine revelation rested. To jettison the scientific method on which Darwinism was erected would be to jeopardize the argument from historical evidence for biblical truth and thereby endanger the veracity of God himself.

Wright's theological acumen also enabled him to pursue the design argument at greater depth than Gray was capable of. He clearly continued to feel that Darwin had not completely invalidated Paley's view of the world, but he also felt it necessary to modify the traditional interpretation. He was bothered on the one hand by the overly anthropomorphic image of the Divine Watchmaker and on the other hand by the evidence from nature that seemed to refute benevolent design. His own solution was to reinvoke the more comprehensive model of the Edwardsian Calvinists who saw the goodness of God in the *ultimate* final cause of creation. Since human beings experienced only part of the cosmic system, this view suggested, it was inevitable that their perception of design was only partial. An enlarged conception of design was needed to account for what seemed on the surface to be waste, failure, and imperfection in nature.

Finally Wright proposed that there was a special relationship between Calvinism and Darwinism. He spelled out five basic parallels in an essay entitled "Some Analogies between Calvinism and Darwinism." Darwinian evolution, he pointed out, in no sense entailed the idea of inevitable progressive development—a point on which it closely paralleled the biblical doctrine of the fall and human depravity. Moreover, both Darwinism and Calvinism affirmed the specific unity of the human race and presumed a direct organic chain linking all humanity together by inheritance. The hereditary transmission of variations and of original sin seemed to Wright a particularly close correspondence. In the Calvinistic interplay of predestination and free agency he saw a mirror image of the Darwinian integration of chance and pattern in the evolutionary system. In addition, advocates of both philosophies were uneasy about a priori methods—Calvinists because of their fear of rampant rationalism, and Darwinians because of their self-imposed restriction to observable rather than ultimate facts. Lastly, the sovereignty of law throughout nature, whether in the history of creation or in the historical transmission of divine revelation, further served to lead Wright to the conclusion that Darwinism was "the Calvinistic interpretation of nature."

As Wright's involvements as a theologian increased, so too did his efforts as a geologist. The glacial geomorphology of New England continued to fascinate him, and he undertook a long trek tracing the great terminal moraine of the last glacial retreat across the North American

GLACIAL GEOLOGY OF THE UNITED STATES, by George Frederick Wright, from *Man and the Glacial Period* (D. Appleton & Co., 1896)

continent. He had already spoken to the Boston Society of Natural History on the subject and had been encouraged by scientists of the stature of Alexander Agassiz, W. M. Davis, Alpheus Hyatt, and Nathaniel Shaler. When Oberlin offered him the professorship of New Testament language and literature in 1881, it gave him the chance to devote his energies to more purely scholarly pursuits, and he gladly accepted the position.

It was not long after he had moved to Oberlin that his work on glaciation brought him to the attention of the Western Reserve Historical Society in Cleveland, Ohio. Fascinated by Wright's evidence for the existence of human beings during the glacial period, they provided him with financial backing to continue his mapping of the glacial boundary. At the same time, Wright's new post allowed him time to get down to more serious writing, and in 1889 he saw the publication of his Lowell lectures in a volume entitled *The Ice Age in North America*. The work was highly acclaimed by at least some leading geologists, and Wright was encouraged to produce a more popular, condensed version. This appeared in 1892 under the title *Man and the Glacial Period*, and it immediately

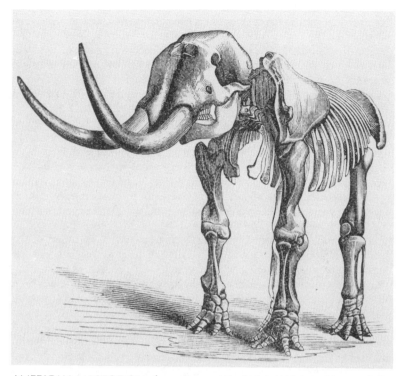

AMERICAN MASTODON, from George Frederick Wright's *Man and the Glacial Period* (D. Appleton & Co., 1896)

caused a stir among the geologists. Wright became the victim of vituperative attacks, particularly from W J McGee, a member of the U.S. Geodetic Survey. His scientific colleagues stood by him, however, defending the scholarly merits of the work.

Wright's doctrinal fidelity and scientific integrity did not fail to impress his Oberlin paymasters. In 1892 they appointed him to the Oberlin Chair of the Harmony of Science and Revelation, though in fact this amounted to no more than placing a formal institutional stamp of approval on what Wright had been doing for years. On the one hand, he had spent his lifetime recommending science to the Christian world by showing that far from undermining religion, it rather had "never found a home outside the nurturing influences of Christianity."[9] On the other hand, he had devoted a lot of time in his later years to defending the

9. George Frederick Wright, "The Affinity of Science for Christianity," *Bibliotheca Sacra* 46 (1889), pp. 701-2.

Scriptures from the encroachments of the new liberal theology. His Stone Lectures at Princeton (delivered in 1904), for example, were entitled "Scientific Confirmations of Old Testament History." And, as we shall later see, he aligned himself with the fundamentalist cause of the early years of the twentieth century. For over forty years, Wright labored to present a Christian Darwinism that was more faithful both to Darwin and to Christianity than was the speculative evolutionism of the liberal theologians. This, of course, is not to say that Wright was a thoroughgoing Darwinian. Christian Darwinism was never the same thing as Darwinian naturalism. But we can say that Wright's version of evolution was closer to the Darwinian model than, say, the Spencerianism then in vogue—and this despite Numbers's suggestion that Wright's attitude to evolutionism progressively hardened during the early years of the new century; even in these later years it was extrapolations beyond Darwin's theory rather than the theory itself that Wright found most irksome. It is true that on occasion he could lapse into "creationist" language when speaking of the special creation of the first human pair, but he also insisted that the human race was "genetically" connected with the higher mammals. However inconsistent these claims may appear, Wright might have been spared the charge of doubletalk if he had come to some form of emergent evolutionary theory.

Along with Gray and Wright, James Dwight Dana was the third member of what could well be called the alliance of evangelical evolutionists.[10] The three knew each other well, corresponded frequently, and encouraged one another. Dana, the son of a saddler and hardware merchant, grew up in a family that was modest, hardworking, and devout. Like a great many other American geologists of the time, Dana had caught the natural history bug under the tutelage of Silliman at Yale. The scientific link between the two men soon became strong and was later reinforced when Dana married Silliman's daughter Henrietta in 1844.

When Dana graduated from Yale in 1830, however, his future was far from certain. As with other college-trained scientists of the day, the prospects for a professional career in science were fairly bleak. But Silliman could sense something quite special in his pupil and saved him for science by offering him an assistantship in Yale's chemical laboratory. Soon Dana was coediting the *American Journal of Science* with Silliman. Asa Gray played his part, too, recommending Dana for a scientific post with the Wilkes expedition of 1838-1842. It was a natural choice, since Dana had published his *System of Mineralogy* the year before the expedition sailed.

The round-the-world survey altered Dana's whole life no less than

---

10. On Dana, see Daniel C. Gilman, *The Life of James Dwight Dana* (New York: Dodd, Mead, 1910); and William Stanton's article on Dana in the *Dictionary of Scientific Biography* (New York: Scribner's, 1971), 3: 549-54.

the *Beagle* trip had altered Darwin's. It provided him with a virtually unmatched breadth of experience in natural history: he was called upon to act as mineralogist, geologist, and later zoologist for the expedition. But it also had another effect. On the eve of sailing Dana underwent a deep personal religious experience that transformed the piety of childhood into a passionate evangelical faith.

As soon as he got back home, Dana set to work on writing up the expedition reports. It took him fourteen years, but the resulting publications on *Zoophytes*, *Crustacea* and *Geology* were quite masterly and served to establish his reputation as America's foremost geologist. Even though the reports were rather specialized, they attracted a wide popular readership. Moreover they showed how thoroughly polished Dana's scientific craftsmanship was at every level from recording observational minutiae to making the grand generalization. Empirically they demonstrated how very fine an observer of nature Dana was. His detailed work on the formation of corals, for example, confirmed Darwin's general theory of corals, and yet he did not hesitate to take issue with Darwin over his chart of areas of subsidence and elevation. Methodologically they revealed him as a consistent uniformitarian in geology and a catastrophist in biology. On the one hand he surpassed even Lyell in emphasizing the geological significance of the ordinary processes of stream erosion, and on the other he was convinced that entire species were periodically destroyed and replaced by creation. Theologically, Dana's works showed him to be profoundly committed to the idea of design in nature. His theory of "cephalization" was just one instance. By this Dana meant that organic progress consists in the mind becoming dominant over the body—the organs of locomotion increasingly being released to the service of the brain. The driving force behind this whole progressive cephalization process, as Dana conceived it, was the supernatural activity of the Creator.

In 1856, the year after he took up the Silliman Professorship of Natural History at Yale, Dana was involved in a theological tussle with the professor of Greek at Union College, Tayler Lewis.[11] As it turned out, Dana later came to embrace Lewis's basic position; nevertheless, a consideration of his defense of science against the assaults of dogma and of the points on which he agreed and disagreed with Lewis is illuminating.

The confrontation between Dana and Lewis was occasioned by the publication of Lewis's book *The Six Days of Creation* in 1855. Dana wrote a four-part response that appeared in the 1856 and 1857 issues of the *Bibliotheca Sacra*, the main organ of Congregationalist evangelicalism. Dana's articles were entitled "Science and the Bible"; Lewis's final rejoinder, *The Bible and Science*, was intended to indicate which deserved

---

11. See Morgan B. Sherwood, "Genesis, Evolution, and Geology in America before Darwin: The Dana-Lewis Controversy, 1856-1857," in *Toward a History of Geology*, ed. Cecil J. Schneer (Cambridge: MIT Press, 1969), pp. 305-16.

precedence. The heart of Lewis's message was abundantly clear: the language of science is defective and its theories transitory, so they should have no bearing on biblical interpretation. "We can get on very well without geology," he insisted; "our intellectual and moral dignity would not have been impaired had no such science ever existed."[12]

Dana felt the sharp sting of Lewis's impatience with those who sought to reconcile Genesis and geology, for he had already borrowed the harmonizing cosmogony of his lifelong friend Arnold Guyot. The dispute was handled with its fair share of confusion and name-calling on both sides, but a couple of central issues stand out clearly nonetheless. Whereas Lewis felt the Hebrew word for "create" did not necessarily mean creation out of nothing, Dana insisted on the classical view of creation *ex nihilo*. Then Lewis proposed that the creation could be sustained only by repeated supernatural interventions, that it would inevitably "die" if left to itself. Dana demurred. He believed that nature is dependent on God's constant sustaining direction. Lewis's major complaint, however, was that biblical exegesis should not proceed with one eye on science. In contrast, Dana argued that science had thrown new light on the Bible. His approach stemmed from his deep devotion to the natural theology tradition, which in principle ruled out any conflict between God's words and God's works. These, then, were the divergences, but just as enlightening were the assumptions and declarations shared by both men. When Lewis, for example, insisted that primary causes and primal forces lay outside the realm of science, Dana agreed. Both held that science was restricted to the scrutiny of secondary causes. They also agreed on the issue of the unity of the human race. Lewis asserted that the human race is descended from a single pair, and Dana's concurrence on the point is clear in his dismissive attack on Nott and Gliddon's *Types of Mankind*, a volume that promoted the theory of the plural origin of mankind.

When the pens were finally laid to rest, compliments began to flood in to Dana from many scientific colleagues. The details of their praise need not detain us here. But it does bear noting that while Agassiz, "creationist" and adopted Unitarian, complimented Dana "for fighting so earnestly the cause of our independence versus clerical arrogance," Gray, the evangelical, later commented in his review of Dana's *Manual of Geology* that "We have faith in revelation, and faith in science, in each after its kind; but, as respects cosmogony, we are not called upon to yield an implicit assent to any proposed reconciliation of the two."[13] So, while

---

12. Lewis, *The Six Days of Creation; or, The Scriptural Cosmology with the Ancient Idea of Time-Worlds in Distinction from Worlds in Space* (Schenectady: G. Y. Debogert, 1855), p. 393. See also Ronald L. Numbers, *Creation by Natural Law: Laplace's Nebular Hypothesis in American Thought* (Seattle: University of Washington Press, 1977), pp. 95-100.

13. Gray, review of *Manual of Geology*, by James Dana, *North American Review* 96 (1863): 375.

JAMES DANA, from George P. Merrill's *The First One Hundred Years of American Geology* (Yale University Press, 1924; copyright © 1952, Mrs. G. P. Merrill)

it is obvious that Gray and Dana were both servants of science and Scripture, it is equally obvious that they understood their joint servitude in quite different ways.

Dana fell ill in 1859, the year Darwin's *Origin of Species* appeared. Incapacitated, he was unable to read it until about 1863. Of course Darwin's theory challenged the very fabric of Dana's natural history in a number of ways.[14] As we have noted, Dana held to a catastrophist position in biology, arguing that in the years from the initial creation of life, various species had been destroyed by catastrophes and replaced by di-

---

14. On this, see William F. Sanford, Jr., "Dana and Darwinism," *Journal of the History of Ideas* 26 (1965): 531-46.

vine creation. His model of the history of life was progressivist not in the sense that it presumed one species progressing into another but rather perceived each new creation being higher than its predecessor in the chain of life. As Dana put it in 1856, "The pre-determined system of Nature thus involved a higher and higher expression of types and new progressing features, adapted to the changing physical conditions."[15] Darwin challenged these conceptions on at least two fronts: on the one hand, his was a thoroughly nonprogressivist theory of organic change, and on the other, it denied that species were immutable.

Not surprisingly, Dana resisted the new theory as soon as he became aware of it. But it is quite vital to point out that his initial disquiet was on scientific rather than religious grounds. He wrote encouragingly to Gray during the early debates with Agassiz, for example, assuring him that a theory of transmutation was certainly not incompatible with religion. He also kept open the *American Journal of Science* (of which he had become the sole editor) to Gray's celebrated review of *The Origin*. And in 1844, on the publication of the pre-Darwinian evolutionary theory contained in the anonymous *Vestiges*, he had written to Gray,

> The supposed grand discoveries in E. Indian History, lengthening the age of the world since it was occupied by man, and those in Egypt, when first brought forward terrified many of the believers in the Bible. But they were the means of setting on foot a train of investigation which resulted in a vast increase of knowledge, and above all in confirming the Bible history in every point—In the same manner I believe that the publication of the Vestiges will be the means of such good to Religion & Science in general. . . . This argument from the internal character of the Bible-system, affords the best possible evidence of the truth of religion. . . . And on this ground I have inferred that the theory of the Vestiges, if proved, would not affect the truths of Christianity.[16]

Rather conveniently, Dana's scientific objections to the theory of evolution are preserved in two letters he sent to Darwin in the early 1860s, even before he had read the *Origin*. First, he noted that geology had provided no clear-cut evidence for the existence of intermediate forms; second, he noted that in some cases higher forms had appeared prior to lower forms, which argued against the idea of linear evolution; and third, he suggested that there was abundant geological evidence for the complete extinction of whole organic races and the sudden appearance of entirely new populations.

Despite these objections, Dana eventually came to accept the theory

---

15. Dana, quoted by Sanford in "Dana and Darwinism," p. 532.

16. Dana, in a letter to Asa Gray dated 27 April 1844 (Historic Letters, Archives, Gray Herbarium Library, Harvard University).

of evolution. It is hard to say exactly when he changed his mind, but during the immediately ensuing years he evidently began to give more and more credence to the theory. In 1874, in the second edition of the *Manual of Geology*, he told readers that the evolution of life had progressed by the derivation of one species from another by natural means and with only occasional instances of supernatural intervention. His advocacy of this new stance apparently defused a certain amount of concern among the more conservative; it may well have been one of the reasons Gray's lectures to Yale divinity students in 1880 caused no disquiet whatsoever. But Dana's most mature reflections were not articulated until 1883, when he initiated a series of lectures on evolution at Yale.

By 1883, Dana had clearly accepted the Darwinian cornerstone of evolution—namely, natural selection. He conceded that as a model for explaining the survival of particular organic characteristics it had great explanatory potential, though he stopped short of accepting the contention that it was the sole mover of evolutionary history. He believed that other factors (notably the Lamarckian idea of the use and disuse of organs) also played a part; he was a good deal more willing than Darwin to acknowledge his debt to Lamarck. Dana also remained disconcerted by the imperfect state of the geological record. The signal absence of paleontological support led him, like many others, to the idea of saltatory evolution—that is, evolution that occurred discontinuously, involving sudden transformations of species rather than gradual incremental changes. On the question of human evolution, Dana sided with Wallace: he was prepared to concede the derivation of the human race from an inferior species, but he insisted that it originated in a special introduction of divine creative energy. This was a view that a number of evangelical theologians, as we will shortly see, were happy to accept. Nor did Dana hesitate to apply the evolutionary principle to society in general or the question of race development in particular. So we find him combining his own theory of cephalization with Darwinian natural selection to suggest that the anthropometric features of the Negro—retreating forehead, longer forearms, and so on—were marks of inferior mental development. Moreover, despite a kindly temperament, Dana was prepared to use this idea to approve (like many other intellectuals of his time, it must be admitted) the imperialistic thrust of the colonial powers.

Clearly the penetration of Darwinism into Dana's thinking was not inconsiderable. It only remains to assess his understanding of how the theory impinged on his religious views. At a personal level it did nothing to diminish the firmness or the fervor of his faith in God. In theological terms, he spelled out his position in full in the first of his eight-lecture course under the title "Relation of Theories of Evolution to Theism." Right from the outset Dana gave assurances that there was nothing atheistic about the terms "development theory," "derivative theory," or "evolution." Rather, since all the terms presumed some orderly process in the introduction of species, some comprehensive law or method, they pointed beyond themselves to a transcendent Lawgiver. Thus he pointed out that evolution, in some form, was consistent with a wide variety of interpretations of the biblical material, ranging from readings implying that every single species had been separately created to readings limiting God's direct intervention to the initial creative act. He said that the very language of the biblical text itself seemed, on occasion, to imply evolution rather than creation. Such phrases as "Let the earth bring forth" and "Let the waters bring forth abundantly," he suggested, made it sound "as if, after the fiat, development went forward through the energies imparted to the earth and waters." And lest this should seem an ad hoc surrender of exegesis to science, he hastily introduced some extracts from Augustine in support of his interpretation. No less compelling, he reckoned, was the theological fact that a God closely bound up with the progressive development of his creation was not a God afar off. Such a deistic conception was the next thing to atheism, he urged, whereas the depiction of a God guiding the whole evolutionary process toward his ultimate goal, a God transcendent yet immanent, was precisely the sort of God Dana found revealed in the pages of Scripture. Both biblically and theologically, he concluded, evolution had much to commend it.

To complete our perusal of Dana's evangelical version of evolution, we will do well to consider his concluding remarks on the bearing of Darwin's theory on Christian theism. He makes the following points:

> (1) That it is not atheism to believe in a development theory, if it be admitted at the same time that Nature exists by the will and continued act of God.
>
> (2) That we cannot tell when we have ascertained the last limit of discovery with regard to secondary causes.
>
> (3) That God is ever near us, ever working in and through Nature, carrying forward his spiritual purpose, and is ever in communion with the Godly man.
>
> These points I have brought forward in order to exhibit the true relation of Nature to God, and, also, to lead you to lay aside all fear of the discussion of development theories.
>
> Let Science dig, and dredge, and work her laboratories. She is searching for God's truth. If her teachers are atheistic, accept still the truth that is well established; but to the atheism give no quarter, for it is to Man the annihilation of hope and of all the higher joys of his being.[17]

Gray, Wright, and Dana constituted the core of a network of American Christians in science whose influence was far from inconsiderable. Gray and Wright collaborated on the construction of a Christian Dar-

---

17. Dana, "Relation of Evolution to Theism," *Lectures on Evolution*, no. 1 (Dana Family Papers, Yale University Library).

winism. Each individually sustained a substantial correspondence with Dana. In turn, Dana published much of their work in the *American Journal of Science*, while Wright printed Dana's essay review of Guyot's *Creation* just as soon as he took up the editorship. There were other figures associated with the network too. Dana penned a long appreciation of Guyot for the National Academy of Sciences and, of course, he had a lifelong contact with Silliman at Yale. Dana's own contributions are recorded in the full-length biography by Daniel Coit Gilman, who wrote to Gray eulogizing Wright's work and recommended his "reconciliation" of science and Christianity to his own students at Johns Hopkins. These informal associations, although not institutionalized, were very powerful and helped to perpetuate a literate, cultured, and scientifically astute evangelicalism during the final decades of the nineteenth century. This is not to say that their message was unified. Indeed, they disagreed with one another on many points, but they helped in large measure to temper the excesses of a few agnostics who strove to wield science in the service of secularism. And they did much to break down the resistance of traditional science to Darwinism; by 1880, evolutionary views prevailed among American scientists at large.

TWO DOUBTFUL DETRACTORS

By 1880 most American naturalists were evolutionists—most, but not all. In fact, that year saw a mini-controversy in the popular press concerning evolution and Christianity. Claims for and against Darwin were made on all sides. The *Popular Science Monthly* challenged the editors of the *Presbyterian Observer* to name two working naturalists in the United States who were not evolutionists. Professor Arnold Henry Guyot of Princeton and Sir John William Dawson of McGill (actually a Canadian) were the two "creationists" nominated and have been regarded since then as opponents of the theory of evolution. Some observations on their stance will certainly be instructive, for their opposition to evolution was far from unqualified, and, just as important, their attitudes changed over time.

We have already traced the pre-Darwinian career of Arnold Guyot up to the publication of his *Earth and Man* in 1849. By the time he was hailed as an antievolutionist in 1880, he was seventy-three years old. Even so, his final book, *Creation; or, The Biblical Cosmogony in the Light of Modern Science* (1884) was still to be published. And in this work, according to James Dana, "he was led to accept, though with some reservation, the doctrine of evolution through natural causes."[18] Undoubtedly Dana

---

18. Dana, "Biographical Memoir of Arnold Guyot," in the *Annual Report of the Board of Regents of the Smithsonian Institution for 1887* (Washington: Government Printing Office, 1889), p. 712.

was stretching the term "evolution" way beyond its customary limits, and yet Guyot's stance did seem to allow for the possibility of some natural development, albeit within strict boundaries. Dana pointed out that Guyot excepted human and the first animal life from this "evolutionary" process because of exegetical considerations having to do with the use of the Hebrew verb *bará* for creation in both these cases. If Dana is even partially correct in sensing an increasing evolutionary stance on Guyot's part, this is significant, because *Creation* was only a moderately enlarged version of a paper (entitled "Cosmogony and the Bible; or, The Biblical Account of Creation in the Light of Modern Science") that Guyot had presented in 1873 to the Sixth General Congress of the Evangelical Alliance—a meeting that incidentally serves to underscore the very pluralistic nature of the evangelical stance on science. At this meeting Guyot was able to hear addresses on science themes delivered by such individuals as William Dawson and James McCosh, whose views will be examined presently.

Guyot's whole discourse was built around his idea of what he called the "great cosmogonic week"—the seven days of creation. It was, in fact, an elaborate harmonization, after the style of Hugh Miller, of the book of Nature and the book of Scripture. Unlike previous concordist schemes, however, Guyot insisted that the days of creation could not be equated with specific geological periods. In his view, the whole of paleontological geology from the beginning of life in the Cambrian through to the Quaternary era was confined to the fifth and sixth Mosaic days. He urged that the whole account should be thought of as an ideal plan that revealed the successive and progressive activity of the Creator. Beginning with the primordial creation, Guyot traced the development of the world from the first cosmic light through the organization of the heavens, the formation of earth and plants, and the appearance of solar light to the creation of animal and human life.

A number of points need to be made about Guyot's scheme. First, it is clear that he did not take the days of Genesis in any literal sense. For one thing, as he pointed out, the absence of the sun during the first three days meant that they could not have been twenty-four-hour solar periods. For another, in his own words, "the geological history of the creation of animals and man demonstrates that they are periods of indefinite time."[19] This alone shows that Guyot was not a creationist in the modern sense of advocating a short earth history. Guyot's statement to the Alliance also reveals his understanding of natural theology: he unambiguously pointed out its theological limitations. A study of God's works,

---

19. Arnold Henry Guyot, "Cosmogony and the Bible; or The Biblical Account of Creation in the Light of Modern Science," in *History, Essays, Orations, and Other Documents of the Sixth General Conference of the Evangelical Alliance*, ed. Philip Schaff and S. Irenaeus Prime (New York: Harper, 1874), p. 280.

no matter how sound and faithful its deductions, he argued, must inherently be a limited exercise, for it could not offer equal substitutes for the great truths of the Christian faith revealed in the Bible. Science could not attend to spiritual needs, he insisted, and Scripture could not answer scientific questions.

Yet we should also keep in mind the fact that Guyot remained enthusiastic about the idealist version of the argument from design. It seemed to him that the archetypal plans typical of each geological age that unified organic structures forced the mind to the contemplation of higher things. The purposive and progressive pattern of the creation attested to the presiding wisdom and power of its ultimate author. In this Guyot was merely perpetuating Owen's pre-Darwinian ideas without evolutionary embellishment. Then again, Guyot's theological conservatism is clearly apparent in his handling of the whole topic. He was, for example, no more patient with those who regarded the biblical story as a mere accommodation to the cultural cosmogony of the time than he was with those who cut the narrative off from the real facts of nature by describing it as "ideal history." Guyot insisted that the author had intended to write real history. "Guided by this view," he insisted, "we shall consider the six cosmogonic days as the organic phases of creation, or the great periods of its history."[20]

So far, of course, Guyot was grappling with problems that had no direct bearing on Darwin's theory of evolution—not surprising, in light of the fact that the general scheme dated from the early 1840s, when he lectured on the subject at Neuchâtel. Nevertheless, in his successive updates of the material he gave several indications of an openness to a theistic account of evolutionary history. For example, he suggested that where the verb *bará* is not used for "creation" in the biblical account, "only transformations are meant" (*bará*, he pointed out, was reserved for the initial creation of matter, of life, and of spirit). Thus he clearly allowed, if only as a possibility, that some biological changes might have taken place by some evolutionary means. At the very least this was a far cry from Agassiz's idea of a separate creation of every species or phylum. And in his 1884 treatment of the material, he slipped in the following additional sentence: "Whether or not we view this order as the result of evolution, God's guiding hand must be discerned, without which nature alone could not have produced it."[21] Finally, Guyot's account of the "creation of man" must be mentioned. The human race is distinguished from the rest of the animal world, he stated, by a spiritual element—the image of God, which he described as being "infused into man, at his creation." And since the image of God has no physiological component, he reasoned,

---

20. Guyot, "Cosmogony and the Bible," p. 278.

21. Guyot, *Creation; or, The Biblical Cosmogony in the Light of Modern Science* (New York: Scribner's, 1884), p. 118.

no traces of it would ever be detected in the fossil record. To look for this "missing link" is pointless, he insisted:

> We often hear of palaeontologists looking sedulously for the missing link between man and the animal. They forget that in the sense of which they speak, there can be no link wanting. The figure and the structure of the ape is as near as need be, to be called a link between man and the animal; the difference between the two beings is not in the shape of a thumb or of any particular bodily organ, but in the moral nature. An animal, as beautiful in form as Apollo Belvidere, but not possessed of the sense of the invisible, would still be an animal and nothing more. A poor misshapen Hottentot, endowed with these spiritual faculties, rendering him capable of becoming a living member of the spiritual world, through faith in Christ, would still be a man, belonging to that upper plane of life, and bound to his Maker by ties of love and adoration.[22]

Guyot did not himself directly link this point to the question of human evolution in any explicit way, but there were theological colleagues at Princeton, as we shall see, who certainly did.

Inasmuch as Guyot's account of creation and science omitted any reference to Darwinian natural selection, he clearly cannot be described as a Darwinian. But given the particular emphases he perpetuated—a kind of pre-Darwinian developmentalism—it would be equally wrong to describe him as a precursor of modern-day creationism.

Guyot's reconciliation of the geological and scriptural records was certainly influential. He had publicly lectured on the topic in New York in 1852, and he had repeated the series at the College of New Jersey (later Princeton University), in a twelve-lecture course at Union Theological Seminary, and for several years in succession to the Princeton seminarians. As we have seen, Dana incorporated Guyot's model into his own *Manual of Geology*. Moreover, when Dana penned his laudatory review essay of *Creation* for the *Bibliotheca Sacra* in 1885, he recalled that while Guyot and he had originally resisted the evolutionary perspective, they had both been compelled by the biological, biogeographical, and geological evidence in its favor. In this Dana was surely overenthusiastic, but it is significant that as a close personal friend of Guyot's since his first coming to America, Dana was happy to describe him as an evolutionist.

What then of Sir John William Dawson, the second nominee for the title of creationist extraordinaire? When Agassiz died in 1873, the mantle of anti-Darwinian leadership fell on Dawson's shoulders. His career therefore bears scrutiny.[23]

---

22. Guyot, *Creation*, pp. 124-25.
23. On Dawson, see Charles F. O'Brien, *Sir William Dawson: A Life in Science and Religion* (Philadelphia: American Philosophical Society, 1971); T. H. Clark, "Sir

WILLIAM DAWSON, from George P. Merrill's
The First One Hundred Years of American Geology
(Yale University Press, 1924; copyright © 1952,
Mrs. G. P. Merrill)

William Dawson, president of McGill University, first president of
the Royal Society of Canada, and president of both the American and
British Associations for the Advancement of Science, had been brought up
in hard circumstances. He was born in Nova Scotia in 1820, the son of a
Scottish immigrant who had had been beset by financial woes during the
economic slump of the 1820s. Continuing domestic hardship eventually
led Dawson to turn his back on the ministry of the Presbyterian Church in

John William Dawson, 1820-1899," in *Pioneers of Canadian Science*, ed. G. F. G.
Stanley (Toronto: University of Toronto Press, 1966), pp. 101-13; and William R.
Shea's introduction to the 1977 reprint of Dawson's *Modern Ideas of Evolution* (New
York: Prodist).

favor of the more lucrative position of teaching at Pictou Academy, where he had received his training. He felt a deep responsibility to help ease his parents' financial burdens; he later recalled that part of his very first wage packet was used to pay off the remains of a twenty-year-old debt incurred by his father.

Even after Dawson had brought this relief to his parents, the family finances remained precarious. He was forced to cut short his geological studies in Edinburgh in the spring of his first academic year in 1842. By then he was a devotee of Lyell, whom he had escorted through the Nova Scotia coal fields in 1841. Soon after he returned home from Scotland, he began contributing geological papers to learned journals. Between 1842 and 1855, when he assumed the principalship of McGill University, he traveled extensively in Nova Scotia in his capacity as superintendent of education. He was deeply dedicated to the work; before he resigned in 1853 he had done much to promote education throughout the Maritime Provinces. Such dedication characterized his whole life. When he suffered an attack of pneumonia in 1892 at the age of seventy-two, he took his first leave of absence from McGill University in thirty-seven years. And his dedication to the world of scholarship was no more intense than his devotion to the things of the spirit. A man of profound Christian faith, he believed, as his biographer Charles O'Brien observes, "that the harmony of the Word and the Work was not simply a device of Sunday School pedagogy." He saw the wisdom, power, and goodness of the Creator revealed in the world of nature. At the same time, he looked on the earth as the theater in which the drama of human redemption is played out.

Dawson averted tension between his geology and theology by adopting the day-age theory and, much to the dismay of his good friend Lyell, the progressivist view of creation. Time after time Dawson expounded his "two theologies"—of Nature and of Scripture—in journals ranging from the old Calvinist *Princeton Review* to the more broadly appealing *Contemporary Review*. Since he stood firmly in the popular tradition of the early nineteenth-century harmonizers, it is evident that his opposition to Darwin's theory had little to do with biblical authority. Dawson rejected the development theory, as he often called it, because it seemed to him an assault on divine design. As we consider his successive treatments of the theme, however, we will discover that as his understanding of evolution changed over the years, and as he found other Christian naturalists interpreting it in terms amenable to design, Dawson relaxed his opposition.[24]

---

24. On this, see John F. Cornell, "From Creation to Evolution: Sir William Dawson and the Idea of Design in the Nineteenth Century," *Journal of the History of Biology* 16 (1983): 137-70. When Dawson addressed the New York meeting of the Evangelical Alliance in 1873, he expressed his confidence in the viability of his "two theologies" in the following terms: "The geological record is so manifestly in accor-

When Darwin's theory first appeared, Dawson assumed, as had Paley and the authors of the Bridgewater Treatises before him, that God's design in nature was directly linked with the idea of the special creation of particular organic structures. This popular assumption had long led naturalists who wanted to defend design to look instinctively to special creations, just as it had led others who denied special creations, like Lamarck and Darwin, to feel that they had explained design away. In keeping with this perspective, Dawson concluded that any theory of evolution or development—not just Darwinian natural selection—was antipathetic to a teleological conception of nature. When he reviewed the *Origin of Species* for the *Canadian Review* in 1860, he condemned natural selection and organic descent as virtually synonymous. Some of the very evidence that Darwin had mustered to serve his own theory (e.g., embryological and morphological similarities) Dawson marshalled in the cause of special creation according to divine plan. Over the next few years, he held rigidly to this interpretation. In his popular *Story of the Earth and Man*, for example, Dawson condemned evolution as hostile to design because it "removes from the study of nature the ideas of final cause and purpose."[25] He repeatedly insisted that "creation and design" constituted a genuine scientific alternative to the theory of evolution. To this extent, he shared Darwin's own assumptions.

To others, however, Dawson's position made rather less sense. Those, for example, who distinguished between evolution and Darwinism sensed ambiguities in Dawson's proposals. Asa Gray pointed this out in his reflections for *The Nation* in 1873 on the attitude of working naturalists toward Darwinism. As we have already observed, Gray himself was assured that the idea of design could be salvaged from Darwin's apparent destruction of it, and others felt Darwin had actually enhanced the picture of design in nature. Moreover, Gray simply could not fathom how Dawson could so steadfastly oppose evolution while conceding that it was not "fair to shut up the argument of design to the idea that [Paley's] watch must have suddenly flashed into existence fully formed and in motion. It would be quite as much a creation if slowly and laboriously made by the hand of the artificer."[26] The difficulty lay in the fact that Dawson insisted on interpreting evolution as, by definition, antidesign.

Despite the close friendship of Dawson and Gray, it was quite some

---

dance with the Mosaic history of creation, that to all those (unfortunately as yet too few) who have an adequate knowledge of both stories, the anticipation of our modern knowledge of astronomy, physics, and geology in the early chapters of Genesis is so marked as to constitute a positive proof of inspiration" ("Primitive Man and Revelation," in *History, Essays, Orations, and Other Documents of the Sixth General Conference of the Evangelical Alliance*, pp. 272-75).

25. Dawson, *The Story of the Earth and Man* (Montreal: Dawson Brothers, 1872), p. 318.

26. Dawson, *The Story of the Earth and Man*, p. 350.

time before Dawson came to see that evolution need not be Darwinian and that design might not be Paleyan. When his *Nature and the Bible* came out in 1875, his position remained substantially unaltered, although he did now feel that some natural development might be part of a supernatural scheme. But over the next few years, as such evangelical figures as R. W. Raymond, Alexander Winchell, and James McCosh corresponded with him and sought to show how evolution did not invalidate a theistic conception of the world, he came to see that evolution could mean something distinct from naturalistic Darwinism. He was not an immediate convert, but he did begin to acknowledge the claims that these theistic evolutionists were making.

There is evidence in Dawson's writing that he was making some conceptual shifts during the 1880s and '90s. In commenting on a paper by Sir George Stokes for the Victoria Institute in 1884, for instance, Dawson was more precise in his objection to what he called *spontaneous* evolution. Then in some reflections entitled "Man in Nature" for the *Princeton Review* in 1885, he maintained that human reason, while far beyond the intelligence of other animals, nevertheless "so harmonizes with natural laws, and acts in such conformity with these, that it is evidently a part of the great unity of nature, and we cannot, without violence, dissociate man from nature."[27] And by the time he issued *Modern Ideas of Evolution* in 1890 he had taken to heart the distinction he had made two years previously in the *Transactions of the Victoria Institute*—namely, that the idea of a process of development in general needed to be disengaged from particular theories of evolutionary causation. Clearly this does not mark any sort of wholesale conversion either to Darwinism or to an unqualified evolution, but it is evidence that he had come to acknowledge conditions under which theistic evolution had validity:

> It is true that there may be a theistic form of evolution, but let it be observed that this is essentially distinct from Darwinian or Neo-Lamarckianism. It postulates a Creator, and regards development of the universe as the development of His plans by secondary causes of His own institution. It necessarily admits design and final cause.[28]

Clearly this was a guarded endorsement. Dawson still felt that reserving judgment on the subject was the safest course both for scientist and theologian. Nevertheless these observations do show his increasing latitude on the subject and a tolerance of divergent views that was less characteristic in his earlier writings.

So it would seem that Guyot and Dawson, who are often characterized as the two leading opponents of evolution in North America in this

---

27. Dawson, "Man in Nature," *Princeton Review* 4 (1885): 218.
28. Dawson, *Modern Ideas of Evolution*, p. 227.

era, are in fact not so single-minded in their rejection of the theory as they are typically presumed to be. Indeed, they shared many assumptions about the geological history of the earth that decidedly distance them from the later creationist movement of the 1920s and '30s. On the most antievolutionary reading of their position, they can at most be described as doubtful detractors.

THE SCIENTIFIC GO-BETWEENS

It seems clear that evangelicals in science during the final decades of the nineteenth century had very little difficulty in coming to terms with evolution in general, if not Darwinism in particular. Nor was their accommodation of the theory limited to the scientific community. Many of them were leading figures in their churches who helped sustain the intellectual life of their religious cultures by contributing to the various denominational journals. As I have pointed out, George Frederick Wright mediated a Christian perspective on Darwinism to the Congregationalists via the *Bibliotheca Sacra*. He was not alone in doing this sort of thing. I want to turn now to two other purveyors of science to the churches— Michigan geologist Alexander Winchell and Princeton biologist George Macloskie, both of whom acted as "scientific go-betweens" for the Methodist and Presbyterian communities respectively.

Alexander Winchell was a Methodist through and through.[29] His parents were cultured people who had taught in the public school in the village of Northeast, New York. They tutored their son thoroughly, and by the time he was fifteen he too was teaching in a one-room district school. This provided a small income that helped sustain him through his formal education at Wesleyan University, from which he graduated in 1847 with a bachelor's degree and in 1850 as a master of arts. Thereafter began a long series of teaching appointments. Winchell and his wife, Julia, found their way first to Alabama, where he was employed in three different educational establishments. In 1853 they moved to Michigan, where he first became professor of physics and engineering and then professor of geology, zoology, and botany at the University of Michigan. During his time there, largely due to his own efforts, the second state geological survey of Michigan was established, with Winchell as director.

By now Winchell had a growing reputation throughout the Midwest not just as a geologist but also as an educationalist, a persuasive public lecturer, and an exponent of a Christian view of science. Invitations to

---

29. On Winchell, see F. Garvin Davenport, "Alexander Winchell: Michigan Scientist and Educator," *Michigan History* 35 (1951): 185-201; and "Scientific Interests in Kentucky and Tennessee, 1870-1890," *The Journal of Southern History* 14 (1948): 500-521. See also H. S. Yoder Jr.'s article on Winchell in the *Dictionary of Scientific Biography*, 14: 439-40.

ALEXANDER WINCHELL, from George P. Merrill's *The First One Hundred Years of American Geology* (Yale University Press, 1924; copyright © 1952, Mrs. G. P. Merrill)

lecture flooded in from many quarters. An eminent figure in American science, Winchell was elected chancellor of the new Syracuse University in 1873. Then in 1876 he accepted a professorship at Vanderbilt designed to enable him to teach there for three months of the year while retaining his links with Syracuse. Here a shadow temporarily crept over his career. In 1878 his Vanderbilt chair was abolished quite summarily. The reason usually given is that his evolutionary views offended Bishop McTyeire, the most influential of the university's trustees. But Winchell had been publishing his evolutionary synthesis since at least 1870, and so a more likely reason was the appearance in 1878 of Winchell's more specific *Preadamites*, to which we will turn in due course. In any event, in 1878 Winchell was recalled to the staff of the University of Michigan, where he remained for the rest of his life as professor of geology and paleontology.

Winchell's impact on the American scientific scene was far from inconsiderable. He played a major role, for example, in organizing geology as a science in the United States. The founding of the American Geological Society was largely due to the efforts of Winchell and his brother, a prominent geologist in Minnesota. Winchell became the society's first president. He was, in addition, one of the founders of the major journal the *American Geologist*. As an apologist for geology in North America, Winchell defended its economic worth to the government, its cultural value to the people, and its theological significance to the churches. A man of many parts, Alexander Winchell wrote poetry, taught subjects ranging from biology to civil engineering, indulged in philosophical reflection, and published profusely on all these topics.

As was the case with the other evangelical scientists we have encountered, Winchell's science was firmly grounded in the British tradition of natural theology. This is plainly brought out in two addresses he delivered before the publication of Darwin's *Origin of Species*. He presented the first, tellingly entitled *Theologico-Geology; or, The Teachings of Scripture Illustrated by the Conformation of the Earth's Crust*, to the Bible class of the Ann Arbor Methodist Episcopal Church in 1857. The second, *Creation: The Work of One Intelligence and Not the Product of Physical Forces*, was a lecture to the Young Men's Literary Association of Ann Arbor given the following year. In these, Winchell's primary allegiance to the Bible as the first and final authority is as obvious as his recognition of the value of Natural Religion. So it is no more surprising to find him lauding the harmonizing practices of Hitchcock and Dana than it is to see him detecting the hand of Providence in the disposition of extractable minerals and metals. It is also interesting to note the degree to which Winchell had gone beyond Paley's traditional system. He saw the design of God most clearly in the reign of natural law guiding the world toward its ultimate destiny and in the perpetuation of the fundamental plans of organic nature first annunciated in primeval times. To Winchell, there was a unity in nature, a cosmic totality binding everything together in an integrated whole. As he put it, "The same identical Succession of Ideas is presented to us in Nature in three ways, 1st, in the Gradations of existing animal forms, 2nd, in the successive phases of the Embryonic Development of animals, 3rd, in the Order of Appearance of subordinate zoological types upon the earth."[30] He elaborated what this might mean in some detail. In some animals, for example, he could find "anticipations" of characteristics exhibited in higher forms. Some fish, he noted, assumed reptilian features just prior to the appearance of reptiles on earth. These "prophetic types" as he called them, pointed to the comprehensive nature of the divine plan as did the same sorts of structure that united so many other

---

30. Winchell, *Creation: The Work of One Intelligence and Not the Product of Physical Forces* (Ann Arbor: Young Men's Literary Association, 1858), p. 13.

plant and animal forms. This was straight Owen anatomy, but even at
this stage, I think, the conceptual foundations of Winchell's later evolutionism were laid. Of course at this juncture he understood the appearance of successive flora and fauna as successive creative acts. But
even so, the point remains that it was in the progressive results of natural
law that Winchell detected God's design.

Winchell's initial hesitancy about the new theory of evolution is
apparent in his *Sketches of Creation*, which appeared in 1870. The aim of
the book, as Winchell made clear, was to update the arguments of natural
theology by expounding the significance of such topics as the unity and
antiquity of the human race, homological design in nature, the harmony
of the Mosaic and geological cosmogonies, and the theory of development. By and large he presented these themes without reference to Darwin, but he did insist that if the evolutionary hypothesis was sustained, it
would be "the duty of the Christian world to embrace it and convert it to
their own uses. To do otherwise is to earn the contempt of those who are
really on the side of truth."[31] The theory of evolution, he further urged,
did nothing to remove God from creation; it simply assumed that he
brought the worlds into existence by secondary causes. Plainly, whatever
reservations Winchell had, they certainly did not spring from religious
sources. They stemmed instead from his continued adherence to Owen's
morphology in its pre-Darwinian guise. In short, Winchell maintained
that every organic individual conformed to one of four fundamental
structural plans—radiate, mollusc, articulate, or vertebrate. And since he
believed each of these could be traced back to a virtually simultaneous
appearance in the geological past, he was disinclined to accept any idea of
development of one form into another. It is interesting to observe, however, that Winchell clearly accepted an evolutionary interpretation of
human society. Every race had its own Stone Age, he asserted; if it advanced sufficiently, it achieved its Age of Bronze; then eventually followed
its Iron Age. He contended that this was an inevitable societal progression, and he went on to propose that different peoples had emerged at
different epochs from what he called "the state of national infancy."

A series of lectures Winchell presented at Drew Theological Seminary in 1873 on the theory of evolution contained some hints of a change
in his outlook. He once again went out of his way to emphasize that the
doctrine of a personal God is in no way imperiled by the admission of any
form of evolution. But now he went further. Both in the physical world
and in organic history, he said, the facts point to some sort of evolutionary
pattern. He was less sure, however, about the specific mechanism. Every
proposal from Lamarck to Darwin, from Spencer to Haeckel had its own

---

31. Winchell, *Sketches of Creation: A Popular View of Some of the Grand Conclusions of the Sciences in Reference to the History of Matter and Life* (London: Sampson
Low, Son & Marston, 1870), p. 47.

difficulties, but he itemized them all under the heading "mediate creation." He was now certain that whatever the cause of change, the developmental relations in the organic world exhibited "a sense of harmonies and correlations which bespeak a co-ordinating intelligence as vast as time and space."[32] Clearly Winchell's thinking now incorporated two distinct motifs: natural theology in its idealist form and the theory of development. Both figured prominently in his lectures on geology at Syracuse University during the mid-1870s. As we have seen, the Neo-Lamarckian theory was best suited to coping with these diverse themes, and indeed, by 1877, when his *Reconciliation of Science and Religion* came out, he had capitulated to "the doctrine of the derivation of species" and more specifically to Edward Drinker Cope's Neo-Lamarckian theory of its cause.

Reconciliation of Science and Religion was a broad-ranging excursus on the philosophies of science and religion set in a historical context and drawing on an impressive range of philosophical, theological, and scientific sources. In this context a number of issues are specially important. First, Winchell for the first time worked out in some detail the interaction of evolution and natural theology. Not surprisingly, he saw the processes of evolution conforming to a general plan and urged the recasting of Owen's work in evolutionary form. In this he went beyond Paley. "We have learned that the intervention of the homological plan is the quickest way to the teleological end," he said. "Homology supervenes on teleology." Instead of arguing watch to Watchmaker, Winchell argued plan to Planner, law to Lawgiver. And all this was supplementary to biblical revelation. The whole import of the volume is that the cultivation of science and philosophy is not only harmless to the faith, but actually leads "the candid mind to a reverent knowledge of God and an implicit faith in the most mysterious utterance of his Sacred Word."[33] Science, archeology, history, geography, and ethnology all confirmed the veracity of Scripture.

The book is interesting in another respect, however. Several of the chapters are reprints of material that had previously appeared in the *Methodist Quarterly Review* during the mid-1870s. These, and a number of other pieces in the journal, give the impression that Winchell had assumed the role of purveyor of science to the Methodist community. By 1876, American Methodism, despite its divided organizational structure, was of one voice in theology. The evangelical Arminianism of John Wesley dominated mainstream Methodist pulpits, and the *Methodist Quarterly Review*, now under the editorship of Daniel D. Whedon, continued to

---

32. Winchell, *The Doctrine of Evolution: Its Data, Its Principles, Its Speculations, and Its Theistic Bearings* (New York: Harper, 1874), p. 110.
33. Winchell, *Reconciliation of Science and Religion* (New York: Harper, 1877), pp. 156, 384.

advocate the Arminianism of its founder, Nathan Bangs.[34] Under
Whedon's editorial management the journal sought to link the essentials
of biblical theism and evangelical Christianity with contemporary intellectual relevance. And Winchell was one of the figures to whom Whedon
turned for scientific guidance.

Winchell's evolutionary theism was well to the fore in his contributions to the *Review*. In a piece entitled "Huxley and Evolution" (1877), for
example, he told the Methodists that it was now far safer to accept the
"doctrine of derivative descent of animal and vegetal forms" than to reject
it. What was safer for the scientist was safer for the Christian. Evidence
from geology, the variability of species, and embryology had pushed him
to the conclusion that Cope and Hyatt's Neo-Lamarckian mechanism was
the best explanation. In other ways too Winchell was willing to harness
the theory of evolution in the service of religion. In "Religious Ideas
among Barbarous Tribes" and "The Religious Nature of Savages," both
printed in the *Review* for 1875, he marshalled the findings of evolutionary
ethnologists and anthropologists—particularly Sir John Lubbock—in
support of the argument from religious experience. The universality of
religious sentiment, he pointed out, was a simple fact, and since it was
shared by human cultures in all ages and in different geographical environments and yet exhibited a strikingly uniform character, he argued,
such elementary theistic ideas must be direct intuitions. In other words,
the idea of God was not so much a deductive argument as an immediate
experience or awareness of divine reality. This, incidentally, was an apologetic move far more Arminian than Calvinist in character. Winchell
drove the argument home with an impressive if not prolix array of empirical evidence, concluding that human beings are religious by their very
nature.

The coming together of biology and anthropology in Winchell's
thinking is most apparent in his *Adamites and Pre-adamites*, which appeared in the spring of 1878 and was re-issued in 1880 under the title *Pre-
adamites; or, A Demonstration of the Existence of Men before Adam*. Here
he resurrected the seventeenth-century idea of the existence of human
beings before Adam. He laid out his case on several levels—theological,
historical, and scientific. Protesting the doctrinal orthodoxy of his thesis,
he urged both that it was consistent with biblical revelation and that the
pre-adamites and their descendants were not excluded from the plan of
redemption. Even Chalmers, he noted, had admitted that the effects of
the atonement could be transferred to other worlds and that such evangelical scholars as Whedon and M'Causland applied it to pre-adamic
humanity.

Several factors had brought Winchell to this position. When he

---

34. See *The History of American Methodism*, 3 vols., ed. Emory Stevens Bucke
(New York: Abingdon Press, 1964).

traced the geographical dispersion of Noachite families, for example, he was struck by the limited extent of their spread around the Eastern Mediterranean, Saudi Arabia, and North Africa. Given the current population distribution and the length of time available from Hebrew chronology, he concluded that the biblical record was more purely concerned with Jewish genealogy than with the whole gamut of human history. Research on Assyro-Babylonian culture, moreover, confirmed the continued existence of pre-Noachites after the Mosaic deluge. Again, anthropological measurements of racial features revealed an amazing variety of ethnic types. Could they all have emerged in the short period from Adam? But then geology had radically questioned Ussherite-type chronology. All evidence pointed to a much longer human history than traditional conceptions had allowed. If the Bible was to be taken seriously, said Winchell, human beings must have existed before Adam.

A number of points about Winchell's book need to be made. We might well ask whether he pressed his pre-adamite theory mainly for ideological purposes. It was a thesis ready made for racist sentiments. The black races, "scientifically" confirmed as inferior by constitution, could be dismissed as pre-adamic stock of a racial lineage different from that of the Mediterranean races of which the white Anglo-Saxons were but one type. Indeed, Winchell was not content to leave such opinions as mere academic reflections; he went on to insist that they had direct implications for United States' national policy. Interracial mixing, he said, was no "more shocking to our higher sentiments, nor more opposed to the native interests of the human being, than it is destructive to the welfare of the nation and of humanity." And yet Winchell also urged that "Preadamitism means simply that Adam is descended from a black race, not the black races from Adam." This shows, moreover, that Winchell repudiated any theory of the plural origin of mankind: the blood of the first humans flows in all our veins, he insisted. He was clearly convinced of the unity, if not the equality, of the whole human race. And yet he remained aloof from the question of the evolution of "man from monkey." "To assert that man has advanced from the lowest condition of humanity," he affirmed, "is not to assert that this condition was reached by advance from the brute."[35]

The idea of pre-adamites did not find its last evangelical representative in Winchell. As we shall see, it was taken up by the fundamentalist propagandist R. A. Torrey. And it has persisted among evangelical writers to the present day. Rendle Short kept the theory alive during the 1940s as a way of combining biblical anthropology and evolutionary biology, and even more recently it has found support from Derek Kidner, E. K.

35. Winchell, *Preadamites; or, A Demonstration of the Existence of Men before Adam, together with a Study of Their Conditions, Antiquity, Racial Affinities, and Progressive Dispersion over the Earth* (Chicago: S. C. Griggs, 1880), pp. 81, 285, 412.

Victor Pearce, R. J. Berry, and John Stott.[36] This is not to say that all these use the idea in precisely the same way. Some picture pre-adamic hominids as "subhuman" judged by the theological standard of lacking the divine image, while others regard them as fully human. Their ways of negotiating the doctrine of the fall are also diverse. In any event, the point is that Winchell was not necessarily going against an evangelical version of the Christian tradition in advocating his pre-adamite theory.

While Winchell was educating the Methodists in the ways of science, George Macloskie was performing a similar task for the Presbyterians. Their journals ran pieces by a number of scientists—Dawson, Joseph Le Conte, Lionel S. Beale, Francis Bowen, Andrew Peabody—but Macloskie's was the most sustained treatment from the evangelical Old School tradition. He made his position known first through the *Presbyterian Review*, then the *Presbyterian and Reformed Review*, and latterly the *Princeton Theological Review*. These three organs of Presbyterian intellectual life were organically related to one another, and the fact that *they* acted as Macloskie's main forum is almost as significant as what he had to say: the medium was as important as the message. The *Presbyterian Review* was originally set up in 1880 to show the spirit of reunion between the Old School and New School forces within the church. While it was under the primary editorship of C. A. Briggs, the well-known New School theologian, he was joined on the editorial board by A. A. Hodge, Francis L. Patton, B. B. Warfield, and Charles Aiken, all of the Old School stance. The journal survived for ten issues, but by then it was plain that the cracks could not be so easily papered over. The internal tensions were too great, and Warfield pulled out, unable to abide what he took to be the doctrinal liberalism of Briggs. The *Presbyterian and Reformed Review* was set up as the *PR*'s immediate successor and was placed under the editorial control of Warfield. In turn it was superseded by the *Princeton Theological Review*, still under Warfield's dominating care.

The Reverend George Macloskie had studied at Queen's College in Belfast during the mid-1850s, when James McCosh was professor of metaphysics there. McCosh was an early convert to Darwinism, and Macloskie looked back with deep appreciation to his old teacher's courage and discernment during the evolution controversies. McCosh, he believed, had averted "a disastrous war between science and faith."[37] And when

---

36. See A. Rendle Short, *Modern Discovery and the Bible*, 4th ed. (London: Inter-Varsity Fellowship, 1954), pp. 114-15; and *The Bible and Modern Research* (London: Marshall, Morgan & Scott, n.d.); Derek Kidner, *Genesis* (London: Tyndale Press, 1967), pp. 26-31; E. K. V. Pearce, *Who Was Adam?* (Exeter: Paternoster Press, 1969); R. J. Berry, *Adam and the Ape* (London: Falcon, 1975); and John Stott, *Understanding the Bible* (London: Scripture Union, 1978), pp. 5-7. I have discussed the history of the pre-adamite theory in "Preadamites: The History of an Idea from Heresy to Orthodoxy," *Scottish Journal of Theology*, 40 (1987): 41–66.

37. Part of this material is drawn from my article "The Idea of Design: The

McCosh assumed the presidency of the College of New Jersey (subsequently Princeton University), Macloskie followed him as Princeton's professor of biology.

Macloskie evidently saw himself in the role of scientific advocate to the theologians. He defended its deductive theorizing, its empirical foragings, and its academic freedom in the denominational journals. In the 1887 issue of the *Presbyterian Review* he affirmed the propriety of "scientific speculation." Here he laid out the methodology of scientific procedure in an interesting reversal of the old Baconian ideal. Bacon insisted that the duty of science was first to observe and register the facts of nature and *then* to generalize about them, but Macloskie could not agree. As he saw it, this was a reversal of the only possible course of research: "Nature is too complex an affair to be analyzed and registered wholesale," he said; "and before going to consult it we must see that we have some idea of the kind of information required." To that extent, he reasoned, scientific speculation is justified—indeed, inevitable. But this does not mean that theorizing is totally detached from empirical reality. Experience of nature is the jury before which speculations are sent for trial. In this way Macloskie hoped to liberate scientific investigation from all forms of authority. He urged that due consideration be given to all hypotheses regardless of whether they conflict with the recognized principles of science, philosophy, or even theology.

Macloskie further suggested that science should be liberated because it had itself been an agent of liberation. It had helped, for example, to excise the multitude of dogmas that medievalism had appended to Christianity—and he saw in this a lesson for the church of his day. The belief in the fixity of species, so authoritatively expounded by Cuvier, had been so closely grafted onto Scripture, said Macloskie, that "a shock was felt when it was assailed by the later speculations of Darwin." The problem in the nineteenth-century church, as in the sixteenth century, was the conflation of cosmological orthodoxy and biblical interpretation. In the end, he turned to Darwinism as a paradigm case of how scientific theory should be negotiated by the Christian. Whatever its problems and irresolutions, he said, the Darwinian theory had reorganized science for the better and had provided fertile soil in which new hypotheses had grown. "Nor was it in any way opposed to religion," he went on, "though some men, by putting atheism into their definition of evolution, are able to get it out again as part of the result. It was only an attempt to show Nature's (or God's) way of doing things." It greatly troubled him that some churchmen had sanctified the position of Agassiz even though he was "not a theologian and scarcely a Christian." The proper course for Christians, he urged, was plain: they must judge the theory on its own merits; they should not weigh the authority of Scripture in Darwinian balances; the Word of God was not "greatly concerned with the fate of evolution."[38]

We should not take these pronouncements to imply that Macloskie had abandoned the idea of biblical inerrancy. On the contrary, in an article on "Concessions to Science" published in 1889—the last issue of the *Presbyterian Review* to appear—he spoke of his conviction that the Bible contained no errors. It is true the he was not thinking of inerrancy in any stark or wooden sense. He maintained that the picturesque, the rhetorical, the stylistic peculiarity all had to be taken into account as such in biblical exegesis. And, interestingly, he asserted that accepting the doctrine of the plenary inspiration of the Bible did not entail adopting the premise that the laws of nature could be deduced from incidental references in the Bible to physical phenomena. Nor did inspiration foreclose the examination of particular scientific questions. "We are not at liberty to erect our science upon the Scripture," he insisted, "and then to turn round and prove the Scripture by our science."[39]

Macloskie evidently needed some means of integrating the light of Scripture and the light of reason. Once again natural theology provided the solution. In the first issue of Warfield's new *Presbyterian and Reformed Review* (1890), he cut his own path between the Scripturalists who believed the Bible contained the fundamental principles of all the sciences, and the Rationalists who argued exclusively from reason. Macloskie argued that the "higher things" could be ascertained only from God's revelation in Scripture but that certain basic axioms could also be discovered from nature. In 1898 he published another article in the journal under the title "Theistic Evolution." In it he found his accommodation of evolution to a Christian view of the world through the use of a reinvigorated version of the design argument. Darwin, he conceded, had abolished coarser forms of teleology but suggested that in his own way, even he had reconciled teleology with morphology. Indeed, Macloskie's understanding of the doctrine of Providence enabled him to incorporate Darwinian "chance" within it. "Whatever chance is," he noted, "we know that it is subject to natural causation, even to mathematical laws; and hence it comes in as included in the order of nature, and obedient to nature's governor, whoever or whatever that may be." The result was that the new biology actually "expounded the old argument for natural theology."[40]

Again and again Macloskie asserted this position. His sympathetic

38. Macloskie, "Scientific Speculation," *Presbyterian Review* 8 (1887): 617, 622, 624, 625.

39. Macloskie, "Concessions to Science," *Presbyterian Review* 10 (1889): 220.

40. Macloskie, "Theistic Evolution," *Presbyterian and Reformed Review* 9 (1898): 7, 8.

review of Newman Smyth's *From Science to Faith* for the *Princeton Theological Review* shows the same perspective, as do his 1903 reminiscences on the historical relations of science and faith. Dismissing as "graphic and rather painful" the harmonizing efforts of such scriptural geologists as J. Pye Smith during the 1830s, he turned to Darwinism with the observation that its implications for Scripture were far less momentous than those of Lyellian geology. Praising the moderating influence of such Christian evolutionists as H. B. Tristram and Asa Gray, Macloskie specifically commended McCosh's detection in Darwin's theory of a clarification of nature's design. Bringing the story up to date, he reported that biologists were increasingly reverting to teleological modes of explanation. "In spite of themselves," he said, "they are forced to assume principles external to science, so as to light their way and render their discoveries intelligible." The need to explain the apparent "goal-directedness" in the evolutionary process had compelled some evolutionary reductionists to "ascribe to the material organism qualities which have usually been regarded as of a spiritual nature, some of them even of a teleological kind, that is indicating effects as if designed, but not admitting any higher implications."[41] Macloskie suggested that the problem was now less how to reconcile Darwin and design than to ensure that ultimate design was not diffused into some sort of vitalistic evolutionism that denied a transcendent Creator. He did not specify precisely who he had in mind as advocating such a stance, but there certainly were biologists (e.g., Dreisch) who had reintroduced the concept of "entelechy" to designate an internal teleological force intrinsic to nature.

Throughout his various assessments, Macloskie remained chary of those "harmonizers" who wanted detailed correlations between biblical statements and scientific explanations. Instead of following them in what he called their "cruel ingenuities," he preferred, for example, "not to fix a rigorous meaning to any of the 'days' [in Genesis]; but rather to regard them as rhetorical marks, much as we use such metaphors as chapter, section, verse, or as the geologists say, period, age, bed, and so on." Clearly such caution was born of his recognition of the inherently provisional nature of scientific theory and therefore of the folly of wedding revelation to "scientific speculation." Of far greater moment than such exegetical detail was the teleological question. He was certain that if the mutation theory of Thomas Hunt Morgan and Hugo DeVries "were established as a general law, it would reinforce the teleological argument that evolution is a divinely organized method of maintaining the Balance of nature by originating new species to replace older forms that have become extinct."[42]

---

41. Macloskie, "The Outlook of Science and Faith," *Princeton Theological Review* 1 (1903): 611.

42. Macloskie, "Mosaism and Darwinism," *Princeton Theological Review*

A brief word finally as to Macloskie's thinking on human evolution. He addressed the subject in the pages of the *Bibliotheca Sacra* for 1903, confirming that biologists were of the opinion, and justly so, that human beings had evolved in some way from lower creatures. The precise genea-logical line was as uncertain as was the mechanism. But he felt sure that some kind of sudden development, or, as he put it, "*per saltum* varia-tion," made sense. This, of course, only applied to the human physical form. The spiritual component, breathed into the first human beings by God, did not fall within the sphere of biology. Carefully sifting the biblical pictures of Adam's creation from the dust of the ground and his receiving the breath of life, Macloskie concluded that

> Evolution, if proven as to man, will be held by the biblicist to be a part, the naturalistic part, of the total work of his making, the other part being his endowment miraculously with a spiritual nature, so that he was created in the image of God. . . . As a member of the animal kingdom, man was created by God, prob-ably in the same naturalistic fashion as the beasts that perish; but, unlike them, he has endowments which point to a higher, namely a supernaturalistic, order of creation.[43]

SUMMING UP THE SCIENTISTS

Enough has been said to this point to illustrate that evangelical scientists in North America experienced relatively little difficulty in ap-propriating the new evolutionary vision. That their response was far from uniform is equally plain. Some kept rigidly to Darwinian biology; some were prepared to flirt with Social Darwinism; others struck out on a more Neo-Lamarckian line. And if some hesitated over human evolution, there were others prepared to allow Darwin to reign even there. Yet all found some form of evolution compatible with evangelical Christianity.

Certainly my survey is far from exhaustive. But the figures I have chosen to illustrate the case are significant either for their major stance in American science or for their popularizing role in postbellum evangelical culture. And there were in addition transatlantic reinforcements. Henry Drummond, for example, sometime associate of Dwight L. Moody, pro-fessor of natural science at the Free Church College in Glasgow, and life-long evangelist, doubtless stretched evangelicalism to the very limits in his attempts to bring natural law into the spiritual world.[44] His thor-

2 (1904): 429, 439.

43. Macloskie, "The Origin of Species and of Man," *Bibliotheca Sacra* 60 (1903): 273.

44. See George Adam Smith, *The Life of Henry Drummond* (London: Hodder & Stoughton, 1899). See also James R. Moore, "Evangelicals and Evolution: Henry Drummond, Herbert Spencer, and the Naturalisation of the Spiritual World," *Scottish Journal of Theology* 38 (1985): 383-417.

oughgoing spiritualistic evolutionism, stressing continuity between the natural and spiritual worlds, was most clearly expressed in *Natural Law in the Spiritual World*, which was surprisingly well received by evangelical reviewers throughout the world. It was translated and reprinted many times and was especially successful in the United States, where it was pirated no fewer than fourteen times between 1883 (the year of its first appearance) and the turn of the century. Drummond was clearly an extreme case, but his position does indicate the lengths to which some evangelicals went in their encounter with Darwin.

Within the British Wesleyan tradition, a notable scientific figure who gave his benediction to the marriage of evolutionary biology and evangelical theology was William Henry Dallinger. Of Anglican parentage, he was converted to Methodism and entered the Wesleyan ministry in 1861. He pursued his pastoral duties with devotion until 1880, when he was elected governor and principal of Wesley College, Sheffield. But he retained his interest in natural science and kept up his research on the biology of micro-organisms and microscopy. For his endeavors he was commended by Darwin himself, was elected to a fellowship of the Royal Society, was four times president of the Royal Microscopical Society, and received several honorary doctorates. Indeed, it was in recognition of his scientific gifts that in 1888 the Wesleyan Conference relieved him of pastoral duties while allowing him to retain the status and prerogatives of a Methodist minister. Throughout his distinguished career Dallinger was a regular contributor on scientific subjects to the *Wesleyan Methodist Magazine*, and it is no surprise that he was invited to deliver the Fernley Lecture to the British Methodist Conference in 1887. His presentation, entitled "The Creator, and What We May Know of the Method of Creation," clearly unveiled his unreserved acceptance of evolution—and just as clearly his rejection of Spencer's materialism and his concern to invest Darwinism with an explicitly idealist design. Two extracts will suffice to give the flavor of Dallinger's union of biology and theology:

> Every instance of what such writers as Darwin are obliged to write of as "contrivance" or "adaptation" throughout the universe as it now is, or that shall yet arise in it through all duration, are, and will be, but factors of related harmony in a stupendously vast interlocked "mosaic" of design, which in its entirety has a "final purpose" too great for man to see.
>
> It is admitted by the fullest and farthest thinkers, that the teleological, and the mechanical views, of phenomena and their origin, are not antagonistic. Instead of mutually excluding each other in thought, they are the complement of each other. . . .
>
> Now modern biological science, guided by the splendid genius and ceaseless research of Darwin, and the whole field of

biologists, for the past quarter of a century, has been able for all
practical purposes to discover and demonstrate a great "law" or
method, according to which all the varieties of living "species,"
animal and vegetable, have arisen; connecting the remotest ages
of the life of the globe with the present flora and fauna in one
unbroken continuity, by one unchanging method.[45]

Even among those decidedly less enthusiastic about evolution on
scientific grounds, many took the trouble to emphasize the very considerable distance evangelical theology could go with the new biology. Take,
for instance, the case of Sir George Stokes, Lucasian Professor of Mathematics at Cambridge from 1849 until his death in 1903, sometime secretary of the Royal Society, and president of the Victoria Institute. Thoroughly evangelical in theology, he remained unambiguously "opposed to
evolutionary theory"[46]—but he also took care on countless occasions to
underscore the fact that it was only the universal applicability of evolutionism that he resisted. He even told the audience of his Gifford lectures
in 1891 that there was no need whatsoever "to assume that each species is
the result of a separate and independent creative act"; moreover, he
stated that "even an extreme adoption of evolution is not inconsistent
with theism." And he suggested that there were good grounds for maintaining that "when it is held so far as real evidence, or even probable
evidence, fairly conducts us to it," the doctrine of evolution exerts "a
wholesome influence even in matters of religious belief." Indeed, though
he remained tentative about human evolution, he did allow for the possibility that "the mental powers of man were conferred upon some previously existing animal form, without more alteration of bodily structure
than was compatible with some sort of evolutionary bodily change—a
supposition as much requiring a creative power as if man had been
formed directly from materials not endowed with life."[47]

My contentions, then, are simple. For evangelicals in science, the
problem with Darwin was not that he challenged the authority of the
Bible but that he had attacked design. And yet, once again, while there

---

45. William Henry Dallinger, *The Creator, and What We May Know of the
Method of Creation* (London: T. Woolmer, 1888), pp. 61-62, 67. Details of Dallinger's
life are available in the *Journal of the Royal Microscopical Society* 32 (1909): 699-702;
Proceedings of the Royal Society 82 (1910): B, iv-vi; and *Nature* 82 (1909): 71-72. See
also William Strawson, "Methodist Theology 1850-1950," in *A History of the Methodist
Church in Great Britain*, 3 vols., ed. Rupert Davies, A. Raymond George, and Gordon
Rupp (London: Epworth Press, 1983), 3: 182-231.

46. David B. Wilson, "A Physicist's Alternative to Materialism: The Religious
Thought of George Gabriel Stokes," *Victorian Studies* 28 (1984): 87.

47. Stokes, *Natural Theology: The Gifford Lectures Delivered before the University of Edinburgh in 1891* (London: Adam and Charles Black, 1891), pp. 45, 51; and
*Natural Theology: The Gifford Lectures Delivered before the University of Edinburgh in
1893* (London: Adam and Charles Black, 1893), pp. 241, 167.

was general agreement that this was a problem, there was nothing approaching an evangelical consensus on a solution. Some wanted to build Darwinism directly into Paley. Others endorsed the reign of natural law. None felt that the problem was insurmountable. And the theologians, as we will see, did nothing to discourage them.

CHAPTER 4

DARWIN AND THE DIVINES

George Frederick Wright thought Darwinism was Calvinism applied to nature. Charles Hodge, Calvinist par excellence, had a different opinion. "We have thus arrived at the answer to our question, What is Darwinism?" Hodge wrote in 1874. "It is atheism." Hodge's thoughtful conclusion, like the ideas of many great individuals, has been reduced to mere slogan by not a few crusaders—more often adopted than examined, more often repeated than explained. For this reason alone, Hodge's case merits reexamination. But in addition, Hodge and the Princeton theological tradition played a formative role in the construction of modern conservative evangelicalism, and so some reassessment of the reaction to Darwinism by the powerful Old School Princetonians is doubly important.[1]

PRINCETON'S PRELIMINARY PERSPECTIVES

Charles Hodge was himself a product of Princeton College. He had gone up from his native Philadelphia to study there in 1812 and soon came under the spell of Archibald Alexander, whose thoroughly Calvinistic outlook provided the framework of Princeton theology for over a

---

1. For the Princeton response to evolutionary theory, I have drawn on my essay "The Idea of Design: The Vicissitudes of a Key Concept in the Princeton Response to Darwin," *Scottish Journal of Theology* 37 (1984): 329-57. See also *The Princeton Theology, 1812-1921: Scripture, Science, and Theological Method from Archibald Alexander to Benjamin Warfield*, ed. Mark A. Noll (Grand Rapids: Baker Book House, 1983); Deryl Freeman Johnson, "The Attitude of the Princeton Theologians toward Darwinism and Evolution from 1859-1929" (Ph.D. diss., University of Iowa, 1968); Joseph E. Illick III, "The Reception of Darwinism at the Princeton Theological Seminary and the College at Princeton, New Jersey," *Journal of the Presbyterian Historical Society* 38 (1960): 152-65, 234-43.

CHARLES HODGE. Reprinted with permission of
the Presbyterian Historical Society

century. Biblical reverence, religious experience, Scottish philosophy, and
Reformed confessions were the warp and woof of Hodge's formal training. They became at once the intellectual furniture of his Presbyterian
mind and the love of his life. In 1822, after ordination and due pulpit
service, Hodge began his lifelong professorial association with Princeton,
broken only by a visit to the great German centers of theology between
1826 and 1828 that served to introduce him to the major currents of
theological thought in Europe. He returned from this trip with a deep
unease about rationalism, mysticism, and ritualism, determined to keep
Princeton pure from these contaminations. He soon stamped the authority of his brilliant intellect on American Protestantism, first through the
pages of the *Biblical Repertory and Princeton Review* and latterly through
his architectonic *Systematic Theology* of 1872-73. Forceful, transparent,
lucid, and zealous, Hodge still casts a long shadow over the theology of
evangelical Christianity.

Hodge's apparently thoroughgoing rejection of Darwinism needs to
be set in the context of his more general philosophical outlook. It was
substantially grounded in the Scottish realism of such individuals as

Thomas Reid and John Witherspoon. Two principles of this Common Sense school of philosophy are particularly relevant here. First, Hodge shared their belief that the universe possesses a rational structure that corresponds with the structure of the human mind. Through the use of reason, the Common Sense philosophers believed, human beings could ascertain the intimate workings and causal processes of the natural world. Mind and nature are presumed to be closely bound together in the order of things. Second, like the Common Sense philosophers, Hodge was an enthusiastic admirer of the inductive Baconian ideal both in science and theology. Put simply, this approach assumed that true knowledge is based on fact gathering, on painstaking data collection without prior recourse to theory.

Hodge's appraisal of Darwinism was structured by these basic convictions. On the one hand, he persistently drew a sharp distinction between fact and theory. He loved to quote Agassiz to the effect that facts are sacred, revelations from God, whereas theories are the mere speculations of fallen humanity. On the other hand, Hodge reserved an important place in his overall theological system for the old theistic arguments, and in particular for the argument from design. Thus, while he followed the Scottish tradition in placing very definite limits on his adoption of natural theology, he remained convinced that the teleological argument was sufficient to establish the existence of God as an intelligent voluntary agent.

Hodge referred to Darwinian evolution only sporadically during the 1860s. In 1862, for example, he mentioned Darwin's "interesting work" in passing in a lengthy footnote appended to an article entitled "Diversity of Species in the Human Race" in the *Biblical Repertory and Princeton Review*. But if he found Darwin's work "interesting," he nevertheless failed to be convinced by it. He was inclined to dismiss as absurd any theory suggesting that life could have developed from a very few original forms. So he left the matter there for the meantime. Indeed, it was not until the publication of his *Systematic Theology* in 1872-73, some thirteen years after the first appearance of the *Origin of Species*, that he gave the subject any considered treatment. And he followed up this analysis the next year in his final book-length work, *What Is Darwinism?*

It was in the second part of his theological magnum opus, dealing with anthropology, that Hodge presented his first systematic rebuttal of Darwin's theory. Under the subject heading "Anti-scriptural Theories of the Universe," he provided a well-informed review of the Darwinian viewpoint, assembling at the same time what he took to be compelling scholarly refutations of the doctrine. The most serious flaw he found in Darwin's theory was that it was a "mere hypothesis . . . incapable of proof." But he also noted its failure to take seriously the distinction between natural and artificial species—that is, between genuinely different species of nature and simple varieties within species. Further, he emphasized its failure to address adequately the sterility of hybrids, the lack of a satisfactory mechanism for inheritance (which, in the absence of Mendel's formula, led to Darwin's problematic theory of pangenesis), and paleontological difficulties in establishing the antiquity of the human race. Throughout his assessment Hodge showed that he had a firm grasp of the relevant scientific material, and he did pay Darwin the compliment of describing him as standing in the first rank of naturalists. Darwin was, Hodge went on, "on all sides respected not only for his knowledge and his skill in observation and description, but for his frankness and fairness."[2]

Such scientifically literate ruminations on the subject, it must be noted, demonstrate just how genuine was Hodge's concern to marry theological reflection to scientific research. After all, he was convinced that in principle there could be no conflict between the established facts of science and those of Scripture. He had already affirmed that biblical hermeneutics should proceed under the guidance of proven scientific findings—though he also made it abundantly clear that the theologian had every right to demand that alleged "facts" be verified beyond the possibility of doubt in view of the fluctuations in scientific theory from age to age and place to place. Still, he was prepared to concede in his 1859 defense of the unity of the human species against the theory of plural origins put forward by Morton, Nott, Gliddon, and indeed Agassiz that if the idea of a long earth history were to be established, then the early chapters of Genesis should be interpreted accordingly.[3] In the 1870s he suggested that the term "day" could be understood as referring to the great geological epochs and went on to remark on the marvelous coincidence between the account of Genesis and the assumed facts of geology. Dana and Guyot, he stressed, had done a great deal to vindicate the biblical record, and for this "the friends of the Bible owe them a debt of gratitude."[4] Apart from anything else, this made any suggestion that the Bible was of human origin "utterly incomprehensible." Hodge was quite understandably delighted, his son Archibald Alexander Hodge recalled, when his younger colleague W. H. Green finally demolished the long-established practice of dating the origin of humanity from the Old Testament chronological records.

Hodge's rehearsal of the various scientific equivocations over Darwinism make it plain that he was much less willing to make the same concessions to the new biology that he was to the new geology. There was a far more fundamental obstacle to his acceptance of Darwinian biology than his reiteration of its scientific inadequacy suggests. It had nothing to

---

2. Hodge, *Systematic Theology*, 3 vols. (1872-73; rpt., London: James Clark, 1960), 2: 12.

3. See Hodge, "Unity of Mankind," *Biblical Repertory and Princeton Review* 31 (1859): 103-49.

4. Hodge, *Systematic Theology*, 1: 574.

do with biblical exegesis or authority. It was, quite simply, that Darwin had overthrown design.

This is unambiguously brought out in Hodge's definition of Darwinism. In his estimation Darwinism comprised three distinct albeit related ideas: evolution, natural selection, and an ateleological mode of explanation. But "neither the first nor the second of these elements," he affirmed, "constitute Darwinism; nor do the two combined." Rather, "the most important and only distinctive element of his theory" was the third—the idea, as Hodge put it, "that this natural selection is without design, being conducted by unintelligent causes." This definition of Darwinism—which was after all the whole point of his book *What Is Darwinism?*—is crucially important for understanding Hodge's apparently resolute conclusion. Darwinism was atheism *precisely* and *solely* because it was inimical to design.

> It is . . . neither evolution nor natural selection, which give Darwinism its peculiar character and importance. It is that Darwin rejects all teleology, or the doctrine of final causes. He denies design in any of the organisms in the vegetable or animal world. . . . As it is this feature of his system which brings it into conflict not only with Christianity, but with the fundamental principles of natural religion, it should be clearly established.[5]

In the remainder of the volume, Hodge sought to demonstrate both from Darwin's own testimony and from the admission of his friends and foes alike that he had left no room for the old Paleyan Watchmaker. The very fact that his long list of witnesses includes such names as Huxley, Haeckel, Buchner, Vogt, Agassiz, the Duke of Argyll, Janet, Flourens, Walter Mitchell, and Dawson itself attests to how widely discussed was the impact of Darwin's theory on the argument from design.

Running through Hodge's analysis are two qualifications that throw much light on his repudiation of Darwinism. First, he emphasizes on several occasions that the theory of evolution is not to be equated with Darwinism. "A man . . . may be an evolutionist," he insisted, "without being a Darwinian." By implication this meant that the rejection of Darwinism did not necessarily mean the repudiation of evolution. "Professor Janet," says Hodge, "does not seem to have much objection to the doctrine of evolution in itself; it is the denial of teleology that he regards as the fatal element of Mr. Darwin's theory."[6] Second, and even more significant, Hodge conceded that the theory of evolution can be interpreted in a theistic as well as an atheistic manner. In his *Systematic Theology*, for example, he states that

> In saying that this system is atheistic, it is not said that Mr. Darwin is an atheist. . . . Nor is it meant that everyone who

---

5. Hodge, *What Is Darwinism?* (New York: Scribner's, 1874), pp. 48, 52.
6. Hodge, *What Is Darwinism?* pp. 50-51, 106.

adopts the theory does it in an atheistic sense. It has already been remarked that there is a theistic and an atheistic form of the nebular hypothesis as to the origin of the universe; so there may be a theistic interpretation of the Darwinian theory.[7]

Again, the crucial point was how the question of design was handled. Hodge accepted the idea that Christians could responsibly believe that one kind of plant and animal had evolved from earlier and simpler forms so long as they also affirmed that everything was designed by God and that it was due to his purpose and power that all the forms of vegetable and animal life are what they are. Moreover, since Hodge defined Darwinism in such a way as to make the rejection of design its cardinal feature, he could with some consistency go on to say that Asa Gray (Darwin's leading American apologist as we have seen) might be an evolutionist, but he was not really a Darwinian at all! Thus, Hodge held that evolution with design was Christian, but evolution without design was atheism.

In some respects Hodge's analysis and instincts were both sound. His reflections on Darwin's concept of "nature" showed just how ambiguous "natural" selection really was. As an antonym both to artificial selection and to supernatural supervision, natural selection was advanced to dispel final cause from biology. Yet the rhetorical cast of his theory, as we have already seen, constantly displayed the teleological vocabulary of purpose, intention, and contrivance. Hodge's distinctions served to throw light on the metaphorical character of Darwin's theory that induced the irrepressible tendency to capitalize and personify Natural Selection. At the same time, Hodge's fearfulness for the future of the old natural theology arguments was not misplaced. As we have seen, the tension between Darwinism and design soon led to the erosion and fragmentation of the Paleyan intellectual tradition. Natural theology was never to be the same again; it was to be salvaged principally by a move to a more holistic conception of design and a new emphasis on the regularity of natural law.

Hodge's doctrine of Providence was certainly sophisticated enough to have encouraged some rapprochement with Darwinism. He already believed that God was working in the processes of life, and it would not have been too foreign to his assumptions to suppose that new species might be introduced by this method. But Hodge's understanding of the argument from design was still cast in the utilitarian terms proposed by Paley, and this, together no doubt with his lifelong suspicion of speculative idealist philosophy, encouraged his intractable concluding dismissal: "The conclusion of the whole latter is, that the denial of design in nature is virtually the denial of God. Mr. Darwin's theory does deny all design in nature, therefore, his theory is virtually atheistical."[8]

---

7. Hodge, *Systematic Theology*, 2: 16.
8. Hodge, *What Is Darwinism?* p. 173.

If Hodge felt that Darwin had subverted design, however, James McCosh felt that he had expounded it. Reminiscing on twenty years as president of the College of New Jersey (subsequently Princeton University), McCosh confessed, "I have been defending Evolution, but, in so doing, have given the proper account of it as the method of God's procedure, and find that when so understood it is in no way inconsistent with Scripture." When McCosh first arrived in Princeton in 1868, determined, as he himself put it, to devote his "remaining life under God to old Princeton and the religious and literary interests with which it is identified,"[9] Hodge, who was then the College's senior trustee, warmly welcomed him. Indeed, during the inaugural celebrations Hodge declared that never in the history of the College had an academic appointment been received with such universal enthusiasm.

Like Hodge, McCosh had drunk deeply of the waters of Scottish philosophy and remained a devotee of such giants in that tradition as Thomas Chalmers and Hugh Miller. During the 1843 disruption of the established Presbyterian Church of Scotland, McCosh had sided with them and soon emerged as a vigorous polemicist for the new self-consciously evangelical Free Church. But whereas Hodge had incorporated the major tenets of the Scottish philosophy into a defensive attack on Darwinism, McCosh "set about to prove that the natural origin of species is not inconsistent with intelligent design in nature or with the existence of a personal Creator of the world."[10] So how, it may well be asked, can we account for these rather different assessments of Darwinian evolution by two such similar men?

I would like to suggest that the foundations of McCosh's evolutionary Calvinism had been laid long before he first crossed the Atlantic to the New World. In 1852 McCosh had seceded from a pastorate in Brechin, Scotland, to occupy the chair of metaphysics at the newly founded Queen's College in Belfast. During his time there, he vigorously threw himself into the life of the Irish Presbyterian Church, eagerly participated in what has come to be known as "the '59 revival," was cofounder and patron of the Bible and Colportage Society of Ireland, and conducted regular Bible classes for mill workers in the poorer parts of the city. His intellectual gifts combined with his evangelical fervor also made him a prominent figure in the Evangelical Alliance.

McCosh's appointment to a professorial chair at Queen's College came largely in recognition of the intellectual stature of his first book, *The*

---

9. McCosh, in *The Life of James McCosh: A Record Chiefly Autobiographical*, ed. William Milligan Sloane (Edinburgh: T. & T. Clark, 1896), pp. 234, 184.

10. Alexander T. Ormond, "James McCosh as Thinker and Educator," *Princeton Theological Review* 1 (1903): 345. The standard biography of McCosh is J. David Hoeveler, Jr.'s *James McCosh and the Scottish Intellectual Tradition* (Princeton: Princeton University Press, 1981).

Method of the Divine Government. It went through some nine editions between 1850, when it was initially published, and 1867. Even in this early work, the conceptual seeds of McCosh's subsequent endorsement of Darwinism can already be detected. He presented his interpretation of the method of divine government in the physical world in the second book of this treatise. He summarized the traditional view of Providential design in what he called "The principle of special adaptation," detailing in a manner worthy of a reincarnated Paley a host of confirming cases. But he hastened to add that this particular scheme was coincident with, and in some ways subservient to, another version, which he named "The principle of Order." Under the rubric "Wisdom displayed in the prevalence of general laws and observable order in the world," McCosh urged that "wherever we find law, there we see the certain traces of a lawgiver." The holistic and idealist form of McCosh's proposals at this point are evident, for example, in his affirmation that "the agents of nature are so arranged into a system, or rather a system of systems, that events fall out in an orderly manner" and in his appreciation of Owen's enumeration of the homologies in the vertebrate skeleton, which he said demonstrate the ideal plan unifying the whole organic order. Speaking of the fundamental numerical order in creation, he noted, "There is a conformity of structure running through the whole vertebrate series, as seen, for instance, in the fore limbs. . . . Thus, the normal or typical number of carpal bones is ten, or five in each row, corresponding to the typical number of digits."[11] So McCosh was already calling for a more thoroughly organic conception of the creation than Paley's system allowed. And, taken as a whole, the book represented his attempt to temper Scottish philosophy's rationalistic tendencies with the evangelical sense of sin and belief in an omnipotent deity.

McCosh perpetuated this same basic argument in his next major work. *Typical Forms and Special Ends in Creation,* which he wrote in 1855 with George Dickie, the Queen's College professor of natural history, was a large synthetic overview, conceived on a grand scale and representative of the greatest strength of pre-Darwinian natural theology. The book was very largely patterned on Owen's morphology. So while McCosh conceded that "the recent discoveries in regard to the homology of parts can never set aside the old doctrine of the teleology of parts, which affirms that every organ is adapted to a special end," he was just as certain that those very illustrations accumulated by earlier British natural theologians were much too restrictive. Far from sensing any expulsion of design in the idea of a "General Order" in nature as some suggested, he felt it actually provided a more secure foundation on which to construct natural theology. Owen's idea of archetypal plans was, it seemed, superior to

---

11. James McCosh, *The Method of the Divine Government: Physical and Moral,* 3d ed. (Edinburgh: Sutherland & Knox, 1852), pp. 136, 115, 123.

Cuvier's special modifications. Even in the idealist writings of such opponents of natural theology as Geoffroy Saint-Hilaire and Lorenz Oken, McCosh found themes that could not "be overlooked in a natural theology suited to the middle of the nineteenth century."[12] Indeed, he suggested, they stood in special need of Christian exposition because they had been ignored by Paley and the successive Bridgewater Treatises alike.

Although the run of this book was ruined by the appearance of Darwin's *Origin*, its mode of analysis was perhaps not so moribund as has sometimes been imagined. For in beginning the transfer of design from utilitarian adaptation to the orderly laws of nature, McCosh was preparing the ground for his subsequent identification of design in the pattern of evolutionary progress. By showing the interconnectedness of all the parts of nature and the presence of an immanent God, McCosh's new idealism prepared the way for a religious understanding of evolution. And the evangelical insistence on inward spiritual experience was not too far removed from these sentiments.

McCosh's first full-length treatment of natural theology after the advent of Darwinism came in a series of lectures at New York's Union Theological Seminary in 1871, later published as *Christianity and Positivism*. The new biology had by now made questions out of former assumptions and plainly necessitated some intellectual adjustments. The fixity of species, for example, could no longer be presumed, and the question of the status of the human race soon came to the fore. On this McCosh cited the anthropological evidence of Lubbock and Huxley to establish a wide gulf between animal and human intellectual capacity. At the same time, he left the matter of the formation of the human body—as opposed to the soul—an open question. And he dismissed the monistic claims of some natural selectionists on the grounds that there were unbridgeable gaps in the natural order, notably between the organic and inorganic, the conscious and unconscious, plant life and animal life. On the significance of human beings as a new evolutionary departure, McCosh sided with such individuals as Wallace, Powell, Cope, and Huxley in emphasizing that the advent of human intelligence inaugurated a new phase in evolutionary history. As he put it, "Man modifies Natural Selection, by bringing things together which are separated in physical geography. . . . The intellectual comes to rule the physical, and the moral claims to subordinate both."[13]

But although he equivocated over and modified the basic Darwinian scheme in these ways, we should not suppose that he had any great difficulty accommodating the new theory of evolution to his version of the

---

12. McCosh and Dickie, *Typical Forms and Special Ends in Creation* (Edinburgh: Thomas Constable, 1856), pp. 5, 27.

13. McCosh, *Christianity and Positivism: A Series of Lectures to the Times on Natural Theology and Christian Apologetics* (London: Macmillan, 1871), pp. 69-70.

argument from design. He held that the laws of organic progression were themselves expressions of Final Cause:

> There is proof of Plan in the Organic Unity and Growth of the World. As there is evidence of purpose, not only in every organ of the plant, but in the whole plant . . . so there are proofs of design, not merely in the individual plant and individual animal, but in the whole structure of the Cosmos and in the manner in which it makes progress from age to age. Every reflecting mind, in tracing the development [McCosh's synonym for "evolution"] of the plant or animal, will see a design and a unity of design in it, in the unconscious elements being all made to conspire to a given end, in the frame of the animated being taking a predetermined form; so every one trained in the great truths of advanced science should see a contemplated purpose in the way in which the materials and forces and life of the universe are made to conspire, to secure a progress through indeterminate ages. The persistence of force may be one of the elements conspiring to this end; the law of Natural Selection may be another, or it may only be a modification of the same. . . .
>
> The accomplishment of all this implies arrangement and co-agency. There are order and progression, we have seen, in the physical works of God: this is said, in modern nomenclature, to be a law. . . . All such laws are complex . . . [but] the law of the progression of all plants and of all animals is a still more complex one, implying adjustment upon adjustment of all the elements and all the powers of nature towards the accomplishment of an evidently contemplated end, in which are displayed the highest wisdom and the most considerate goodness.[14]

When the Evangelical Alliance met in New York during October 1873, McCosh shared the platform of the Philosophical Section with Arnold Guyot and William Dawson. He chose as his subject "Religious Aspects of the Doctrine of Development." Here he stressed the complementarity of religious and scientific accounts of the same phenomena. What on the one hand was ascribed to the orderly workings of the Creator, he argued, could on the other hand be interpreted as the results of natural law; each account expounded the plans of the great Lawgiver in its own way.

Here too McCosh insisted that it was useless to tell younger naturalists that there was no truth in the theory of evolution. Whatever its limitations, he said, "they know that there is truth, which is not to be set aside by denunciation. Religious philosophers," he went on, "might be more profitably employed in showing them the religious aspects of the doctrine of development; and some would be grateful to any who would help them to keep their new faith in science." In his own address, McCosh

---

14. McCosh, *Christianity and Positivism*, pp. 90-92.

tried to do just that—to show the religious value of the theory. Waxing lyrical in his analogy between creation and the "new creation," he spoke of a continuity of divine purpose running throughout the created order. "Just as in the prehistoric ages there had appeared a plant life, and an animal life, and an intellectual life, and a moral life, so now we have a spiritual life—it is the dispensation of the Spirit." This idea of plan and purpose governed McCosh's reinvigoration of the design argument. For he was only too aware that the world was a place of conflict, misery, struggle, and suffering. These realities had been glossed over in the writings of Newton, Cuvier, Paley, and Chalmers, he said. Only in the recognition of an overarching plan, a more ultimate whole, could it be seen that "there *is* order in the world, but it is order subordinating conflicting powers."[15] The idea of development was not just compatible with design, he maintained; it augmented and clarified it.

In its theoretical posture, McCosh's 1885 booklet *Development*—the third in his Philosophic Series—offered the same basic synthesis of Darwinism and design. Order, beneficence, and design were all to be detected in the evolutionary process, he said; "chance" variations were ultimately misnamed; and the idea of the production of new species by natural law was not intrinsically irreligious. Only in his understanding of the nature of the processes involved does there seem to be any reappraisal. Already suspicious about the universal efficacy of natural selection, McCosh's approving citation of Cope's belief that "psychical powers modify and strengthen development," together with his according a more active role to the external environment, suggest an increasing predilection toward Neo-Lamarckism.[16]

As we have already seen, a Lamarckian renascence was by now well under way in the United States under the influence of such individuals as Cope, Hyatt, Packard, Le Conte, Powell, and King. This movement gave renewed impetus to the old idea of the inheritance of acquired characteristics and the directive evolutionary significance of consciousness and will. The compatibility of Neo-Lamarckism with idealism, a spirit of progress, and emergent evolution made it particularly attractive. So when McCosh gathered together his mature reflections on the subject in his Bedell lectures for 1887 (published the following year as *The Religious Aspect of Evolution*), he listed natural selection, the use and disuse of organs, and direct environmental modification as causes of biological transmutation. Such a tripartite formula would have been welcomed by almost any Neo-Lamarckian. Indeed, McCosh's tributes to the work of

---

15. McCosh, "Religious Aspects of the Doctrine of Development," in *History, Essays, Orations, and other Documents of the Sixth General Conference of the Evangelical Alliance*, ed. Philip Schaff and S. Irenaeus Prime (New York: Harper, 1874), pp. 264-71.

16. McCosh, *Development: What It Can and Cannot Do*, Philosophic Series, no. 3 (Edinburgh: T. & T. Clark, 1885), p. 38.

such prominent Neo-Lamarckians as Henry Fairfield Osborne (a former student of his who had risen to the post of professor of comparative anatomy at Princeton) and Joseph Le Conte (a Presbyterian and professor of geology at the University of California) further attests to his increasing enthusiasm for that theory. His references to Cope and Hyatt's Neo-Lamarckian mechanism as "undoubtedly acting everywhere in nature" only confirms this suggestion.[17]

All in all, McCosh's thirty years of efforts to work out an evolutionary natural theology brought him to an assessment of Darwinism quite at variance with that of his colleague Charles Hodge—though, as I have tried to show, Hodge was really opposed only to a Darwinian theory opposing teleology. Their different appraisals stemmed from the way in which each framed the argument from design. Indeed, more than anything else, their divergent interpretations of that philosophical question determined their evaluations of the "evidence" for Darwinian science. Yet for both of them, the idea of a designed universe constituted both the foundation and fabric of a truly biblical philosophy of science. Their assessments of the precise character of the relationship between natural history and natural theology might have been different, but they were both convinced that it was a marriage made in heaven.

The agreement between Hodge and McCosh on the need for union between natural history and natural theology remained quite central in the Princeton theological tradition. Indeed, in 1865 a special Princeton professorship of the harmony of science and religion was created for Charles Woodruff Shields, a Princeton graduate and Presbyterian minister of some sixteen years' standing. Shields's magnum opus, the two-volume *Philosophia Ultima*, was designed to fulfill what he took to be his appointed task as a Princeton professor—namely, providing "a systematic illustration of the harmony of Biblical and scientific truth."[18] The sublimity of Shields's vision to survey the entire gamut of human scientific knowledge, and his prolixity in making the attempt, recalled for James R. Moore the work of Herbert Spencer.[19] While it is true that Shields was of the opinion the union of science and religion amounted to something of a marriage under strain, he was in no doubt that scientific discovery and divine revelation were ultimately mutually reinforcing. Thus in geology and anthropology—the disciplines he surveyed that were most subject to evolutionary reinterpretation—he wrote,

---

17. McCosh, *The Religious Aspect of Evolution*, rev. ed. (New York: Scribner's, 1890), p. 17. See also the second booklet in his Philosophic Series, *Energy: Efficient and Final Cause* (Edinburgh: T. & T. Clark, 1884).

18. Thomas Jefferson Wertenbaker, *Princeton 1746-1896* (Princeton: Princeton University Press, 1946), p. 285.

19. See Moore, *The Post-Darwinian Controversies: A Study of the Protestant Struggle to Come to Terms with Darwin in Great Britain and America, 1870-1900* (Cambridge: Cambridge University Press, 1979), pp. 358-59.

Take away this revealed portion and there would be left nought but a blind evolution of chaotic matter and force without rational cause or aim; successive dynasties of life supplanting one another in one long, fierce struggle for supremacy; and an issuing medley over the globe of change and design, life and death, pain and pleasure. Take away the discovered portion, and that eternal Jehova, with whom a thousand years are but as one day, will appear crowding the creative energy of ages into a few hours merely to enforce a lesson of Sabbath observance, and then maintaining a rule throughout animate nature as impotent and malevolent as that of some all-devouring Saturn or tyrannical prince. But combine the two portions of knowledge, and the creative epochs of Genesis become illustrated by the cosmogonic eras of geology in one growing argument for the power, wisdom and goodness of that Creator whose tender mercies are over all his works, and unto whom are they known from the beginning of the world.

Or again,

Take away these revealed truths and civilized man could see in himself only a developed animal; his highest and purest culture would be accepted as but the gradual outcome of savage bestiality; and the image of God be lost in the image of an ape. Take away the discovered facts, and that marvellous frame, whose members were all written in God's book when as yet there was none of them, would seem to have been wrought as a mere Promethean statue of clay in the midst of living nature.[20]

With this in mind, let us turn now to an assessment of the way in which the theory of evolution was regarded by later Princeton theologians.

THE PRINCETON SUCCESSION

The respective theological estimates of Darwinism by Hodge and McCosh symbolize in many ways the two phases of Archibald Alexander Hodge's evaluation of the Darwinian theory. Son of and academic successor to Charles Hodge, the younger Hodge studied physics in 1841-42 under the distinguished Joseph Henry, later director of the Smithsonian Institution, before devoting his energies more exclusively to theology. The successive editions of his *Outlines of Theology* provide a convenient point of departure. The first edition, published in 1866, displays an almost

---

20. Shields, *Philosophia Ultima; or, Science of the Sciences*, 2 vols. (London: Sampson Low, Marston, Searle & Rivington, 1889), 2: 444-45. See also the articles on Shields in the *Dictionary of American Biography*, 17: 104-5, and *Appleton's Cyclopaedia of American Biography*, ed. James Grant Wilson and John Fiske (New York: D. Appleton, 1888), 5: 509-10.

slavish adherence to the position already articulated by his father. Like him, A. A. Hodge was prepared to accept, for example, the nebular hypothesis as a working theory of the origin of the universe as long as it was interpreted as a description of the divine *modus operandi*. But he was suspicious of any new theory that implied a suspension of the assumption that the universe is divinely designed and providentially controlled. In his opinion, Darwin's theory fell into this category, and he was glad to be able to draw on Lyell's attempts to refute the idea of species transformation. By the time Hodge produced an enlarged revision of his book in 1878, however, the intellectual climate had significantly shifted. Louis Agassiz was gone, and with him the teeth of scientific objection to Darwin; Lyell had changed his mind; and James Dana at Yale, Asa Gray at Harvard, and George Wright at Oberlin, all scholars with impeccable scientific and theological credentials, were publicly advocating a Christianized Darwinism. Even those unhappy with the specifically Darwinian formula (e.g., the Neo-Lamarckians) were nonetheless convinced that evolution had occurred.

The crux of Hodge's reevaluation, it once again seems to me, lies in his understanding of the design argument. He couched his whole discussion in terms of the charge that the teleological argument had been impaired, if not invalidated, by Darwin's theory. Thus, while he reaffirmed the old view that the argument from order and adaptation in the universe was obfuscated in Darwin's resort to "*accidental* variations occurring through unlimited time," he did concede that the natural theologian had only the most "friendly interest" in evolutionary theories that did not deny divine immanence and providence.[21] This not inconsiderable change of heart and tone doubtless reflects Hodge's shift to a more idealist interpretation of the design argument. He had, after all, already told his students that Christendom was in need of "another Paley, to rewrite the argument from design in view of the advance of science."[22] Now he felt sure that even if continuous evolution were to be proved, the teleological argument could be salvaged.

As his subsequent telling review of Asa Gray's *Natural Science and Religion* clearly shows, Hodge had come to see a "more comprehensive and ultimate teleology" in the ideas of "Continuity of causation throughout the universe" and "the universal law of the Uniformity of Nature." Here, too, we should note in passing, Hodge characterized Gray as "a thorough evolutionist of the Darwinian variety, and at the same time a thoroughly loyal theist and Christian"—a description rather different from his father's earlier designation. If the universe is the manifestation

---

21. A. A. Hodge, *Outlines of Theology*, rev. ed. (New York: A. C. Armstrong, 1891), p. 40.

22. Hodge, quoted by Johnson, in "The Attitude of the Princeton Theologians toward Darwinism and Evolution from 1859-1929," p. 140.

of a coherent plan of God, said Hodge, then the concept of "an ideal evolution, a providential unfolding of a general plan, in which general designs and methods converge in all directions to the ultimate end of the whole" is far from incompatible with Christian theism.[23] And, it must be added, Hodge was now prepared to allow that the human physical form had undergone its own evolutionary history.

Further perusal of Hodge's viewpoint need not detain us longer. Suffice to say that in his introduction to Joseph Van Dyke's *Theism and Evolution* (1886), he confirmed that "Evolution considered as a plan of an infinitely wise Person and executed under the control of His everywhere present energies can never be irreligious; can never exclude design, providence, grace or miracles." Certainly Hodge's innate conservatism prevented him from wholeheartedly embracing the new evolutionary biology. Much of the scientific groundwork still had to be laid. And there was always the danger that the theory would be elevated to a comprehensive philosophy that would squeeze out the God of the Bible. But his reassessments do reveal a concern to take the sting out of the "Science or Scripture" propaganda by showing how a reconstituted natural theology with a holistic conception of design could provide a point of convergence for scientist and theologian alike.

Joseph Van Dyke, in fact, was no less half-hearted in endorsement of evolution than was Hodge. The two men, of course, were exponents of the same tradition. Van Dyke had already had a long association with Princeton, as a graduate first of the college and then of the seminary. He had, moreover, just received a D.D. from the college two years before his book appeared and had done some teaching there as well. His real goal in writing *Theism and Evolution* was to protect the faith from collapse should the Darwinian theory come to be vindicated. In strategy he did little more than repeat the efforts of McCosh and A. A. Hodge. Darwinian natural selection did not subvert design, they all argued; it strengthened it. A newer teleology had emerged to win the day by incorporating within it such apparently purposeless processes as overproduction, the struggle for existence, and the survival of the fittest. This was, at best, a guarded endorsement, but as Moore has quite rightly said of Van Dyke's volume, "Its significance lay rather in its deliberate openness to Darwin and in its calculated departure from the anti-Darwinism of the elder Hodge."[24]

A broadly similar evaluation of the theory was made by Francis Landey Patton, who in 1888 succeeded McCosh as president of Princeton University. Patton had returned to the seminary in 1881 to occupy a chair specially created for him, and subsequently, on his resignation from the university, he returned to the seminary to become its president in 1902.

---

23. A. A. Hodge, review of *Natural Science and Religion*, by Asa Gray, *Presbyterian Review* 1 (1880): 586-89.

24. Moore, *The Post-Darwinian Controversies*, p. 245.

His loyalty to the Old School traditions is evident not only in his institutional affiliations, however, but also in his eulogy for Charles Hodge, in such publications as *Fundamental Christianity*, and in the fact that J. Gresham Machen dedicated his book *What Is Faith?* to him in 1925. The ultimate ambivalence of Patton's Darwinian judgments is plainly brought out in an article entitled "Evolution and Apologetics" that he wrote for the *Presbyterian Review* in 1885. On the one hand, he dissociates himself in this article from Charles Hodge's conclusion, arguing that even if his evaluation was valid for a particularly restrictive version of evolution theory, it was possible—in fact, it was inevitable—that one would construe it teleologically.

> There is a teleology immanent in the very nature of the organisms providing for the existing order of biological development. This, again, only shows that the doctrine of evolution cannot be made rational without invoking the idea of design, and that instead of being antagonistic to the theistic proof which builds upon design, the idea of design is woven into the very web of nature.[25]

And yet, like A. A. Hodge, Patton wanted incontrovertible scientific proof. With missing links, hybrid sterility, and gaps in the chain of being still obstacles to be removed, Patton insisted that theologians need not feel compelled to embark on any doctrinal reconstruction. In the end, he simply affirmed that if Darwinism should be verified, apologetics could easily accommodate its philosophical implications.

If Hodge's and Patton's endorsement of evolution was ultimately tentative, B. B. Warfield was decidedly more partisan. By his own admission a "Darwinian of the purest water" even before the arrival of McCosh at Princeton, Warfield nonetheless recalled his coming as "distinctly the most inspiring force" he had encountered during student days.[26] And indeed, at key points his judgments on Darwinian biology betray the infiltration of McCosh's natural theology. It goes without saying that Warfield's endorsement of Darwin was not unqualified, however. He held that any scientific theory that in principle subverted providence or occasional supernatural interference must ultimately prove unacceptable. But within those limits, Warfield, in pointed contrast to both of the Hodges, said he would "raise no question as to the compatibility of the Darwinian form of the hypothesis of evolution with Christianity."[27]

The context of this particular ratification of Darwin's theory is itself important, for it shows Warfield's capacity to distinguish central issues

---

25. Patton, "Evolution and Apologetics," *Presbyterian Review* 6 (1885): 140.
26. Warfield, "Personal Reflections of Princeton Undergraduate Life," *The Princeton Alumni Weekly*, 6 April 1916, pp. 650-53.
27. Warfield, "Charles Darwin's Religious Life: A Sketch in Spiritual Biography," in *Studies in Theology* (New York: Oxford University Press, 1932), p. 548.

B. B. WARFIELD. Reprinted with permission of the
Presbyterian Historical Society

from peripheral issues. He made the statement in an article entitled
"Charles Darwin's Religious Life," in which he reviewed the three-volume
Life and Letters of Charles Darwin. As the subtitle "A Sketch in Spiritual
Biography" suggests, Warfield focused on what has come to be known as
Darwin's "affective decline"—that is, his increasing distaste for art, music, literature, and religion. Warfield certainly lamented the spiritually
disruptive effects of the theory of evolution on its chief advocate, and he
expressed his annoyance at Darwin's absolutist claims for his natural
selection mechanism. But this must not be allowed to conceal the fact
that Warfield remained enthusiastic about the theory as a natural law
operating under the control of Providence—an interpretation supported
in various ways, he noted, by such scientists as Carpenter, Dallinger, and
Gray. Warfield held that Darwin's aesthetic atrophy and spiritual dis-
affection could be traced on the one hand to an inability to conceive of
God as immanent in the universe (which resulted in a misapprehension

of the doctrine of Providence) and on the other hand to an unsophisticated understanding of teleology. It was Warfield's concern, therefore, to articulate a theological defense of divine design and providential government of the world in evolutionary terms.

Warfield's sustained interest in the evolution controversies is evident first in his numerous reviews of literature on the subject and then in the "Anthropology" lectures he delivered annually from 1888 to 1907. As for the reviews, Warfield looked favorably on the proevolution sentiments in George Matheson's *Christianity and Evolution* and in McCosh's *Religious Aspect of Evolution* but was rather less happy with what he took to be the pantheistic savor of Joseph Le Conte's evolutional idealism.[28] Much greater enthusiasm was reserved for James Iverach's *Christianity and Evolution*, to which we will presently turn, and for J. N. Shearman's *Natural Theology of Evolution*.[29] Both of these had sought to integrate evolution and the theistic argument through a renewed emphasis on the uniformity of natural law.

That Warfield particularly endorsed these attempts to rescue natural theology from the Darwinian onslaught (he announced that "an evolutionary Paley" had arrived in Shearman) is not surprising. In his "Anthropology" lectures he repeatedly emphasized the point that theists could consistently hold to a virtually mechanistic theory if they believed natural laws were the expression of divine supervision. This is also clearly brought out in his extended review of Vernon L. Kellogg's monumental *Darwinism Today*, published in 1908. Warfield was lavish in his praise for Kellogg's expository skill and critical penetration, stating that readers interested in biological theory "cannot do better than to resort to his comprehensive and readable volume." But on one major point Warfield demurred—namely, Kellogg's antiteleological prejudice. "Some lack of genuine philosophical acumen must be suspected," he said, "when it is not fully understood that teleology is in no way inconsistent with—is rather necessarily involved in—a complete system of natural causation. Every teleological system implies a complete 'causo-mechanical' explanation as its instrument."[30] As far as Warfield was concerned, it was possible to explain any given phenomenon in terms of either a religious cause or a scientific cause. This idea of "concursus" was central to his theological project; it also enabled him to take into account the human and divine elements in biblical inspiration. Clearly, therefore, Warfield was just as willing as McCosh to relocate design in the orderly laws of nature.

---

28. See the *Presbyterian Review* 9 (1888): 355, 510-11.

29. See the *Presbyterian and Reformed Review* 6 (1895): 366; and the *Princeton Theological Review* 14 (1916): 323.

30. Warfield, review of *Darwinism Today*, by Vernon L. Kellogg, *Princeton Theological Review* 6 (1908): 640-50. He made the same point in his review of *Naturalism and Religion*, by Rudolf Otto, *Princeton Theological Review* 7 (1909): 106-12.

Of course this should not be taken to mean that Warfield had kicked over the traces of divine intervention or hastily jettisoned the miraculous. For if miracle was not crucial to *natural* theology, it was foundational to *biblical* theology. In his "Anthropology" lectures he insisted, contrary to Darwin and Romanes, that it is impossible to give a purely naturalistic account of mentality and morality, not least because of the importance of a period of moral probation prior to the fall; contrary to Joseph Le Conte and Freeman Hove Johnson in particular, he insisted on the need for holding to the immediate creation of the soul; and he acknowledged the evolutionary difficulty posed by the Mosaic account of the creation of Eve. In light of the fact that Warfield was so passionately dedicated to the idea of biblical inerrancy, it is remarkable that he saw the latter description as the "sole passage" that seemed to bar the way to an acceptance of an evolutionary viewpoint. Nevertheless, as he put it himself, "I am free to say, for myself, that I do not think that there is any general statement in the Bible or any part of the account of creation, either as given in Gen. I & II or elsewhere alluded to, that need be opposed to evolution." As to the question of Eve's creation, Warfield conceded that it was "possible that this may be held to be a miracle (as Dr. Woodrow holds), or else that the narative [*sic*] may be held to be partial & taken like the very partial descriptions of the formation of the individual in Job & the Psalms, to teach only the general fact that Eve came of Adam's flesh & bone." He himself felt, however, that these construals ran against the natural reading of the text.

Besides, Warfield made it clear at this stage in 1888 that evolution theory did not pass muster as "proof" in either the Newtonian or probabilistic sense, and for good empirical reasons. There were simply too many unresolved geological, paleontological, embryonic, and physical problems, which he did not hesitate to itemize. Still, for all that, he did conclude in the following manner:

> The upshot of the whole matter is that there is no *necessary* antagonism of Xty to evolution, *provided that* we do not hold to too extreme a form of evolution. To adopt any form that does not permit God freely to work apart from law & wh. does not allow *miraculous* intervention (in the giving of the soul, in creating Eve &c) will entail a great reconstruction of Xian doctrine, & a very great lowering of the detailed authority of the Bible. But if we condition the theory by allowing the ~~occasional~~ [*sic*] constant oversight of God in the whole process, & his occasional supernatural interference for the production of *new* beginnings by an actual output of creative force, producing something *new* ie, something not included even *in posse* in preceding conditions,— we may hold to the modified theory of evolution & be Xians in the ordinary orthodox sense.
>
> I say we may do this. Whether we ought to accept it, even

in this modified sense, is another matter, & I leave it purposely an open question.[31]

Warfield left the matter an "open question" in 1888, but there is no mistaking his increasing acceptance of evolutionary theory over the years. It is particularly evident in his reflections on two issues of burning contemporary significance—the origin and the unity of the human race. First, his anthropology lectures already reveal that he followed McCosh in seeing no need for divine intervention to produce the human physical form; the origin of soul, mind, consciousness—call it what you will—was his only concern in this regard. His review of James Orr's *God's Image in Man* further presses home this point. I shall want to return to Orr's viewpoint presently, but in this context I simply want to note that he argued for the entirely supernatural origin of Adam, body and soul, on the grounds that the complex physics of the brain necessary for human consciousness made it impossible to postulate a special origin for the mind distinct from the body. To this Warfield countered that Orr's objection would be ineffective against the idea of evolution by sudden mutation, thereby proposing a kind of emergent evolutionary solution to the problem. As Warfield put it, "If under the directing hand of God a human body is formed at a leap by propagation from brutish parents, it would be quite consonant with the fitness of things that it should be provided by His creative energy with a truly human soul."[32] As he had already made clear in his "editorial notes" for *The Bible Student* a few years earlier, the need for divine intervention to create the image of God was in itself no "denial of the interaction of an evolutionary process in the production of man."[33]

It is clear that Warfield believed he was perpetuating orthodox Calvinism even while conceding the possibility of a human evolutionary history. In his 1915 exposition of Calvin's doctrine of the creation for the *Princeton Theological Review*, for example, he made much of Calvin's insistence that the term "creation" should be strictly reserved for the initial action of creation. Subsequent "creations," he argued, were not technically creations out of nothing but rather modifications of the primeval "indigested mass" by "means of the interaction of its intrinsic forces." The human soul was the only exception: Calvin held to the Creationist (as opposed to Traducianist) view that every human soul throughout the whole history of propagation was an immediate creation *ex nihilo*. As Warfield understood it, Calvin's doctrine of the creation

31. Warfield, Lectures on Anthropology (Dec. 1888), Speer Library, Princeton University.

32. Warfield, review of *God's Image in Man*, by James Orr, *Princeton Theological Review* 4 (1906): 557.

33. Warfield, "Editorial Note," in *The Bible Student* 8 (1904): 243.

opened the door to a controlled "naturalistic" explanation of natural history, including the human physical form, in terms of the operation of secondary causes. These of course were directed by the guiding hand of Providence, but that did not prevent Warfield from concluding that Calvin's doctrine of creation was "a very pure evolutionary scheme."

One other small point is important here: somewhat surprisingly, Warfield's insistence on plenary inspiration and the complete inerrancy of the Bible did not pose any problems for his view of science. In the article on Calvin's doctrine of the creation, he makes a point of noting that while Calvin naturally understood the six days of creation in a literal sense, he himself believed that Moses, "writing to meet the needs of men at large, accommodated himself to their grade of intellectual preparation" and that the Mosaic record was nothing like an exhaustive account of the whole process. To retain the spirit of Calvin's doctrine, he suggested, "it was requisite that these six days should be lengthened out into six periods,—six ages of the growth of the world. Had that been done," he continued, "Calvin would have been a precursor of the modern evolutionary theorists . . . for he teaches, as they teach, the modification of the original world-stuff into the varied forms which constitute the ordered world, by the instrumentality of secondary causes,—or as a modern would put it, of its intrinsic forces."[34]

Although Warfield dilated on the problem of human origins, he felt that the widely debated question of the antiquity of the human race was really theologically irrelevant, that the time factor was in itself of no religious significance. Of far greater importance was the ideologically laden controversy over the unity of mankind. On this Warfield was uncompromising: both Bible and science taught the organic solidarity of the human species. To appreciate the import of Warfield's contribution fully here, we need to consider it in the context of the longstanding feud between the monogenists and the polygenists, a debate antedating the Darwinian episode by several decades.

The chief scientific point at issue was whether mankind as a species was of single or multiple origin. But this apparently innocuous question had a more sinister dimension, for many of those who assumed a multiple origin also assumed that the different races were totally different biological species. The plainly monogenetic implications of biblical anthropology had earlier been challenged by S. G. Morton and J. C. Nott, whose pre-Darwinian writings set the style for American polygenism. Already convinced that certain races were inherently inferior, some individuals interpreted their scientific "findings" as a scholarly defense for the institution of slavery. Indeed, some Christians, such as the Rev. Alexander McCarne, were prepared to defend slavery on biblical grounds, and

---

34. Warfield, "Calvin's Doctrine of the Creation," *Princeton Theological Review* 13 (1915): 208, 209, 196.

such scientific polygenists as Agassiz went so far as to declare that the different races were the separate, special creations of God. Despite its implications of a common ancestry, Darwin's theory did not immediately dispel the polygenist tradition. It persisted among the ranks of physical anthropologists well after the appearance of the *Origin*, particularly in North America, perhaps because of fears arising from mass immigration. Moreover the codification of American racism in Madison Grant's *The Passing of the Great Race* in 1916 reveals that the issue was not laid to rest even by that late date.[35]

A longstanding champion of the blacks, Warfield directly confronted this question in his 1911 paper "On the Antiquity and the Unity of the Human Race." He ably reviewed the relevant scientific literature and argued that the strong tendency to deny the unity of mankind sprang from a deep-seated racial pride. He maintained that the unity and common origin of the human race was a direct, necessary corollary of the theory of evolution. What is more, he affirmed that on this issue science and Scripture clearly corroborated each other. The unity of the race was to Warfield a prerequisite for the biblical doctrine of salvation. "The prevalence of the evolutionary hypotheses," he wrote, "has removed all motive for denying a common origin to the human race, and rendered it natural to look upon the differences which exist among the various types of man as differentiations of a common stock." Warfield's discussion serves to illustrate not only his adoption of an evolutionary model for explaining aspects of human development but also his uncompromising conviction that the whole doctrinal structure of biblical redemption is rooted in the assumption that "the race of man is one organic whole."[36]

The significance of Warfield's proposals is not inconsiderable, especially in view of his defense of biblical inerrancy. He plainly held that there was no conflict between evolutionary science and belief in scriptural infallibility. If there was any conflict between science and Christianity, it was centered on the issue of design. And it was Warfield's willingness to renegotiate the design argument along the idealist lines suggested by McCosh that facilitated his presentation of a Christian evolutionism that had theological as well as apologetic value.

It is clear that the advocates of the old Princeton theology, scientists as well as theologians, had by the middle of the first decade of the twentieth century achieved a tolerably comfortable accommodation of organ-

---

35. On scientific racism in the period, see Thomas F. Gossett, *Race: The History of an Idea in America* (Dallas: Southern Methodist University Press, 1963); Mark Haller, *Eugenics: Hereditarian Attitudes in American Thought* (New Brunswick, N.J.: Rutgers University Press, 1963); and John S. Haller, Jr., *Outcasts from Evolution: Scientific Attitudes of Racial Inferiority, 1859-1900* (Chicago: University of Illinois Press, 1971).

36. Benjamin B. Warfield, "On the Antiquity and the Unity of the Human Race," *Princeton Theological Review* 9 (1911): 18.

ic evolution. Via the reinterpretative impetus of idealistic and holistic natural theology, Princetonians were prepared in varying degrees to concede to science a long earth history, the transmutation of species by Darwinian, Lamarckian, or Mendelian means, and an evolutionary past for the human physical form. Again and again the compatibility of science and Scripture was affirmed in the Warfield-controlled *Princeton Theological Review*. Writing for the *Review* in 1903, for example, W. H. Johnson argued that belief in God's immanence in the world did not absolve psychologists or biologists from the task of reconstructing a *natural* history of life and mind. He contended that the idea of evolution as "the gradual and progressive unfolding of a plan" was liberating for science and theology alike—because it presented nature as an orderly system of natural forces and at the same time avoided the extremes of deism and pantheism.[37] Hugh Scott of Chicago Theological Seminary, writing in the same journal, insisted that all scientists now accepted evolution even if they were divided as to the actual mechanisms involved.[38] He was, of course, pleased to report that such philosophical evolutionists as Lotze, Wundt, Paulsen, Von Hartmann, Romanes, and Reinke all rejected materialist attempts to eliminate purpose from nature. With science now moving from monism toward dualism, he reckoned, the doctrine of divine immanence was in a splendid position to overthrow what Rudolf Otto once called this *Darwinismus Vulgaris*.

Caspar Wistar Hodge, Jr., too, while perhaps rather more keen to catalogue the discontinuities in evolutionary history itemized by such individuals as Virchow, DuBois-Reymond, Fleischmann, and Kellogg, was nevertheless prepared to concede that the evolution of the human body solely by secondary causes was compatible with Scripture. In his basic outlook, he closely followed the interpretations of his predecessor Warfield. Even Henri Bergson's controversial work *Creative Evolution* was commended by S. A. Martin in the pages of the *Princeton Theological Review* for its "splendid contribution" to the understanding of evolutionary processes. Whatever its drawbacks, Martin saw the book as a telling illustration of the radical shift "from materialism toward spirituality and biblical conceptions of the universe." If the idea of creative volition was substituted for Bergson's "Vital impulse," and the immanence of divine efficiency for the "inner directing principle," said Martin, then Bergson's version of evolutionary theory was strikingly harmonious with the Christian view of the world.[39]

---

37. Johnson, "Evolution and Theology Today," *Princeton Theological Review* 1 (1903): 403-22.

38. Scott, "Has Scientific Investigation Disturbed the Basis of Rational Faith?" *Princeton Theological Review* 4 (1906): 433-53.

39. Martin, review of *Creative Evolution*, by Henri Bergson, *Princeton Theological Review* 10 (1912): 116-18.

EVANGELICALS AND EVOLUTION IN AMERICA: A TRADITION IN TRANSITION

Among the Princeton theologians we can readily detect a broad transition from hesitantly opposing the theory of evolution to tentatively submitting to it and eventually to positively assimilating it. This pattern, I think, is equally discernible in the more general response of American evangelical theologians to evolution during the latter part of the nineteenth century. To illustrate this I want to trace the reception of Darwin's theory by three systematic theologians from different branches of the Reformed tradition—Robert L. Dabney from the Presbyterian, William G. T. Shedd from the Congregationalist, and Augustus Hopkins Strong from the Baptist. I choose these particular individuals because their writings were widely influential not just within their own ecclesiastical groups and denominational colleges but also within the general body of evangelical scholarship. Reprints of their works, moreover, are still widely available today. Their writings reveal, I suggest, a move from dismissal in the case of Dabney to absorption in the case of Strong.

Robert L. Dabney, perhaps the leading figure in the Southern Presbyterian Church, was born and reared in Virginia. He served as a minister of the church from his ordination in 1847 until 1853, when he was called to the chair of Ecclesiastical History and Polity at Union Seminary in Virginia. In 1859 he transferred to the department of systematic theology. As we shall see, his views closely paralleled those of Charles Hodge, and it is no surprise that in 1860 Hodge urged him to join the Princeton faculty. Dabney refused this invitation, however, answering instead the call of Stonewall Jackson to serve as adjutant-general during the Civil War. Apart from this military break, Dabney taught at Union until 1883, when, at the age of sixty-four and with broken health, he moved to teach in the new University of Texas and to cofound the Austin School of Theology.

Dabney was defensive about science from the start, and this stance remained unchanged throughout his life. In 1861, for example, he set out his thoughts on "Geology and the Bible" for the *Southern Presbyterian Review*. After outlining the several prevalent theological strategies for coping with the new geology—Chalmers's gap theory, Miller and Lewis's day-age theory, and so on—he went on to stress the inherently provisional nature of scientific theory and therefore the folly of pinning biblical exegesis on one current interpretation. Yet this did not prevent him from pressing his own solution to the problem. It was what could be called the "mature creation theory." He argued that if scientific investigators were able to study, say, a tree that had just been created by God, they would find it had all the traces of apparent age, even though it was only a few seconds old. So too with Adam: his bone structure would reveal to the anatomist every mark of growth from natural infancy to maturity. Apparently Adam did have a navel even though he was created, not born! As

Dabney expressed it, "any creative act of God, producing a structure which was intended to subsist under the working of natural laws, must produce one presenting some of the *seeming* traces of the operation of such laws."[40]

Perhaps not surprisingly, Dabney's assaults on what he called "anti-Christian science" in 1871 did not sit well with James Woodrow, uncle of Woodrow Wilson and Professor of Natural Science in Connection with Religion at the Southern Presbyterian's Columbia Theological Seminary. Something of a fracas ensued between the two men in the pages of the *Southern Presbyterian Review* during 1873 with a lamentable excess of charges of incompetence, willful misunderstanding, and misinterpretation on both sides. Woodrow, happy to accept evolution as a description of second causes, could not countenance Dabney's charge that the materialist philosophy of Lamarck, Chambers, Darwin, Hooker, Huxley, and Spencer was the prevalent interpretation. Large numbers of scholarly witnesses were called into the dock by both parties. And if both conducted the argument with a pretense of recognizing the sincerity of the other, it is nonetheless the case that neither experienced a change of heart.

The Dabney-Woodrow incident did serve to show that while Presbyterians could hold divergent views about the subject in the 1870s, the situation in the conservative South had substantially hardened by the mid 1880s. Woodrow was dismissed from his professorship in 1886 after two years of controversy that began when he described evolution as the plan of God's creation. Indeed, the Southern General Assembly in 1888 recorded its verdict decidedly against human evolution by insisting that "Adam's body was directly fashioned by Almighty God of the dust." The symbolic significance of this incident has quite rightly attracted the attention of George Marsden, who contends that it typifies the antievolution sentiments that were much more prevalent in the southern states than in the north. No doubt this had as much to do with cultural differences as anything else. Southerners were already defensive about what they viewed as Northern liberalism in matters of slavery, and they were naturally inclined to be quick to spot any signs of doctrinal laxity and to root out compromisers at the first sign.[41] The facts of the case would seem to support the contention that opposition to evolution was mainly a southern phenomenon.

Given these machinations, Dabney's attitude toward Darwin is quite predictable. He held stringently to the Hodge line, thereby cementing the Southern Presbyterian links with Old School Princeton that pre-

---

40. Dabney, "Geology and the Bible," *Southern Presbyterian Review*, July 1861; reprinted in vol. 3 of *Discussions* (Edinburgh: Banner of Truth, n.d.), p. 145.

41. On this, see Gary S. Smith, "Calvinists and Evolution, 1870-1920," *Journal of Presbyterian History* 61 (1983): 335-52; and George M. Marsden, "A Case of the Excluded Middle: Creation versus Evolution in America," forthcoming.

dated the Civil War. Again he cited as obstacles the evolution of human beings from animal forebears and the dangers of rampant materialism. But his chief objection was that "the bearing of the hypothesis is towards an utter obliteration of the teleological argument." Evolution was to his mind necessarily atheistic in spirit. Typically, Dabney went on to bolster his case by outlining what he saw as the major scientific and philosophical defects of the theory, rehearsing standard objections: Kelvin's doubts about the available time scale, the sterility of hybrids, the problem of accounting for the evolution of mind, evolution's status as a mere hypothesis, and, most importantly, the assertion that natural selection "is giving us metaphor in the place of induction." Dabney's review, in other words, was competent if uncompromising. But he did go one stage further. Should Darwinian theory come to be vindicated, Dabney planned out the route evangelical theologians should take. It was precisely what the Princeton men had already begun to do.

> I remark that if the theory of the evolutionist were all conceded, the argument from designed adaptation would not be abolished, but only removed one step backward. If we are mistaken in believing that God made every living creature that moveth after its kind; then the question recurs: Who planned and adjusted these wondrous powers of development? Who endowed the cell-organs of the first living protoplasm with all this fitness for evolution into the numerous and varied wonders of animal life and function, so diversified, yet all orderly adaptations? There is a wonder of creative wisdom and power, at least equal to that of the Mosaic genesis. That this point is justly taken, appears thus: Those philosophers who concede (as I conceive, very un-philosophically and unnecessarily) the theory of "creation by law," do not deem that they have thereby weakened the teleological argument in the least.[42]

Dabney was clearly very reactionary in his attitude toward science. But he did show a firm grasp of the nature of Darwinism and pointed the way to reconciliation should his inductivist doubts be shown to be without foundation.

In the writings of William G. T. Shedd, the tensions of a transitional figure are clearly exposed. "Like a delicate barometer," Cushing Stout has noted, "the mind of Shedd registers the intellectual storms of the age with remarkable sensitivity. In his speculations are revealed the tradition of orthodox Puritan Congregationalism, the Romantic reaction to Enlightenment empiricism, the new emphasis on historical consciousness, and the prophetic foreshadowing of evolutionary naturalism." Shedd does indeed figure prominently in the traditional hagiography of Re-

---

42. Dabney, *Lectures in Systematic Theology* (1878; rpt., Grand Rapids: Zondervan, 1980), pp. 27, 28, 37.

formed evangelicalism, and not without some justification. Thoroughly respectable in the best New England conservative tradition, he had effortlessly followed the path from the University of Vermont via Andover Theological Seminary and a short ministerial career to Union Theological Seminary, where he taught sacred rhetoric and systematic theology for a quarter of a century until his death in 1894. His writings reveal the attempts, says Stout, of "a cultured and agile mind to meet the nineteenth-century challenges to traditional New England Congregationalism."[43]

Paradoxically, it is precisely because of the sophistication and contemporaneity of Shedd's scholarship—he was already using the term "evolution" some years before the publication of Darwin's *Origin* in his work on the philosophy of history—that we must take special care in our assessment of his stance. In his historical reflections, notably the *Lectures upon the Philosophy of History* (1856), Shedd had managed to integrate reason and revelation in a creative reinvigoration of orthodox Calvinism. The precise details need not detain us here; it is enough in this context to note that it was the idea of evolution that provided Shedd with a new conceptual tool by which to interpret the historical process. It was a truly novel approach, prefiguring that of such historians as Herbert B. Adams, Henry Adams, John Fiske, and Frederick Jackson Turner. Shedd's sense of history represented an important departure from traditional Edwardsian Calvinism, which had done little to encourage historical consciousness because of its rather determinist assurance that history is ultimately a fait accompli. In contrast, Shedd approached the subject in dynamic, genetic terms, contending that there is in history a steady, serene growth that reveals the progressive development of the world under the guiding hand of Providence.

Two important points arise from Shedd's historical discussions. First, he insisted that without the interpretative idea of evolution, history becomes a mere catalogue of events, incoherent, lacking any vital link between past, present, and future. To this extent Shedd's approach to the science of history was something of a departure from traditional Baconian induction. Defending the necessity for an a priori theory of history, he asked in a truly deductive spirit,

> Does the scientific mind start off upon its inquiries in every direction, without any preconceived ideas as to where it is going, and what it expects to find? Is the human understanding such a *tabula rasa*, that it contributes nothing of its own towards the discovery of truth . . . ? We have only to watch the movements of our minds to find that we carry with us into every field of investi-

---

43. Cushing Stout, "Faith and History: The Mind of W. G. T. Shedd," *Journal of the History of Ideas* 15 (1954): 153. Although Shedd was nominally a Presbyterian while he was at Union, he carried on the Congregationalist traditions.

gation an antecedent idea, which gives more or less direction to
our studies, and goes far to determine the result to which we
come. . . . The demand therefore so constantly made by the
rationalist of every century, that the mind be entirely vacant of
a priori ideas and initiating preconceptions; in his phraseology,
free from "prejudices"; in order that it may make a truly scientific examination, is a demand that cannot be complied with,
even if there were a disposition to do so on the part of the inquir-
er, and is not complied with even on the part of him who makes
it.[44]

Second, Shedd's 1856 paper "The Philosophy of History" (revised
and reprinted in 1873 with the significantly different title "The Idea of
Evolution Defined, and Applied to History") shows his essentially pre-
Darwinian understanding of evolution. Here, for example, he distanced
his own conception from Spencer's version. In fact, he understood evolution to be precisely the opposite of the Spencerian "development of the
homogeneous into the heterogeneous." He used the metaphor of the
organic sequence of growth in an individual corn plant from seed into
blade, then into ear and finally into full corn in describing the history of
his two kingdoms—the material and the mental, the physical and the
spiritual. In his revised preface to a later 1877 reprint of this paper, he
lamented the "misuse to which the doctrine of evolution has been put by
the sceptical physics of the day." He stated that his purpose in reproduc-
ing the earlier paper was to contend that "evolution is never creative, or
originant from nothing," and that the concept is as applicable to deterio-
ration as it is to improvement.

Shedd's major treatment of evolutionary biology and geology in the
post-Darwin era appeared in the seventh chapter of his 1889 *Dogmatic
Theology*. His assessment is clearly framed in terms of a pre-Darwinian
conception of evolution. He was prepared to allow for evolution of varieties only within species (i.e., within homogeneous, not heterogeneous
groups). But again, this avowal is not so simple as it might appear. What,
we need to ask, did Shedd mean by "species"? A clue to the answer is, I
think, found in his discussion of the first chapter of Genesis, in which he
isolates four (perhaps five) creative fiats—namely, the creation of vegetable species, lower animal life, higher animal forms, and human beings.
These, he says, were the limits, or "species," within which evolution could
take place. For as he confirmed, "No mere evolution of that which was
created by the first fiat will yield that which was created by the second; in
other words, no one of these distinct species can be transmuted into
another by merely natural causes." This implies that, depending on
where the line is drawn between the organic kingdoms, "it would not

44. Shedd, "The Idea of Evolution Defined, and Applied to History," in *Theological Essays* (New York: Scribner, Armstrong & Co., 1877), pp. 122-23.

contradict the Mosaic physics to concede that reptiles have developed from fishes, and even birds from reptiles."

Clearly Shedd had moved quite significantly beyond Dabney on the question of evolution, as he also had regarding the interpretation of the Genesis "days." Indeed, he went so far as to propose that biblical exegesis during the patristic and medieval periods had made them long periods of time, not twenty-four-hour days, suggesting that this latter interpretation had "prevailed only in the modern church." His own position was unambiguous: "There is nothing in the use of the word 'day,' by Moses, that requires it to be explained as invariably denoting a period of twenty-four hours; but much to forbid it."[45]

Whereas Dabney opposed evolution and Shedd allowed it, Augustus Hopkins Strong embraced it. What is more, Strong showed how a conservative theologian could ply evolutionary philosophy in the service of Christian theism. A graduate of Yale University and Rochester Theological Seminary, Strong served as a Baptist preacher from 1861 until 1872, when he became president and professor of systematic theology at his theological alma mater, a position he held until 1912. During a long life, Strong achieved wide renown as a conservative theologian comparable to P. T. Forsyth in Britain and Martin Kahler in Germany through his propagation of what has been called "progressive orthodoxy." At the same time, he retained a deep and lasting interest in the Baptist missionary endeavor, serving as president of the American Baptist Missionary Union from 1892 to 1895. His 1917 book *A Tour of Missions* amounted to a scathing denunciation of theological liberalism both at home and abroad.[46]

A. H. Strong reveals the creative potential that Darwin's doctrines held for an orthodox theologian whether considering geology, teleology, anthropology, or eschatology. In his interpretation of the Mosaic story, for example, Strong was equally unhappy with allegorical, mythological, and hyperliteral interpretations. He urged that such approaches should be scrapped in favor of what he called the "pictorial-summary interpretation"—in essence a synthesis of the harmonizing tactics advanced by Guyot and Dana, built on Augustinian foundations, and structured according to Owen's archetypal forms. All this, of course, was by that time conventional wisdom.

Strong's reconstruction of the teleological argument was more sus-

45. Shedd, *Dogmatic Theology* (New York: Charles Scribner's Sons, 1889), pp. 485, 486, 475.

46. On this, see Irwin Reist, "Augustus Hopkins Strong and William Newton Clarke: A Study in Nineteenth Century Evolutionary and Eschatological Thought," *Foundations* 13 (1970): 26-43; and George M. Marsden, *Fundamentalism and American Culture: The Shaping of Twentieth Century Evangelicalism, 1870-1925* (New York: Oxford University Press, 1980).

tained. His reflections typically display a profound and broad-ranging grasp of both the philosophical and scientific literature. Initially he argued out that evolution is only the method of God's activity. "It has to do with the *how*," he suggested, "not the *why* of phenomena, and therefore is not inconsistent with design, but rather is a new and higher illustration of design." Along with Henry Ward Beecher, he rejoiced that "design by wholesale is greater than design by retail." But Strong was keen to go even further. Evolution was not just compatible with design, he said; it actually enriched design by removing some traditional objections to the teleological argument. Some, for example, had urged that the imperfections in nature militated against the possibility of benevolent design. Strong asserted that "The doctrine of evolution answers many of these objections, by showing that order and useful collocation in which the system as a whole is necessarily and cheaply purchased by imperfection and suffering in the initial stages of development. The question is: Does the system as a whole imply design?"

Nor did these convictions remain isolated from Strong's solidly Christocentric theology. With a firm insistence on immanence and incarnation, divine revelation in nature and redemption, he could go on to say that "the attraction of gravitation and the principle of evolution are only other names for Christ." In Strong's theology, of course, there was no danger of the idea of divine immanence eating up the doctrine of transcendence. In *Christ and Creation* (1899), for example, he had already stressed the importance of discontinuities in the evolutionary process, because, apart from anything else, "absolute continuity is inconsistent with progress. If the future is not simply a reproduction of the past, there must be some new cause of change." What was needed for a truly comprehensive evolutionary theory, he felt, was a combination of "increments of force *plus* continuity of plan." And herein lay the superiority of evangelical theism over deism. A theological account of the miraculous intervention of a transcendent God in the natural evolutionary process was possible only in a theology that held immanence and transcendence in creative tension. His conclusion may well seem revolutionary for an early fundamentalist:

> If we were deists, believing in a distant God and a mechanical universe, evolution and Christianity would be irreconcilable. But since we believe in a dynamical universe, of which the personal and living God is the inner source of energy, evolution is but the basis, foundation and background of Christianity, the silent and regular working of him who, in the fulness of time, utters his voice in Christ and the cross.[47]

---

47. Strong, *Systematic Theology: A Compendium* (1907; rpt., London: Pickering & Inglis, 1956), pp. 75-76, 78, 123.

Since Strong accepted the principle of evolutionary progress as the ground and grammar of Christian theology, it is not surprising to find that, following in the tradition of McCosh and Warfield, he accepted the idea of a human evolutionary history from brute ancestors. Like them, he resisted monistic accounts of natural selection but still saw in evolution more generally powerful scientific evidence for the unity of the human race. Further, drawing on Drummond's speculative evolutionism, Strong spoke of an evolutionary advance in what he saw as the social progression from egoism to altruism—or, as he put it, from "selfism to otherism." To this extent, therefore, evolution was "not a tale of battle, but a love-story."

One other dimension of Strong's theology that received impetus from the theory of evolution was his eschatology. Since evolutionary development is nothing less than the purposive method of God, he said, the whole process of history is the manifest outworking of a transcendent and immanent agent directing the grand cosmic drama toward its ultimate destiny. Not that this implies any mechanical or automatic progress. History, like nature, displays its own cases of degeneration and atrophy. But with the permeating influence of immanent divine government, any retrogressive evolution is merely incidental to the ultimate purpose of universal history. Here, then, was the basis for Strong's robust optimistic eschatology, which looked for the postmillennial invasion of Christ's consummated kingdom at the end of time. In his subtle interweaving of eschatology and evolution, of the transcendental and the immanent, Strong found a synthesis of science and Scripture that was as conceptually enriching as it was theologically sophisticated.

In the half century from 1860 to about 1910, the Calvinist outlook in the United States in general, and the Princeton Old School tradition in particular, underwent a gentle revolution. The hesitancies and doubts about evolution in the 1860s had progressively given way to confident and assured assimilation by the turn of the century. The changeover was, as I say, gentle. The acrid polemics that were to characterize the fundamentalism of the 1920s and '30s are conspicuous by their absence, largely because both those who remained unconvinced and those who were persuaded by Darwin and evolution had carefully sifted the scientific and philosophical arguments. Where prejudice remained, it was well concealed beneath a daunting layer of scholarly footnoting. But this is not to say that the transition was uniform. There was no clear consensus about what constituted the orthodox Calvinist line. Some, such as McCosh, Warfield, and Strong, were willing supporters; others, such as A. A. Hodge, Patton, and Shedd, were more tentative; still others, including Dabney and Charles Hodge, remained unconvinced, if not hostile. Nor I think was the Baconian ideal prized quite so universally as is sometimes thought. In the case of Shedd and, as we saw earlier, Macloskie, the need for a priori theory was unambiguously presented. Nevertheless, a general picture clearly emerges: American evangelicals in the Reformed mold absorbed the Darwinian shock waves fairly easily.

Naturally this is not the whole story. Reformed Americans were not the only evangelicals to find the middle ground attractive, nor was evangelical opposition entirely absent. On both sides of the Atlantic there were those who took up the cudgels against the underrated menace of Darwin while others were zealous in their defense of the evolutionary naturalists. While their names may lack the theological luster of the figures we have been considering, a brief examination of their reactions is not out of place.

THE WIDER SCENE: CRITICISM AND CONCESSION

The style for much antievolution rhetoric in the immediate aftermath of the Darwinian revolution was set by Francis Orpen Morris. An amateur ornithologist and Anglican rector in West Yorkshire, he kept up a barrage of assaults on Darwinian evolution for a quarter of a century. In such pamphlets as "Difficulties of Darwinism" (1869), "All the Articles of the Darwin Faith" (1875), and "The Demands of Darwin on Credulity" (1890), Morris exercised no rhetorical discipline in his acerbic denunciation of the Darwinian delusion. It was "ten thousand times worse than childish absurdities," he asserted; it deserved only "ineffable contempt and indignation"; it was a "criminal injury" that had brought "miserable infidelity" to the minds of its adherents. "If the whole of the English language could be condensed into one word," he insisted, "it would not suffice to express the utter contempt those invite who are so deluded as to be disciples of such an imposture as Darwinism." The fatal flaw that undermines the whole Darwinian system, Morris stated, is the assumption that because species vary they could be descended from each other.[48]

From north of the border, William Miller issued a far more multifaceted critique some time around 1900. Unambiguously entitled *God, . . . or Natural Selection?* the book is little more than a compendium of extracts from a variety of sources on subjects ranging from rudimentary organs to geographical distribution, from geology to embryology. Miller extracted hesitancies, doubts, queries, and half-questions from the works of many naturalists (many of whom were evolutionists themselves), pieced them together with the writings of more hostile critics, and added a pastiche of anti-Darwin gobbets. In the end, however, it is evident that he presented these scholarly reservations merely to confirm his own repugnance for the theory on other grounds: "Ah! here the secret has come

---

48. My discussion and these citations are drawn from Moore, *The Post-Darwinian Controversies*, pp. 196-97.

out. Evolution has been adopted by its authors in order to get quit of the supernatural or miraculous, in which they have no faith. Will this not open the eyes of good credulous people?" Nor indeed was his language always so restrained. The effect of reading Romanes's *Darwin and after Darwin*, for example, was to make him "question the sanity of the writer, and also to conclude that the theory which required the support of such egregious nonsense, must be a pure hallucination."[49]

Between Morris and Miller stood many other anti-Darwinian clerics whose message was expressed in more or less similarly strident tones. T. H. Birks, evangelical Anglican in the Edward Bickersteth mold, produced two "exceedingly illiberal" books on evolution during his tenure as Knightsbridge Professor of Moral Philosophy at Cambridge. To Birks, evolution was as philosophically moribund as it was antiscriptural. In the United States, L. T. Townsend took a similar line. He had already achieved a reputation as a popular evangelical apologist through several book-length works, numbered among which were *The Mosaic Record and Modern Science* (1881) and *Evolution or Creation* (1896). A graduate of the Congregationalist seminary in Andover and a teacher at Boston Theological Seminary, Townsend dismissed Darwinism first for its merely hypothetical character and then because it was "not supported as a whole or in any of its parts by a single well-established fact in the whole domain of science and philosophy."[50]

Not all the anti-Darwinians, as we have seen, were so caustic in their dissent. Edinburgh's New College professor of systematic theology, John Laidlaw, turned to the *Biblical Doctrine of Man* for his Cunningham Lectures while he was still ministering to the West Free Church in Aberdeen. When the lectures were reissued in a revised form in 1895, Laidlaw took full advantage of the rising tide of doubt over Darwinism. The theory, he freely conceded, had provided a viable explanation of a large range of biological facts. But on the question of origins in general and human origins in particular it had been overextended. How much more dignifying, Laidlaw mused, was the biblical story of man made in the image of God than the coarse speculation of human development from bestial savagery.[51] Within these Calvinist citadels, John William Dawson became the scientific luminary of the anti-Darwinians, giving scholarly support not only to Laidlaw but also the American Presbyterian minister John Duffield—who nevertheless maintained that technical queries were less important than the need to determine independently what the biblical view of human origin really was. The message, he felt, was unambiguous.

---

49. Miller, *God, . . . or Natural Selection?* (Glasgow: Leader Publishing Company, n.d.), pp. 152, 84.

50. On Birks and Townsend, see Moore, *The Post-Darwinian Controversies*, pp. 201, 199.

51. Laidlaw, *The Biblical Doctrine of Man* (Edinburgh: T. & T. Clark, 1895).

Reflecting on the passage dealing with the creation of Eve, he confirmed that if the "language is to be taken as a literal record of an historical fact, it is utterly irreconcilable with Evolutionism."[52] More philosophically inspired was E. F. Burr, a Congregationalist minister in Connecticut and an amateur astronomer of no mean achievements. His fears were less over scientific ambiguity and biblical exegesis than over the implicit materialism of a theory that reduced all reality, including the spiritual, to mere forces and laws.[53]

If Darwin's evangelical critics displayed a wide range of polemical styles, their rhetorical skills, as we have already seen, were not sufficient to win over all of their fellow evangelical theologians and clergymen. Beyond the powerful American exponents of traditional Calvinism, some conspicuous supporters can be readily identified. Henry Baker Tristram, evangelical canon of Durham between 1874 and 1906, is only one early case in point. A lifelong supporter of the Church Missionary Society and a first-rate ornithologist, Tristram distinguished himself through numerous publications on Palestine in which he displayed an unrivaled knowledge of the geology, geography, and natural history of the Holy Land. For his scholarly work he was elected to a fellowship of the Royal Society and presided over the Biological Section of the British Association at its 1893 meeting in Nottingham. Tristram, in fact, had supported the Darwinian theory even before the publication of the *Origin!* He had eagerly read the joint Darwin-Wallace communication to the Linnaean Society and found that it matched his own ornithological observations in North Africa. Subsequently, according to Bernard Cohen, he was persuaded by Wilberforce's arguments at the British Association and became an anti-Darwinian. But even if he felt that Darwin's theory remained largely hypothetical and in need of further empirical corroboration, he nevertheless could write in 1866 that it was "beautiful, ingenious, and self-consistent," and that should its most daring speculations about human origins come to be vindicated, it should still be welcomed by any lover of truth. Tristram was sure that idealist natural theology would continue to be supported by the findings of natural science, for, as he put it, "Nature is full of plan, yet she plans not; she is only plastic to plan. The plan has its warp, indeed, as well as its woof. The exquisite variety of exhaustless specialities of adaptation are engrafted on a pervading unity of type."[54]

At a more general level, the Baptist D. W. Faunce popularized the harmonizing schemes of the Christian geologists in his 1877 volume *A*

52. Duffield, "Evolutionism Respecting Man, and the Bible," *Princeton Review* 1 (1878): 155.

53. See Moore, *The Post-Darwinian Controversies*, pp. 197-98.

54. Tristram, "Recent Geographical and Historical Progress in Zoology," *Contemporary Review* 2 (1866): 124. See also the article on Tristram in the *Dictionary of National Biography*, Second Supplement, vol. 3, pp. 535-36; Cohen, *Revolution in Science* (Cambridge: Harvard University Press, 1985), p. 290.

Young Man's Difficulties with His Bible. In a chapter entitled "Difficulties from Geology," he stressed that in method and language, science and revelation operate with quite different standards, and he went on to outline his own reconciliation based on the work on Miller, Dana, Guyot, and Winchell. Like them, he found Owen's idealism highly congenial and used it to emphasize the unity of the organic world and the plan of the progressive creations in each succeeding geological period. Moreover, he remained open on the question of human evolution: "If it should ever be proved that, before Adam, there were creatures having man's physical form, and that at length it pleased God, in Eden, to take this being, whose body centuries before had been 'formed out of the dust of the earth,' and then and there to breathe into him a higher kind of life . . . all this would not be in any necessary conflict with the Scripture story." Indeed, he concluded that this would enable the doctrine of the moral unity of the human race to be defended on both scriptural and scientific grounds. It is especially interesting that this chapter was singled out for special praise by the *Sunday School Chronicle*, which heartily commended the book "as one that all teachers of senior classes should get for themselves, and, if necessary, put in the way of their scholars."[55]

Support for an open-minded approach to Darwinism was also forthcoming from Joseph Cook and Oren Root, both influential figures in late nineteenth-century American evangelicalism. Cook's oratorical skills and wide-ranging knowledge made his Boston Monday Lectures a national event for almost a quarter of a century. Self-consciously orthodox in the face of a trendy Transcendentalism, Cook perpetuated the old Andover theology of Edwards Amasa Park, retaining with it a high regard for the scientific enterprise. This is not really surprising in light of the fact that Cook remained buoyantly enthusiastic about the intellectual power of the argument from design. He took it upon himself to clarify the claims of evolution and mediate between Christianity and Darwinism. And if in his desire to press biology into the service of theology he allowed his imagination to run riot—as with his "proof" of the doctrine of immortality from the supposed independence and immateriality of the mind— he nonetheless performed a much-needed service in distinguishing the diverse strands of evolutionary thinking whether atheistic or theistic. His conclusion was unmistakable: if by "natural" was meant "habitual divine action," then "it cannot be dangerous to religion to inquire whether the origin of species is attributable wholly to natural causes; that is to habitual Divine action."[56] So, even if he remained vague in his positive

---

55. D. W. Faunce, *A Young Man's Difficulties with His Bible* (London: Hodder & Stoughton, 1877), p. 168, frontispiece.

56. Cook, *Biology, with Preludes on Current Events* (Boston: James R. Osgood, 1877), p. 30. My discussion of Cook has been significantly informed by Steven R. Pointer's "Apologetics and Science in the Career of Joseph Cook," a paper presented at

proposals, Cook was still sure that a theisized version of evolution was a viable evangelical option.

For Oren Root too, a Presbyterian minister and sometime Pratt Professor of Mathematics at Hamilton College in upstate New York, the need to keep alive the marriage of reason and revelation was a dominating concern. At least in part this concern sprang from his own deep commitment to the nationalistic and capitalistic tincture of American civil religion. If science was to play a leading role in the ideology of post-Darwinian society, with its "professional" ethos, he reasoned, it would be crucial to prevent hostilities between biology and theology. This goal, however socially opportunistic it seems, grew naturally out of a reverence for things scientific he had had since childhood. His father had been a "regular friend of Asa Gray" and "an early advocate of Darwinism," and years later it seemed perfectly natural for Root, Jr., to describe evolution as the "progressive dealings of God with man." Indeed, like Gray, he could coolly contemplate natural selection as "the outworking of intelligent purpose to a clearly discerned end."[57]

Within the conservative Wesleyan tradition, support for a modified theory of evolution can also be traced among some of its most prominent theologians. Consider, for example, William Burt Pope, tutor in systematic theology at Didsbury College and holder of an honorary D.D. from the University of Edinburgh. Born in Nova Scotia, Pope rose to prominence among British Wesleyans through his editorship of the *London Quarterly Review*, his biblical expositions, his translation of German anti-rationalist works, and his three-volume *Compendium of Christian Theology*. His scholarly conservatism goes some way toward explaining the slow infiltration of liberal theology within Wesleyanism generally, and yet his openness to evolutionary theory is conspicuous both in the *Compendium* and in his later *Higher Catechism of Theology* (1883). While Pope made it clear that evolution was not necessarily associated with pantheistic, dualistic, or materialistic heresies, he was just as certain that it was *discontinuous* evolution that most accorded with Christian theism. The gaps between the inorganic and organic, and between animal and human life were as yet unbridged; in Pope's mind, they were unbridgeable. And yet he felt that evolutionists should be thanked for drawing attention to the principle of development within certain ideal types—traces of Owen once again. "They have also taught us," he continued, "to appreciate the wonderful relations in which man is placed to the creatures whose all is bound up with the earth; that, as created out of the dust, he is a develop-

---

the American Society of Church History Conference, Denver, Colorado, March 1984. See also his Ph.D. dissertation, "The Perils of History: The Meteoric Career of Joseph Cook (1838-1901)," Duke University, 1981.

57. Win Winship, "Oren Root, Darwinism and Biblical Criticism," *Journal of Presbyterian History* 62 (1984): 115.

•

ment of older physical types, a final development on which evolution has spent itself, found worthy at last to be the receptacle of an immortal spirit." Thus Pope held that a true theory of human evolution merely required "that something was superadded to the physical and immaterial life that lay behind it in the history of the creation."[58] It should come as no surprise to find him answering the question of how "evolution [might] be made consistent with our own doctrine" in the following terms:

> The scriptural account of the secondary creation or formulation of all things combines creation and providence; there are the creative epochs, in the intervals of which providence works ceaselessly by the development of types. Natural selection, heredity, and the survival of the best types are terms which are all but used in the scriptures: the middle one is used. Under the seventh secular day of Moses we now live: there is no longer creative intervention; but the Creator still works in a regular development which preserves the original types.[59]

Another Wesleyan scholar who shared Pope's conviction that evolution and creation could be harmonized was S. J. Gamertsfelder, president and professor in the Evangelical Theological Seminary. Gamertsfelder is interesting because he represents another stream of the Wesleyan tradition, because he was much closer in time to the early twentieth-century controversies, and because his major work in systematic theology was widely used by those Wesleyans who consciously wanted to preserve the evangelical riches of their own tradition. In his observations on the origin of the human species, for example, he insisted that the Christian theologian "should not ruthlessly ignore the light that natural science may throw on the inquiry." Indeed, he went on to confirm that "a rational theory of theistic evolution does not necessarily contradict the Biblical account of creation" and that evolutionists had demonstrated that in terms of anatomy and physiology "the broad line of distinction between man and the lower animals is removed." Moreover in advocating the Traducianist theory of the origin of the soul—the doctrine that the soul is inherited from the first human pair and not separately created every time—he found that it agreed in "many points" with the "teaching of theistic evolution on the origin of man."[60]

Of course the stance taken up by Pope and Gamertsfelder does not

---

58. Pope, *A Compendium of Christian Theology: Being Analytical Outlines of a Course of Theological Study, Biblical, Dogmatic, Historical*, 2d ed., 3 vols. (London: Wesleyan Conference Office, 1880), 1: 405, 432.

59. Pope, *A Higher Catechism of Theology* (London: T. Woolmer, 1883), pp. 111-12.

60. Gamertsfelder, *Systematic Theology* (1921; rpt., Harrisburg, Pa.: Evangelical Publishing House, 1938), pp. 376, 377, 379, 380.

entirely represent the substance of the Wesleyan encounter with Darwin. In 1874, for instance, Asa Mahan had made it plain that "Theologians do not deny evolution because it is opposed to religion but because there is, undeniably, no valid evidence whatever of its truth."[61] And yet he couched even this rebuttal in scientific rather than theological terms—no doubt because he deeply respected the "scientific method" as exemplified in the endeavors of Kepler, Newton, and Galileo.[62] Others had less refined objections. But their unease, if George Lyon is anything to go by, stemmed not from doubts about the principle of evolution itself but from its application to the human species. "Nothing can be more certain," he told readers of the *Northwestern Christian Advocate* in 1872, "than, if the Darwinian hypothesis be true as to the origin of man's physical structure, that of the Bible is false."[63] And yet even at this early date, there were those less theologically nervous. E. O. Haven told the readers of the same Methodist journal that "so far . . . as the Darwinian hypothesis pertains to the origin of vegetables and animals or even man's physical structure, it is a matter of supreme indifference to Christianity."[64] Another Wesleyan, reflecting the growing influence of Asa Gray, contended in 1879 that the "theologian need not fear an enlargement of the sphere in which God works through laws"—that, on the contrary, evolutionary design both deepened and heightened the Christian understanding of the Creator.[65] At the same time, James Lisle was arguing for a scientifically informed reading of the early chapters of Genesis, urging that the "doctrine of genetic evolution is not necessarily antagonistic to revealed truth."[66]

As we will presently discover, this openness to Darwin was soon to be muted, if not displaced, within the evangelical Wesleyan tradition, as it was within its Calvinistic counterpart. But before we turn to that "great divide" in the evangelical mind, I want to make some concluding observations on the attitude of the powerful group of Scottish Calvinists to the theory of evolution around the turn of the century.

SCOTTISH REINFORCEMENTS

The intellectual vitality of Scottish culture throughout the entire nineteenth century can scarcely be underestimated. We have already

---

61. Mahan, "Evolution and Theology," *Northwestern Christian Advocate*, 4 March 1874, p. 1.

62. See Mahan, "The Self Glorification of Modern Evolutionists," *Northwestern Christian Advocate*, 10 December 1873, p. 393.

63. Lyon, "Supreme Indifference of Christianity," *Northwestern Christian Advocate*, 24 April 1872, p. 129.

64. Haven, "Darwinism and Christianity," *Northwestern Christian Advocate*, 27 March 1872, p. 102.

65. "The Present Aspect of the Evolution Controversy," *The Methodist*, 16 August 1879, p. 3.

66. James Lisle, "Evolution," *Northwestern Christian Advocate*, 12 November 1879, p. 1. See also Robert E. Bystrom, "The Earliest Methodist Response to Evolution," M.A. thesis, Northwestern University, June 1966.

noted the formative influence of Calvinist theology on the outlook of such scientists as Miller and Fleming and such theologians as Chalmers and McCosh. Their openness to the scientific enterprise continued to characterize the Scottish Presbyterian tradition throughout the second half of the nineteenth century. Like many others, George Matheson (author of the hymn "Make Me a Captive, Lord") found it easy to absorb Spencer's evolutionism within his synthetic Christian Hegelianism. In *Can the Old Faith Live with the New?* Matheson discovered Almighty God lurking behind Spencer's "Unknowable," while at the Belfast 1884 meeting of the world Alliance of Reformed Churches, he urged that if "we agree to call [Spencer's] Force an inscrutable or unsearchable Will, we shall have already established a scientific basis, not only for the belief in a guiding Providence, but for the possibility of an efficacious prayer."[67] Likewise, A. B. Bruce, a Free Church professor in Aberdeen, found it possible in his 1897 Gifford Lectures to absorb the entire gamut of evolutionary history within what he called *The Providential Order.*[68]

My purpose here, however, is not cite a multitude of such cases within the broad sweep of Scottish Calvinism but rather to focus on two figures within that general tradition who were more closely identified with the evangelical wing, one of whom—James Orr—was to play a key role in the growth of early fundamentalism. First, however, some observations on the Free Church professor of apologetics James Iverach are in order.

Iverach had followed the now well-worn path from science education in Edinburgh by way of the Free Church parish ministry to a theological professorship in Aberdeen during the last quarter of the nineteenth century. Weaving his way among the "monstrous self-consciousness of the Hegelian school," the immanence theology of Spinoza's World Soul, and Herbert Spencer's "Unknowable," he held to an impeccably orthodox theological line and sought to integrate it with the intellectual concerns of his day. In several monographs on subjects ranging from Spencerian philosophy and evolutionary ethics to more general considerations of the relationship between theology and science, Iverach tirelessly distinguished Darwin's biological theory from Spencer's evolutionary speculations as Gray and Wright were doing on the other side of the Atlantic. The general parameters within which he issued his approval of Darwinism are now quite predictable. He dismissed universal schemes erected on naturalistic evolution as both im-

---

67. Matheson, "The Religious Bearings of the Doctrine of Evolution," in *Alliance of the Reformed Churches Holding the Presbyterian System: Minutes and Proceedings of the Third General Council, Belfast 1884* (Belfast: Assembly's Offices, 1884), p. 86. See also Matheson's *Can the Old Faith Live with the New? or, The Problem of Evolution and Revelation* (Edinburgh: William Blackwood & Sons, 1885), and "Modern Science and the Religious Instinct," *Presbyterian Review* 5 (1884): 608-21.

68. Bruce, *The Providential Order of the World* (London: Hodder & Stoughton, 1897).

possible and illegitimate; only when the whole process was enlivened by the sovereign purposes of God could any universal implications be drawn. But given this qualification, he went on to insist that theists should not interfere with the methodology of mechanical science.[69] Iverach's most detailed treatment of the evolution question appeared in his *Christianity and Evolution*, first published in 1894. A brief review of its main themes will suffice to demonstrate Iverach's evolutionary stance. The heart of his message lay in the renewed emphasis he placed on the theological value of natural law and the uniformity of nature. Every "fresh proof of the universal reign of law" was to be welcomed within the halls of theology, for here were traces of divine footsteps just as surely as in Paley's adaptations. How foolish therefore, he felt, to be constantly looking about "for imperfections in a mechanical or other theory in order to find a chink through which the theistic argument may enter." Natural law was itself natural theology. And this applied a fortiori to natural selection. In a highly competent review of Darwin's theory, Iverach noted that variations seemed to proceed along increasingly definite lines and not just in a random fashion. The issue therefore was "not between 'evolution' and what our friends call 'special creation.' It is between evolution under the guidance of intelligence and purpose, and evolution as a fortuitous result."[70]

As with many of the other figures we have discussed, it was Iverach's capacity to reconstrue the design argument in more dynamic, holistic terms that encouraged this rapprochement with Darwinism. The "old fixed static way" of thinking about the history of life was gone forever, he insisted; in its place was a new set of dynamic interrelationships so beautiful and marvelous that they inevitably revealed the shallowness of those who thought they could merely substitute Darwin for Paley. So committed was Iverach to this new vision of the world that he was prepared to go even further than Warfield on the question of human origin. He was unhappy with Wallace's dualistic separation of mind and body, as he was with proposals reserving special creation for the mind but allowing evolution for the body. In his opinion, the idea of a superadded soul destroyed the unity of the human constitution. He preferred "to trace the origin of man, body, soul, spirit, as a unity, to the creative power of God."

Are we, then, to deny even in the case of man "special creation"? Yes and no, as we understand the meaning of the term. To me

---

69. Iverach, *Is God Knowable?* (London: Hodder & Stoughton, 1884), p. 49; and *Theism in the Light of Present Science and Philosophy* (London: Hodder & Stoughton, 1899). See also Moore, *The Post-Darwinian Controversies*, pp. 253-59.

70. Iverach, *Evolution and Christianity* (London: Hodder & Stoughton, 1894), pp. 18, 26, 104.

creation is continuous. To me everything is as it is through the continuous power of God; every law, every being, every relation of being are determined by Him, and He is the Power by which all things exist. I believe in the immanence of God in the world, and I do not believe that He comes forth merely at a crisis, as Mr. Wallace supposes. Apart from the Divine action man would not have been, or have an existence; but apart from the Divine action nothing else would have an existence.[71]

What is especially interesting is that it was Iverach's thoroughgoing Reformed orthodoxy that energized his espousal of the theory of evolution. "The Christian view of the world," he contended, "is the only view which does justice to all the factors of evolution, and recognizes all its complexity."[72] Certainly human beings can see through the glass of nature only darkly, but what they can see points them to the immanent second person of the Trinity in whom and through whom all things were made.

James Orr, a professor in the United Free Church College in Glasgow, earned a well-deserved reputation as a scholarly apologist for historic evangelicalism on both sides of the Atlantic. His sensitive treatment of Old Testament higher criticism, his analysis of the dominant Ritschlian theology, and his defense of such cardinal doctrines as revelation and resurrection made him a major force within the evangelical movement. As we will see later, he contributed several essays to the twelve-volume *Fundamentals*, from which the fundamentalist movement got its name. Here I want to consider Orr's not insubstantial treatment of the evolution question in its application to biology, anthropology, and theology.

Orr was repeatedly at pains to point out that the theory of evolution ought not to be equated with its specifically Darwinian formulation. He never for a moment doubted that evolution had occurred and that it operated under the universal reign of natural law. The idea of the "genetic derivation of one order or species from another" had found wide support among practicing scientists, and Orr saw no reason to dispute the general principle.[73] The Bible, he said, was no *"anticipative text-book* of natural science" and should not be treated as such.[74] But writing during a period when Darwinism was in eclipse, Orr exploited to the full the rival evolutionary alternatives arising in many quarters.[75] He set out some of

---

71. Iverach, *Evolution and Christianity*, p. 175.

72. Iverach, *Evolution and Christianity*, p. 231.

73. Orr, *God's Image in Man and Its Defacement in the Light of Modern Denials* (London: Hodder & Stoughton, 1905), p. 88.

74. Orr, *The Faith of a Modern Christian* (London: Hodder & Stoughton, 1910), p. 206.

75. A good introduction to these various schools can be found in Peter J. Bowler's *The Eclipse of Darwinism: Anti-Darwinian Evolution Theories in the Decades around 1900* (Baltimore: The Johns Hopkins University Press, 1983).

JAMES ORR, from Stewart R. Scott's *East Bank Church, Hawick: Its Origin and History, 1773-1923* (Hawick: J. Edgar, 1923)

the major schools of evolutionary thought in his monumental *Christian View of God and the World*. It is apparent that he himself was increasingly attracted to the version proposed by the Dutch biologist Hugo DeVries, whose mutation theory stressed the sudden appearance of quite new organic forms—what were called "saltations." Orr felt that this theory overcame many of classical Darwinism's greatest problems, such as missing links in the fossil record, reversion to type, and hybrid sterility. It was, moreover, more compatible with the Christian view of divine intervention at key points in the creation of the chain of life. As we have seen, other Calvinists, including Macloskie and Warfield, had also found DeVries's version attractive.

What Orr objected to most in Darwin's theory was, as we might expect, its antiteleological bias. But he felt that he could sense in the more recent work of certain evolutionary naturalists a greater openness to directed evolution. To redeem the evolutionary vision, he felt, it was only necessary to relocate divine purpose within the natural order instead of restricting it to external interference:

> Assume God—as many devout evolutionists do—to be imma-nent in the evolutionary process, and His intelligence and pur-pose to be expressed in it; then evolution, so far from conflicting with theism, may become a new and heightened form of the theistic argument. The real impelling force of evolution is now from *within*; it is not blind but purposeful; forces are inherent in organisms which, not fortuitously but with design, work out the variety and gradations in nature we observe. Evolution is but the other side of a previous *in*volution and only establishes a higher teleology.[76]

With these qualifications to naturalistic Darwinism already worked out, Orr approached the question of human development in his Stone Lectures at Princeton in 1903-04. They were subsequently published as *God's Image in Man*. Two important points arise from his discussions. First, Orr devoted quite a lot of space to establishing the discontinuity between human and animal life in both physical and mental terms. Calling on the testimony of the evolutionary biologists themselves, he demonstrated to his own satisfaction the "enormous distance that sepa-rates man from the highest animals, alike in a bodily and in a mental state." He could have left the matter there, applying a saltatory theory of evolution to human emergence, but he seems to have wanted to go fur-ther. For him, the ideas of mind, soul, and the image of God were so closely bound together as to be almost conflated. He obviously felt the need to postulate an entirely supernatural origin for them, not least to preserve the biblical doctrine of the fall. And since the mind and brain were so intimately related, he had to push on toward an entirely super-natural creation of the first human being in toto. "I confess," he said, "it has always seemed to me an illogical and untenable position to postulate a special origin for man's mind, and deny it for his body. I base here on the close relation which every one now admits to subsist between man's mental and physical organisation. Mind and body constitute together a unity in man. Mind and brain, in particular, are so related that a sudden rise on the mental side cannot be conceived without a corresponding rise on the physical side. . . . You could not put a human mind into a simian brain." And yet he did go on to note that this was a direct creation "in a peculiar sense," perhaps allowing it to have taken place by an evolution-ary jump. Let us remember that he had opposed the polarization of

---

76. Orr, *God's Image*, pp. 95-96.

evolution and special creation, looking instead for "some higher notion which will be seen to be the synthesis of both."[77]

A second interesting feature of Orr's study is the way in which he felt the need to yoke together the Lamarckian idea of the inheritance of acquired characteristics and the inheritance of original sin. He was, of course, well aware of the hot debate on the Lamarckian issue currently engaging Weismann and Spencer. But he held out hope that the inheritance of at least some acquired characteristics would be scientifically verified. Physical changes arising from mutilations and so on were, he admitted, "ordinarily not inherited." But in increasing measure, aspects of intellectual, emotional, and moral life could well be passed on to succeeding generations. The inheritance of Adam's first sin—the inherent sinful bias—fell into the latter category, and so the doctrine of original sin was umbilically tied to Lamarck's evolutionary scheme.[78] B. B. Warfield, it is worth noting, took up this very point in his review of the book for the *Princeton Theological Review*. He complained about what he called Orr's "over-emphasis of the fact of 'heredity,' taken in the strict sense," which he felt unnecessarily involved Orr in the difficulty of needing to defend Lamarckian evolution. Warfield, by contrast, maintained that the doctrine of original sin relied solely on the *representativeness* of Adam, not the inheritance of his guilt. So whereas Warfield held to a decidedly more conservative line on the question of biblical inerrancy than did Orr, their positions were reversed on the question of human evolution. Again, no simple categorizations are possible.[79]

Whatever scruples Orr may have had about Darwinism did not prevent him from using the idea of evolution as a model for reconstructing historical theology. When he was invited to give the Elliot lectures at the Western Theological Seminary Allegheny in 1897, he took as his theme "The Progress of Dogma." His solid allegiance to the cardinal doctrines of evangelical Christianity did nothing to blind him to the genuine progress that had characterized theological scholarship. "I plant myself here, in truth," he said, "on the most modern of all doctrines—the doctrine of evolution." He reserved his objections for the speculations of those theologians who cut off their dogmatics from the great doctrinal traditions of the church embodied in Scripture and the Reformation creeds. Any search for the genuine doctrinal content of Christianity, he insists, must

---

77. Orr, *God's Image*, pp. 126, 152, 87.

78. See Orr, *God's Image*, pp. 235-40. Orr also discusses the implications of science for theology in *Christian View of God and the World as Centring in the Incarnation* (Edinburgh: Andrew Elliot, 1893); and *The Bible under Trial: Apologetic Papers in View of Present-Day Assaults on Holy Scripture* (London: Marshall Brothers, n.d.), especially pp. 199-226, on "oppositions of science."

79. Warfield, review of *God's Image in Man*, by James Orr, *Princeton Theological Review* 4 (1906): 555-58.

give prima facie weight to these ancient credal formulations—because, after all, the doctrines they embodied had been subjected to "natural selection":

> They represent the "survival of the fittest" in doctrine under the severest possible strain. Not one of these doctrines but has been hacked and hewed at till, if it had not been founded on God's word, and felt to be true to Christian experience, the breath would have gone out of it long ago. Yet men fling it aside as if this simple fact that it is old—has survived all this brunt of battle—were sufficient without further ado to condemn it! It is not explained why, in every other sphere, the surviving product in an evolutionary process should be the fittest, and dogma alone should be an exception.[80]

Clearly Orr saw Darwin's principle as a two-edged sword that could be used either to fight in the cause of militant agnosticism or to fight the good fight in defense of historic Christianity.

These individuals do not exhaust the range of Scottish responses to evolutionary theory of course. The reception of the new biology at New College, Edinburgh, would merit detailed investigation. Suffice it to note here that while John Duns, the New College professor of natural science from 1864 to 1903, balked at natural selection as a substitute for the "theory of design" in the 1870s, Robert Rainy, the New College principal, chose the topic "Evolution and Theology" for his inaugural address in 1874. To him the question of "whether man's animal constitution could conceivably be developed from lower forms" was not one "of any great theological interest," while the supposed effects of evolution on the arguments of natural theology had been much overrated. Should evolutionary theory come to be verified, Rainy was sure that "the argument of the Theist, and the just impression of a God on the mind of a reverent spectator of nature, would be exactly where they were." So long as room was left for divine intervention in the development of human spiritual nature, Rainy, like his Edinburgh colleague Henry Calderwood, professor of moral philosophy in the University and evangelical exponent of the Scottish philosophy in its anti-Hegelian guise, would raise no obstacles to embracing evolutionary theory.[81]

---

80. Orr, *The Progress of Dogma*, 4th ed. (London: Hodder & Stoughton, 1901), p. 18.

81. See Duns, *Creation According to the Book of Genesis and the Confession of Faith: Speculative Natural Science and Theology* (Edinburgh: Maclaren & Macniven, 1877); and *On the Theory of Natural Selection and the Theory of Design* (London: Victoria Institute, n.d.). See Rainy, *Evolution and Theology: Inaugural Address* (Edinburgh: Maclaren & Macniven, 1874), pp. 32, 9; and *Faith and Science: A Sermon* (Edinburgh: Macniven & Wallace, n.d.). And see Calderwood, *Evolution and Man's Place in Nature* (London: Macmillan, 1893).

TAKING STOCK

As we have reflected on the reaction of evangelical churchmen to the Darwinian onslaught, a number of things have become increasingly clear. That there was no uniform response to Darwin must now be beyond doubt. Some few outrightly rejected both Darwinism and the more general theory of evolution; others carefully discriminated between the two, dismissing the former while courting the latter; still others were prepared to go most of the way with Darwin. But it is just as clear that evangelicals throughout the latter part of the nineteenth century and the first two decades of the twentieth generally found the theological resources necessary to absorb the implications of the new biology. Various methods of salvaging natural theology were proposed. And if, as Alvar Ellegård observed, "a direct synthesis of idealistic philosophy and Biblical orthodoxy . . . was evidently very widespread among the early opponents of Darwin's theory," we have found a considerable number of evangelicals using just that synthesis for quite the opposite end.[82] On the question of human origin, too, an equally willing accommodation to evolutionary anthropology was sensitively negotiated. All this goes to show a quite surprising diversity within the evangelical movement in the decades before 1920. Yet, this pluralism did not degenerate into factionalism. The channels of communication between individuals who evaluated evolution quite differently remained open. And this in turn suggests some degree of coherence within a diversified tradition. Surely most of those we have discussed would have given their assent to the diagnosis P. T. Forsyth made in 1905:

> Everything turns on the kind of teleology and the range of its lines. There is nothing in evolution fatal to the great moral and spiritual teleology of Christianity, whatever may happen to the antiquated, and what I ask pardon for describing as even the paleyological, forms of design. . . . It is not in nature at all that we can find nature's end. . . . In Jesus Christ we have the final cause of history, and the incarnation of that kingdom of God which is the only teleology large enough for the whole world.[83]

---

82. Ellegård, *Darwin and the General Reader: The Reception of Darwin's Theory of Evolution in the British Periodical Press, 1859-1872* (Göteborg: Act Universitatis Gothenburgensis, 1958), p. 203.

83. Forsyth, "Some Christian Aspects of Evolution," *The London Quarterly Review*, October 1905, pp. 217-19.

CHAPTER 5

THE GREAT DIVIDE

By the time of the outbreak of the First World War, evangelicals in science and theology had found the necessary resources to accommodate evolutionary biology to their evangelical outlook. In some cases they had gone a good deal further, marshalling the central themes of evolution theory in the cause of Christian apologetics and finding in it clarification of the biblical doctrines of creation and humanity. This in itself might seem strange given the popular notion that science and Christianity were at war with one another, but the years that followed were to prove yet more conclusively that that notion was illusory. This part of the story is all the more remarkable because it was precisely in the decades around 1900 that Darwinism was in eclipse within the scientific community at large as a host of alternative biological theories were advanced. And yet, despite the fact that there were resources in abundance for turning the tables on Darwinian evolution, the evangelical reaction during even these years was, overall, both thoughtful and tolerant.

The measured response of an evangelical theologian to these new currents of scientific thought is nowhere more conspicuous than in the case of B. B. Warfield. In a pamphlet entitled "The Present Day Conception of Evolution" issued some time around the turn of the century, he reviewed the state of play in the rapidly changing field of evolutionary science. Certainly Warfield objected to the apparent reductionism of Cope and Le Conte's recent proposals. The idea that evolution is an "all-inclusive self-production" he designated *"a philosophy of the universe,"* which for that reason had "no claim to be called 'science.'" He was insistent that the theory be judged solely by its theoretical and empirical adequacy. Evolution, he said, had helped unravel some exceptionally difficult problems, but that surely did not mean that it could account for all facts. He urged caution and humility on the part of proponents of the theory, especially in light of the fact that there was little consensus within the scientific fraternity itself. Nevertheless, as he made it plain right from the outset,

> There seems to be an impression abroad that the adherents of the doctrine of evolution have hopelessly fallen out among themselves, and threaten to destroy by internecine conflict the hold which this doctrine has obtained upon scientific thought. This impression is an erroneous one. Evolutionists do differ gravely from one another on such subordinate matters as the causes of variation, the classes of variation which may be preserved by heredity, and the selective factors at work in the gradual moulding of organic forms. . . . But it is obviously not a difference fundamental to the conception of evolution itself, but one which has reference only to the modes of its working. Evolutionists appear to be entirely and even increasingly at one in their fundamental conception of the doctrine.[1]

Warfield, however, was not the only proto-fundamentalist to keep an open mind on the evolutionary hypothesis. Other key figures in the movement were equally considered in their judgments on the issue. To illustrate this I want to turn now to some of the contributors to *The Fundamentals* to ascertain their reaction to Darwinism. This is especially important because of the rampant antievolution crusade that in the 1920s became the grand cause of the fundamentalists, culminating in the infamous "Monkey Trial" at Dayton, Tennessee.

THE EARLY FUNDAMENTALISTS

At heart, *The Fundamentals,* a twelve-volume paperback series published between 1910 and 1915, was "an interdenominational expression of the anti-modernist movement" in theology.[2] It drew together a wide range of theologically conservative writers whose aim was to reaffirm the traditional Christian doctrines about Christ and the Bible. Successively edited by A. C. Dixon, Louis Meyer, and R. A. Torrey, and sponsored by two wealthy Californians, some three million copies of the documents were eventually distributed to "every pastor, evangelist, missionary, theological student, Sunday School superintendent, Y.M.C.A. and Y.W.C.A. secretary in the English-speaking world, so far as the ad-

---

1. Warfield, *The Present Day Conception of Evolution* (Emporia, Kans.: The College Printing Office, n.d.), p. 2.
2. So writes George M. Marsden in his *Fundamentalism and American Culture: The Shaping of Twentieth-Century Evangelicalism, 1870-1925* (Oxford: Oxford University Press, 1980), p. 119. In developing this section, I have drawn on my essay "B. B. Warfield, the Theory of Evolution and Early Fundamentalism," *Evangelical Quarterly* 58 (1986): 69-83.

dresses of these [could] be obtained."[3] Of course the fundamentalist movement insofar as it already existed, and certainly as it subsequently developed, was a very complex social movement,[4] and *The Fundamentals* cannot be simply taken as the manifesto of the whole tradition. Nevertheless, the plurality of scientific views expressed by the contributors to the series does throw into significant relief the subsequent evolution phobia, which, as I have said, later became the movement's cause célèbre.

The most pointed consideration of Darwin's theory appeared in the seventh volume of the series. It was prepared by the aging George Frederick Wright, whose promotion of a Calvinistic version of Darwinism has already attracted our attention. That *he* was invited to write on the topic is surely highly significant. Nor was he in any sense an unwilling recruit. His heart was clearly in the movement, for in addition to this essay on evolution he contributed other articles to the series—one to the second volume entitled "The Testimony of the Monuments to the Truth of the Scriptures" and one to the ninth entitled "The Mosaic Authorship of the Pentateuch."

The burden of Wright's contribution to the seventh volume of *The Fundamentals* was to discriminate between evolution as a scientific theory of species transmutation and evolutionism as a metaphysical worldview. The word *evolution*, he noted, "has come into much deserved disrepute by the injection into it of erroneous and harmful theological and philosophical implications. The widely current doctrine of evolution which we are now compelled to combat is one which practically eliminates God from the whole creative process and relegates mankind to the tender mercies of a mechanical universe the wheels of whose machines are left to move on without any immediate Divine direction."[5] Clearly Wright's dissatisfaction with evolutionary theory centered less on exegetical questions about the early Genesis narratives than on the materialistic reductionism that had shorn natural history of any teleological element. But Wright was quick to point out that "Darwinism was not, in the mind of its author, a theory of universal evolution" and that in fact Darwin rarely used the term. Wright argued, moreover, that Darwin had rested his theory on the assumption that "the Creator in the beginning breathed the forces of life into several forms of plants and animals"—a suggestion that has led at least some historians of science to identify him as an evolutionary deist. Of course, as we have already seen, this amounted to a kind of methodological atheism inasmuch as, after the initial act of creation, the evolutionary process proceeded according to the laws of nature. It was Darwin's postulation of such a *modus operandi* that

---

3. *The Fundamentals*, 12 vols. (Chicago: Testimony Publishing Company, 1910), 1: 4.

4. In addition to Marsden's excellent *Fundamentalism and American Culture*, see Ernest Sandeen's *The Roots of Fundamentalism: British and American Millenarianism, 1800-1930* (Chicago: Chicago University Press, 1970).

5. Wright, "The Passing of Evolution," in *The Fundamentals*, 7: 5.

encouraged some critics to suggest that he had merely substituted Nature for God, natural selection for natural theology.

But Wright was eager to use Darwin's tentative admission to pry open the theory just enough to squeeze in the old Paley Watchmaker, and so he contended that "by no stretch of legitimate reasoning can Darwinism be made to exclude design." To support his own version of the argument from design, he enlisted the support of such savants as Agassiz, Owen, Mivart, Shaler, Dawson, Kelvin, Wallace, Virchow, and Cope, all of whom, in different ways, expressed dissatisfaction with the way Darwin had formulated his proposals. Even now, well into his eighth decade, Wright kept abreast of current developments in science and hence was able to review the internal evolutionary debates engaging the Neo-Lamarckians and the Neo-Darwinians as well as post-Darwinian developments in the new science of heredity. But Wright's intention in summoning this not insubstantial body of opinion was not to reject the scientific validity of Darwin's original theory; rather, it was to spotlight the naivety of inflating such a contested scheme into a universal principle and to urge that to posit an evolutionary history "without the intervention of the Supreme Designing Mind is to commit logical 'hara-kiri.' Such chance combinations are beyond all possibility of rational belief."[6]

Wright's comparatively latitudinarian attitude to scientific evolutionism mirrored the earlier discussion of the theme by James Orr, whose major contributions we have also already reviewed. A staunch and scholarly apologist for historic evangelicalism from the perspective of a modified Calvinism, Orr supplemented his book-length treatments of basic Christian theology with several contributions to *The Fundamentals*. In two of these, "Science and Christian Faith" (vol. 4) and "The Early Narratives of Genesis" (vol. 6), Orr touched on issues directly impinging on the evolution question. In the former he was again at pains to highlight what he termed "the unwarrantable confusion or identification of evolution with *Darwinism*." While he was quite open to evolutionary explanations, he itemized three areas in which he believed the conventional Darwinian model had been found wanting on scientific grounds.

First, Orr assured his readers that the Darwinian idea of natural selection involving fortuitous biological variations was being superseded in the scientific community by theories suggesting that such changes occurred "along definite lines, and [were] guided to definite ends."[7] Orr did not specify which particular scientific theories he had in mind, but as we have seen, there were indeed schools of biological opinion (notably the Neo-Lamarckian) advocating this viewpoint. He was certainly correct in saying that many scientists were unhappy with Darwin's crucial dependence on the ideas of "chance" and random variation.

6. Wright, "The Passing of Evolution," p. 16.
7. Orr, "Science and Christian Faith," in *The Fundamentals*, 4: 102.

Second, Orr questioned whether natural selection could in fact account fully for organic diversity. He was not alone in this judgment; many in the scientific fraternity balked at the exclusivist temper of Darwin's theory, whether applied to organic or moral development. Darwinians such as Wallace and Lamarckians such as Powell both wanted to supplement natural selection with other evolutionary processes, while T. H. Huxley, for one, argued that ethically superior conduct entailed opposition to the struggle for existence. Ethics and evolution were pulling in opposite directions.

Third, Orr maintained that the slow and insensible rate of the changes by which new species were supposed to be produced was being challenged by the new idea of "mutations"—the belief that new species originated in rapid and sudden changes. Orr almost certainly had in mind the mutation theory of Hugo DeVries, whose work, as we have seen, attracted several evolutionary Calvinists.

In effect, then, Orr's approach was rather like that of Wright, involving as it did a cataloguing of challenges to the spirit of Darwinism made by evolutionists themselves in order to confirm his conclusion that " 'Evolution,' in short, is coming to be recognized as but a new name for 'creation,' only that the creative power now works from *within*, instead of, as in the old conception, in an *external*, plastic fashion."[8] By thus advocating a sort of emergent evolutionism in which radically new evolutionary departures—life, consciousness, rationality, and morality—illustrated the essential discontinuity of the process, he presented his own evangelical rapprochement between science and the Bible.

Orr also pursued this reconciliation of science and Scripture in another *Fundamentals* essay on the Genesis narratives. Since he was trying to construct an evolution theory that was providentialist in character and teleological in spirit, he affirmed the religious significance of the doctrine of creation in terms of the assurance it gave to belief in a purposeful universe under the control of a sovereign Creator. So it is no surprise to find him reaffirming his conviction that the "Bible was never given us in order to anticipate or forestall the discoveries of modern twentieth century science,"[9] leaving open the question as to how the six creative days should be understood and stressing the popular culture-specific character of biblical language. What he objected to was the identification of evolution with what he took to be a materialistic Darwinism.

The decision of the compilers of *The Fundamentals* to include these contributions from Wright and Orr is in no sense evidence of misjudgment on their part. It is true, as we will see, that the series included two vehemently antievolution tracts. But before we turn specifically to these I want to make one or two observations on the scientific thinking of R. A.

---

8. Orr, "Science and Christian Faith," p. 103.
9. Orr, "The Early Narratives of Genesis," in *The Fundamentals*, 6:94.

Torrey, who edited the final two volumes of the series. In many ways, Torrey, a close associate of D. L. Moody, was the archetypal fundamentalist; but he was for all that a graduate of Yale and had studied in Germany for a year—experiences that, as Marsden puts it, made him "one of several leaders who represented the direct tie between fundamentalism and the New England tradition in which learning was so revered."[10]

Certainly Torrey was not prepared to go as far as Warfield, Orr, or Wright on the Darwin question. "Whatever truth there may be in the doctrine of evolution as applied within limits to the animal world," he insisted, "it breaks down when applied to man."[11] Nevertheless, a number of not insignificant concessions to science—first to geology and then to anthropology—are clearly evident in his 1907 book *Difficulties and Alleged Errors and Contradictions in the Bible*. On the question of the Genesis "days," Torrey unequivocally confirmed that "Anyone who is at all familiar with the Bible and the Bible usage of words knows that the use of the word 'day' is not limited to periods of twenty-four hours. It is frequently used of a period of time of an entirely undefined length." To rebut the accusation that such exegesis was merely a capitulation to the pressures of modern science, he simply pointed to the supporting witness of Augustine. Yet for all that, he was pleased to report the harmony of science and Scripture on the chronological order of creation. He felt himself in a position to make this claim, moreover, because it had been his "privilege to study geology under that prince of geologists, who has been pronounced by competent authority to be the greatest scientific thinker of the nineteenth century with the exception of Charles Darwin, namely Professor James D. Dana, of Yale." Torrey's laudatory aside on Darwin, incidentally, speaks for itself.[12]

Torrey's second concession, this time to prehistoric anthropology, is apparent in his support for the idea of the existence of pre-adamic human beings. He claimed, of course, to base this judgment on purely internal exegetical criteria. And it is true that the theory was first proposed long before the challenge of modern primitive anthropology, by Isaac de la Peyrère in 1655. In any event, Torrey's interpretation of the vocabulary of Genesis 1:2 provided "a brief but suggestive account of how the earth became involved in desolation and emptiness, presumably through the sin of some pre-Adamic race."[13] But he did not fail to notice the value of his exposition for reconciling biblical discourse and scientific discov-

10. Marsden, *Fundamentalism and American Culture*, p. 47.

11. Torrey, *What the Bible Teaches: A Thorough and Comprehensive Study of What the Bible Has to Say concerning the Great Doctrines of Which It Treats* (Chicago: Fleming H. Revell, 1898), p. 249.

12. See Torrey, *Difficulties and Alleged Errors in the Bible* (London: James Nisbet, 1907), pp. 30, 31.

13. Torrey, *Difficulties and Alleged Errors*, p. 32.

ery. He took the archeological findings then being excavated in the region of Nineveh to be "the remains of the pre-Adamic race already mentioned." Such evidence, he urged, together with the scholarly consensus that it is not possible to calculate the antiquity of mankind from biblical genealogical tables, encouraged a more positive outlook on prehistoric archaeology:

> No one need have the least fear of any discoveries that the archaeologists may make; for if it should be found that there were early civilizations thousands of years before Christ, it would not come into any conflict whatever with what the Bible really teaches about the antiquity of man, the Adamic race.[14]

The cautiously proevolution stances of Wright and Orr and the comparatively open attitude of Torrey to science are matched by two decisively and aggressively anti-Darwin statements in the eighth collection of *Fundamentals* papers. It is immediately apparent that the contributors of these pieces (one of them remained anonymous; the other is the relatively unknown Henry Beach) lack the theological and scientific standing of the senior evangelicals we have been discussing. I may risk a charge of sarcasm if I describe this transition as a shift from pineapples to crabapples, but it is nonetheless important for us to note that the authors of these pieces are significantly less distinguished in the ranks of evangelicals than such figures as, say, Wright, Orr, and Warfield. We would doubtless do well to view this part of the story in terms of what Marsden calls the "remarkable shift from moderation to militancy" that typified the fundamentalist cause during the half decade or so before 1920; after that date fundamentalists threw all reserve to the winds and became "engaged in holy warfare to drive the scourge of modernism out of church and culture."[15] Antievolutionism constituted one important chapter in that history.

In the "Decadence of Darwinism," to return to the subject at hand, the Rev. Henry H. Beach of Grand Junction, Colorado, objected to the theory of evolution on the grounds that the organic world exhibits three distinct levels of being—vegetable life, animal life, and human life—and that "these three kinds of life touch each other, but never merge." He also questioned the theory because of Darwin's idea of reversion—the idea that evolutionary history is sometimes retrogressive. Beach protested that there "are no retreatings or abortions in the Divine economy, but God adjusts every feature to present and future conditions, and causes all to march regularly forward in the grand procession of eternal processes."[16] This objection is especially interesting in light of the fact that evangelicals

---

14. Torrey, *Difficulties and Alleged Errors*, p. 36.
15. Marsden, *Fundamentalism and American Culture*, p. 141.
16. Beach, "Decadence of Darwinism," in *The Fundamentals*, 8: 38, 40.

have subsequently objected to Darwinism precisely because of its sup-
posedly *progressivist* philosophy implying human perfectibility—"moving upwards and working out the beast."

Beach further bolstered his objections to the theory with the implicit accusation that it is bad science—that, according to Bonnier, Darwin had no idea of the experimental method, that he had presented a
concept of selection without a selector, and, fundamentally, that evolution was merely an unproven, speculative hypothesis. This tends to confirm Marsden's argument that the ideals of an inductive Baconian outlook
provided the conceptual parameters for much scientific and theological
endeavor in the period. But Beach resorted to scientific authorities merely
to confirm his moral distaste for the theory, a repugnance expressed with
prolix and dismissive zeal: Darwin's theory degrades God and humanity;
it is "ridiculous"; it is "immoral"; for it to "be true, black must be white,
and wrong must be right, and God an Ivan the terrible."[17]

Beach's pugnaciously anti-Darwin sentiments were more than
matched in a parallel essay entitled "Evolutionism in the Pulpit," an
anonymous reprint from the November 1911 issue of the *Herald and
Presbyter* that rivals the exuberance of Beach's rhetoric. This full frontal
attack both on the theory of evolution and on those Christians who accepted it was frank and untempered. Darwinism contradicted the plain
reading of Scripture, the author of the piece argued, and those who salved
their consciences by saying that the Bible was not intended to teach
science were perpetuating a half-truth "more misleading than a down-
right untruth."[18] It has to be pointed out, however, that the author's own
citation of scholarly authorities was at best undisciplined and at worst
deceptive. For example, he cited Dr. Shaler of Harvard as affirming that
the Darwinian theory had not a single fact to confirm it; but Shaler was in
fact deeply committed to the Neo-Lamarckian version of the theory, and
while he was not prepared to extend the natural selection mechanism to
human development, he nonetheless felt it had great explanatory power.
And he cited Virchow regarding the failure of anthropologists to find
paleontological confirmation of a link between "man and monkey,"
thereby neatly obscuring Virchow's longstanding commitment to
Lamarckian evolution.[19]

In the final analysis, however, scholarly authority was immaterial
to the author of "Evolutionism in the Pulpit." The problem was that
Darwinism, as he understood it, contradicted the Bible, and those Chris-

17. Beach, "Decadence of Darwinism," p. 44.

18. "Evolutionism in the Pulpit," in *The Fundamentals*, 8: 28.

19. For more on Shaler's evolutionary thinking, see my *Nathaniel Southgate Shaler and the Culture of American Science* (University, Ala.: University of Alabama Press, 1987); on Virchow, see F. B. Churchill, "Rudolf Virchow and the Pathologist's Criteria for the Inheritance of Acquired Characteristics," *Journal of the History of Medicine and Allied Sciences* 31 (1976): 117-48.

tian ministers who accepted any form of a theory "conceived in agnosticism, and born and nurtured in infidelity" (including presumably fellow contributors to *The Fundamentals*) were, he said, "cowardly," "grossly inconsistent with their Christian profession," and "of low moral quality." He concluded, "Far better would it be for all concerned if these ministers had the courage of their convictions, and sense of honor enough to compel them to leave the Christian Church."[20]

MOUNTING TENSION

This split in the ranks of the protofundamentalists was, I think, symbolic of a growing tension within the evangelical community more generally. Nowhere, perhaps, is this more clearly manifest than within the pages of the *Princeton Theological Review*. In the early years of the twentieth century, as we have seen, contributors to this prestigious periodical had found the conceptual resources for a robust assimilation of at least some form of Darwinism; by the 1920s, however, the complexion of the journal had rather dramatically altered. Of course, there is no sense in which the various statements on the subject of evolution appearing in the *Review*, once the chief organ of Princeton theology, indicated Princeton's official line—after all, with the single exception of W. B. Greene, none of the contributors on the subject in question held a full professorship at Princeton; several were not even members of the faculty. The intricately complex controversies and debates within Princeton during the 1920s that resulted in the exodus of J. Gresham Machen and other junior faculty members to form Westminster Theological Seminary in 1929 doubtless provides an important backdrop to our discussion insofar as it attests to the wide spectrum of theological opinion within the seminary. But for our present purposes it will be enough to note that the increasing number of antievolution tracts published in the journal shows how successful was the infiltration of fundamentalist sentiments into one of the major evangelical theology journals of the day.

William Brenton Greene's progressive withdrawal from a genuine engagement with the Darwinian model provides a useful starting point. He quickly followed the short path from doubt to denial. When he reviewed William North Rice's *Christian Faith in an Age of Science* in 1904, Greene objected to Rice's reinterpretation of Christian dogma in the light of scientific theory. In its place he advocated a hermeneutic that would "interpret the Bible in accordance with all the facts of science; and . . . control the theories, and especially the hypotheses, of science by the plain meaning of the word of God."[21] Yet at this stage in his thinking Greene did

---

20. "Evolutionism in the Pulpit," p. 34.
21. Greene, review of *Christian Faith in an Age of Science*, by William North Rice, *Princeton Theological Review* 2 (1904): 506.

no more than object to Rice's thoroughgoing evolutionism on the grounds that it suppressed the genuine scientific difficulties in bridging the gaps between the nonliving and the living, the nonhuman and the human. By 1908 Greene still held to the theological propriety of a God immanent within the evolutionary process, though he predictably insisted on the need for divine intervention at unspecified points in the history of life. But even at this stage, Greene's sense of irresolution can be detected in his introduction of a distinction between the terms *development* and *evolution*. Since the former, he pointed out, traced the "continuity of progress not to forces resident in nature, but to the Supreme Person who is author of nature," it was certainly compatible with Christian orthodoxy. The latter, however, at least as promulgated by its leading advocates, found "the cause of the progress of nature in nature."[22] Greene's linguistic concerns here are, I believe, doubly interesting. First, they show the degree to which the design question was still the key factor in evangelical evaluations of evolution; and second, they represent the seeds of a return to that restrictive definition of Charles Hodge that found expression in cries of "atheism."

By 1922 Greene's position had substantially hardened. Now he typified contemporary evolution theory as a priori godless because of its contention "that the universe is a 'continuous development' and 'a continuous development' *only*."[23] Like Hodge a half century earlier, Greene now specified as the distinctively Darwinian element in the theory of descent its refusal to allow "for the intervention of mind anywhere." And once again he bolstered his case with reports of scientific inadequacies in the formula and numerous alternative proposals. On the other hand, Greene *was* prepared to accept a supernaturalistic version of the theory, though with tenets that went far beyond the mere reintroduction of design. He advocated the idea of an "evolution within limits"—that is, "evolution within the type." This supernaturalistic evolution, according to Greene, "holds, for example, that while God created the different species, he formed and perfected varieties within those species by providential development, and it allows that many so-called species are but varieties and so have been developed."[24] When the extent of evolutionary penetration into the thinking of men like A. A. Hodge, Warfield, McCosh, and Macloskie is remembered, Greene's substantive return to Charles Hodge's recommendations read as though fifty years of Princeton reflection on the subject had never happened.

In even more strident tones George McCready Price, a Seventh-day

22. Greene, review of *The Religion of Evolution*, by Carma, *Princeton Theological Review* 6 (1908): 119.

23. Greene, "Yet Another Criticism of the Theory of Evolution," *Princeton Theological Review* 20 (1922): 544.

24. Greene, "Yet Another Criticism," p. 549.

Adventist to whom we will presently return, typified the evolutionary principle of uniformity as "essentially pagan or atheistic" and promised "that the whole of evolution is crumbling to pieces, and that a literal Creation of all the great primal types of plants and animals, including man, is the only fact left for men who are acquainted with the progress of scientific discoveries in modern times."[25] Then Floyd E. Hamilton—currently at Princeton—presented a long inventory of deficiencies in the theory of evolution drawn from the fields of genetics, comparative anatomy, embryology, and taxonomy—though again he presented them only to substantiate his basic distaste for the theory on the grounds that it had "become in the eyes of so many a universal law of nature, a religion, a philosophy seeking to place its interpretation upon all things seen and unseen." Theistic evolution, he insisted, is not a viable alternative, because its "tendency is to make the Bible harmonize with evolution; and there are many things involved in the theory which it is difficult, if not impossible, to present in a truly Christian form."[26]

We will presently have occasion to return to the maneuvers of Price and Hamilton in the cause of the newly emerging scientific creationist movement. For the meantime let us just note that the *Princeton Theological Review* allowed them latitude in the expression of their views. Others took the same line. In 1928, for example, Ambrose J. Wilson promised to tell his readers "What Darwin Really Found," but merely reiterated the same old arguments against the theory—evolutionary discontinuities, the restriction of natural selection to intraspecific evolution, missing links, and anthropometric differences between "man and ape."[27]

There were, it must be pointed out, some detractors. But their concessions to Darwinism were far more guarded than those of their predecessors a decade earlier. David Clark, who had graduated with a bachelor's degree from Princeton almost forty years earlier, is a good example. He discussed the relevance of evolution for the theological understanding of doctrines of God, creation, humanity, sin, salvation, Scripture, and so on. Certainly he was unhappy about the pantheistic and deistic tendencies of some evolutionists, and he did not hesitate to cite the contemporary Mendelian challenge to Darwinian gradualism, but he did insist that the "Scriptures do not say *how* God created man, whether instantaneously by fiat, or by a process of slow development." And yet he did confess that the evolutionist's idea of the development of human

---

25. Price, "Modern Botany and the Theory of Organic Evolution," *Princeton Theological Review* 23 (1925): 51-65.

26. Hamilton, "Modern Aspects of the Theory of Evolution," *Princeton Theological Review* 24 (1926): 447, 448.

27. Wilson, "What Charles Darwin Really Found," *Princeton Theological Review* 26 (1928): 515-30.

mental and moral capacity from animal instinct "decidedly strains the interpretation of the record that God made man in his own image."[28]

CREATIONISM LAUNCHED

By the mid-1920s the evangelical tradition as represented in the *Princeton Theological Review* had become progressively alienated from Darwinian evolution. This at least in part reflects the infiltration of the antievolution stance of those with a highly literalistic approach to the Bible. Initially this outlook was particularly associated with the Missouri-Synod Lutherans and with premillennialist groups such as the Seventh-day Adventists, Jehovah's Witnesses, and dispensationalists who exhibited a fascination with exact predictions about the future. Their literalistic reading of biblical prophecy, with its emphasis on numbers and dates, was inevitably extended to the interpretation of the first chapter of Genesis, which they were convinced contained the exact record of the world's creation in six twenty-four-hour days.[29]

George McCready Price's 1926 article in the *Princeton Theological Review* has already attracted our attention. But by the time he penned this piece he had already acquired some notoriety among professional scientists for his "creationist geology." In his case, creationist science and premillennial prophecy went hand in hand. His career, in fact, was devoted to confirming the vision of Ellen G. White, who claimed divine inspiration for her belief that the world's geological features were the result of the Genesis flood. Price had much to thank White for. Apparently she had rescued him from near capitulation to the evolutionism of the local doctor in the remote part of Eastern Canada where Price was the principal of a small high school.

Price was a Seventh-day Adventist and had received his formal education during a two-year course at an Adventist college in Michigan followed by a teacher training curriculum at New Brunswick's provincial normal school. The schoolteaching career on which he subsequently embarked was not to be his life's work, however. In 1902 his *Outlines of Modern Science and Modern Christianity* appeared; in 1906, at the age of thirty-six, he had come to be employed as a handyman in an Adventist sanitarium in southern California. His antievolutionism was full grown by that time, as evidenced by the publication that year of his *Illogical Geology: The Weakest Point in the Evolution Theory*. Price was never one to

---

28. Clark, "Theology and Evolution," *Princeton Theological Review* 23 (1925): 199-200, 203.

29. The following discussion draws substantially on Ron Numbers, "Creationism in 20th-Century America," *Science* 218 (1982): 538-44. See also his essay "The Dilemma of Evangelical Scientists," in *Evangelicalism and Modern America*, ed. George M. Marsden (Grand Rapids: Eerdmans, 1984), pp. 150-60.

mince his words. He said what he thought—as did his reviewers. According to Price, Darwinism was "a most gigantic hoax"; on the other hand, David Starr Jordan, paleontologist president of Stanford University, expected no professional geologist to take the book seriously.

Undeterred, Price pressed ahead with the job at hand. Moving from one Adventist school to another, he still found the energy to push out six more volumes attacking evolution. By the 1920s he was beginning to receive national notice. *The New Geology* of 1923 placed him squarely before the evangelical mind. His argument was staggeringly simple: the Genesis flood had so disturbed the geological strata that neither rhyme nor reason could be found in the fossil record. Needless to say, the geologists were not impressed. Charles Schuchert of Yale told the readers of *Science* that Price was "harboring a geological nightmare." But fundamentalist friends were close at hand to offer support and encouragement. Harry Rimmer described the book as "a masterpiece of REAL science," and Price soon found his way from Adventist obscurity into the solemn pages of the *Princeton Theological Review*.

Rimmer was the other mainspring of creationist science. Numbers colorfully introduces him thus:

> Rimmer, a Presbyterian minister and self-styled "research scientist," obtained his limited exposure to science during one term at a small homeopathic medical school, where he picked up a vocabulary of "double-jointed, twelve cylinder, knee-action words" that later served to impress the uninitiated.[30]

In the midst of his full-time evangelistic work, Rimmer found time to establish his Research Science Bureau in the early 1920s. This venture grew out of his homemade laboratory specifically constructed to carry out embryological and related research. The institution's purpose—defined and promoted by Rimmer himself—was to prove the compatibility of biological, paleontological, and anthropological science with a literal reading of the Bible. He planned what turned out to be an abortive mission to Africa to delineate the anthropometric chasm between gorilla and human, and, ever energetic, embarked on a tireless round of lectures and debates throughout the United States. His style was distinctive and engaging. Who, after all, would not find high entertainment in the challenge of a $100 reward to anyone finding a scientific error in the Bible? Rimmer neither lost his money nor his nerve. Creationism's gestation period was almost over.

Two other figures helped translate this antievolution mood into a movement. William Jennings Bryan, three-time Democratic candidate for the United States presidency, looked forward in 1922 to the time when Darwinism would be driven from the school curriculum. In his case it

---

30. Numbers, "Creationism in 20th-Century America," p. 539.

was disillusionment about the future of Christian civilization that compelled him to meditate on the depravity of human nature. He attributed evils of every sort, from seared consciences to German militarism, to the influence of Darwinian biology. Any theory based on struggle, he felt, must inevitably glorify war. Darwin's ideas thus inspired pan-Germanic jingoism; more, it destroyed the faith of America's youth by undermining confidence in the sacred oracles. "Armed with this information about the case of the world's and the nation's moral decay," Numbers writes, "Bryan launched a nationwide crusade against the offending doctrine."[31] He was joined in the crusade by William Bell Riley, a Baptist pastor in Minneapolis, who threw his weight behind the cause. Here again biblical literalism, premillennialism, and antievolutionism went together. Bell founded the distinctively premillennialist World's Christian Fundamentalist Association in 1919.

During the early 1920s, however, the creationists remained a disparate coalition of scientific skeptics. What they needed was a public spectacle to rally the troops. The infamous Scopes trial of 1925 provided just such a spectacle. The story has been told so often in print and on film that a detailed recapitulation is scarcely necessary here. Briefly, what happened was that John T. Scopes, a teacher in Dayton, Tennessee, confessed to violating the state's new law forbidding the teaching of human evolution in public schools. The ensuing trial attracted worldwide attention as Bryan for the prosecution and Clarence Darrow for the defense battled it out beneath a barrage of press coverage. The creationists emerged to Pyrrhic victory.

The trial, there can be no doubt, has been subjected to more than its fair share of close scrutiny. It has been variously seen as a florescence of cult paranoia and redneck anti-intellectualism; as a desperate battle between God and Satan, faith and infidelity; as the inevitable clash between the rural and the urban, the rustic and the sophisticated, the past and the future. But whatever the explanations, the issue focussed the fundamentalist agenda wonderfully. It drew lines with the precision of a surgeon's knife. Whoever was not for the cause was against it. And, as it drew lines through the national community, it also cut clean through the minds of individuals. Bryan himself found the need to develop a public and a private face. In private he admitted that he had no objection to "evolution before man"; in public he said theistic evolution was just "an anaesthetic administered to young Christians to deaden the pain while their religion is being removed by the materialists." This ambivalence on Bryan's part is indicative of a general failure of the fundamentalists to assemble a coherent strategy for assaulting the menace of Darwinism. While Bryan joined Riley in conceding that the days of creation were much longer than

---

31. Numbers, "Creationism in 20th-Century America," p. 538.

twenty-four-hour days, Price described the day-age theory as the devil's counterfeit.

I would argue that these disagreements among the early antievolutionists do more than simply betray the lack of a consistent public face: they point to the plural origins of the antievolutionary movement. It was born principally of the contributions of such fundamentalists as Price who adopted a highly literalistic approach to the Bible. The objection of this contingent was simply that Darwin went against Moses. But this was not Bryan's dominating concern. His project was thoroughly *ideological*. Bryan, we need to remember, was "The Great Commoner" who saw politics as "applied Christianity." As Durant puts it, "In religion as in politics Bryan was a democrat, and he opposed a biblical criticism which would make theological truth the exclusive property of intellectuals on exactly the same grounds that he opposed a monopoly capitalism which would make economic wealth the exclusive property of industrialist 'robber barons.' Truth, like wealth, he believed, should be equally accessible to all." Bryan rejected Darwinism on the grounds that it was ethically repugnant, subversive of Christian morality and American civilization, and redolent with elitism and the cult of the superman. His opposition to Darwin, therefore, focussed on the theory of human evolution by the heartless, cutthroat processes of natural selection. If anything, it was Social Darwinism that revolted him. Indeed, Durant suggests that this made him "unsuited to leadership of the fundamentalist cause. . . . His religion was too temperate, and his politics were far too progressive. However, on the issue of evolution and morality he found himself in sympathy with a genuinely populist movement; and by becoming its spokesman he gave it a focus and a national significance that it would never otherwise have achieved."[32]

When the fuss died down and realism again surfaced, it became clear that the creationist dream of converting the world was not going to be realized. The fundamentalists were forced into a rearguard action. But a lack of scientific credibility or indeed any coherent theoretical alternative to the theory of evolution thwarted the emergence of any signifi-

---

32. Durant, "Darwinism and Divinity: A Century of Debate," in *Darwinism and Divinity*, ed. John Durant (Oxford: Blackwell, 1985), pp. 24, 26. See also the discussion in Ferenc Morton Szasz's *The Divided Mind of Protestant America, 1880-1930* (University, Ala.: University of Alabama Press, 1982), pp. 106-35. Szasz emphasizes that "the soothing words of the late nineteenth-century 'reconcilers' enabled many Protestants to accept [evolution] without difficulty. Consequently, it did not become a matter of serious public debate until World War I, and its emergence was largely due to William Jennings Bryan. Almost single-handedly, Bryan revived the issue of evolution and brought it to the attention of the American public. With the 1925 trial of John Thomas Scopes in Dayton, Tennessee, it assumed national proportions" (p. 137). Szasz is also of the opinion that the evolution issue was crucial to the development of fundamentalism because it "came to be seen as central to all elements of religious conservatism" (p. 107).

cant coalition until Henry Morris, who spearheaded the modern creationist revival, rediscovered Price's work in the 1940s. This is not to say that the creationists were without a voice during the 1930s, however. Price kept up whatever pressure he could, and Floyd Hamilton, who as we have seen contributed to the *Princeton Theological Review* in the mid '20s, helped keep the flame alive.

In 1931, Hamilton, now professor of Bible at Union Christian College, Korea, published *The Basis of Evolutionary Faith*, following it up shortly afterward with *The Basis of Christian Faith*. He anticipated in a striking way the approach later taken by the modern scientific creationists. He catalogued, for instance, such obstacles to Darwinian inheritance as the nonheritability of small variations, the failure of the Neo-Lamarckians to demonstrate induced hereditary modifications, and the particulate nature of Mendelian inheritance. In geology he pointed to the gaps in the paleontological record, inverted geological strata, and the absence of an actual as opposed to a theoretical geological column. He suggested, moreover, that many geological problems—such as rapid fossilization—could be accounted for by a universal flood. All these considerations pressed Hamilton to the conclusion that "if the evolutionary hypothesis has no foundation in fact, however much we may dislike special creationism, it is the only alternative left for us."[33]

This scientific strategy of Hamilton's was to become, as I have said, the hallmark of creation science. In his case, the Neo-Darwinian synthesis associated with the research of such individuals as R. A. Fisher, J. B. S. Haldane, and Sewall Wright in the 1930s would soon undermine many of his objections. But Hamilton had another more subtle strategy. He dedicated *The Basis of Evolutionary Faith* to "the late Reverend Professor B. B. Warfield . . . my beloved teacher and guide." If this was designed to tell his readers that he was perpetuating Warfield's scientific outlook, he was either mistaking his mentor's viewpoint or manipulating his reputation.

Price's influence also found expression in another volume published in the immediate aftermath of the Scopes trial. Frank Allen, a minister in the Reformed Presbyterian Church, Winnipeg, Canada, issued his *Evolution in the Balances* (1926)—a collection of essays drawn from material that had previously appeared in *The Presbyterian,* *Herald and Presbyter*, and *The Christian Nation*—through the publisher Fleming H. Revell, the company that had already published *The Fundamentals*. Indeed, judging from the content of the material and its original place of publication, Allen may well have been the anonymous author of the *Fundamentals* article "Evolutionism in the Pulpit." His strategy was identical to that of Price, whose name litters the pages of the book and whose *New Geology* Allen describes as "an epoch-making work . . . thor-

---

33. Hamilton, *The Basis of Christian Faith* (London: Marshall, Morgan &
Scott, n.d.), p. 85.

ough, scientific and true to the record of creation as found in the Scriptures." Specifically, Allen made full use of the rising tide of scientific
doubt about Darwinism, haphazardly calling in witnesses to testify to
this or that loophole in the Darwinian formula, although invariably ne-
glecting to mention their acceptance of some form of evolution. Thus, to
give a single example, Allen's perfectly accurate claim that Weismann
"gave up the theory which Lamarck had held to be true" subtly ignores
Weismann's role in the construction of Neo-Darwinism. He employed
similar tactics in the cases of William Bateson, Joseph Le Conte, Hugo
DeVries, and Thomas Hunt Morgan.[34]

The currents of creationism soon began to be felt on the other side
of the Atlantic, though at first without the exuberant rhetoric of Price or
Rimmer. In 1931 the Evolution Protest Movement was founded in Britain,
the eighty-two-year-old Sir Ambrose Fleming serving as its first president.
The British antievolutionists numbered among their ranks some eminent
individuals, notably Fleming himself, a Fellow of the Royal Society; James
Knight, a Fellow of the Royal Society of Edinburgh; Douglas Dewar, a
lawyer and amateur ornithologist; and Sir Charles Marston, an industrialist. But again the problem of presenting a united theoretical front
was soon evident. As Sir Arthur Keith pointed out in his attack on the
doctrine of special creation, *Darwinism and Its Critics,*

> Sir Ambrose ventures the opinion "that there have been pre-
> Adamitic races of beings, whom I call hominoids in my address,
> which may have had more than animal intelligence and powers,
> but were not 'man' in the psychical and spiritual powers or
> possibilities in the Biblical sense of the word." He even ventures
> the opinion "that between true man and anthropoid apes there
> *may* have been some species of hominoids created." Is not Sir
> Ambrose taking an unwarranted liberty with the inspired word
> by introducing acts of creation and types of humanity of which
> there is no mention in the Mosaic record?[35]

Telling though Keith's assault may be, his criticisms themselves
point to a liberalism of interpretation by Fleming later to be expunged by
the more strident creationists. After all, Sir Ambrose had made it clear in
his *Evolution or Creation?* (first published some time around 1920) that
his objections to the theory of evolution were grounded in its failure to
provide a cogent account of the appearance of animal life, mind, and
humanity: it was the universal claims of evolutionists that most troubled
him. Besides he readily conceded that "We do not deny that there has

34. Allen, *Evolution in the Balances* (New York: Fleming H. Revell, 1926), pp.
18, 36. Peter J. Bowler discusses the evolutionary outlook of some of these other
figures in *Evolution: The History of an Idea* (Berkeley and Los Angeles: University of
California Press, 1984).

35. Keith, *Darwinism and Its Critics* (London: Watts & Co., 1935), p. 20.

JOHN AMBROSE FLEMING
M.A., D.SC., F.R.S.
From a pen and ink portrait sketch by Mr. Robert Kastor

AMBROSE FLEMING, from Sir Ambrose Fleming's *Memories of a Scientific Life* (Marshall, Morgan & Scott, n.d.)

been such gradual development; but what we do emphatically deny is that this development did not start with an act of Creation, but is due to a spontaneous, intrinsic, and innate power in matter itself, having no dependence upon a self conscious creative Intelligence and Will."[36] If some space were allowed for the input of divine energy to fill the unbridged gaps and to control the historical process, he would rest content with some developmental scheme.

Even this latitude, however, was soon to be abandoned. The extent to which the positions had become polarized in the 1930s is nowhere more apparent than in the response of a London journalist, Newman

---

36. Ambrose Fleming, *Evolution or Creation?* 2d ed. (London: Marshall, Morgan & Scott, n.d.), p. 60. Fleming's life story is recorded in his autobiography, *Memories of a Scientific Life* (London: Marshall, Morgan & Scott, 1934).

Watts, who took up the cudgels against Keith for the popular reader, claiming at the same time to put the record straight on what had really happened in Dayton, Tennessee. The spirit of his book can be detected from its title, *Why Be an Ape—?* The details of his message need not delay us. It was simply the mirror image of its American counterparts, of which he was well aware. He condemned evolution for its association with decadence and immorality and for its scientific inadequacy, which had been demonstrated by numerous working scientists.

The influence of such anti-Darwinian sentiments on the more serious evangelical spirit was far from inconspicuous. Take the Calvinist wing as represented by J. Gresham Machen, for instance. Unlike his Princeton predecessors, he remained ambivalent on the evolution question. He affirmed that it was quite unnecessary to take the six days of Genesis literally and that they could be thought of "as very long periods of time." He even cited Warfield's evolutionary interpretation of Calvin's use of the term "creation." But just at the point where he seemed to be following closely the early Princetonians, he distorted the significance of

Left, "MODERN IDOLATRY"; *right*, "WHERE 'EVOLUTION' LEADS TO": illustrations by "A London Journalist" in *Why Be an Ape—?* (Marshall, Morgan & Scott, n.d.)

Warfield's exposition by merely saying that Calvin regarded the origin of man as "a work of creation in the very strictest sense of the word." There he left the matter, making no mention of the body-soul duality so crucial to Warfield's interpretation.[37]

E. J. Carnell too, otherwise leader in the intellectual reawakening of evangelicalism after the Second World War and president of Fuller Theological Seminary, remained equivocal about the subject. His strategy was to advocate what he called "threshold evolution." By this he intended to allow for evolutionary transformation at the species level while drawing back from acknowledging evolution at the higher level of the "kinds originally created by God"—by which he seems to mean orders. Changes at this higher level, he suggests, could have occurred only through divine creative intervention. And, like Machen, he insisted that the human species is one of these "kinds" and therefore that "man"—both body and soul—had originated by an act of special creation.[38]

As Paul Bassett notes, a "fundamentalist leavening" of the conservative Wesleyan tradition was also taking place at this time.[39] Consider, for example, H. Orton Wiley, a chief apologist for conservative Wesleyanism. In his *Introduction to Christian Theology* of 1947 he never really grasped the issue of the implications of evolutionary theory for biblical creation or biblical anthropology. He simply pointed to its failure to span the gaps between animate and inanimate, vegetable and animal life, animal and human life. "Only the creative activity of God could have originated vegetable, animal and personal life," he concluded.[40] There he too left the matter, giving no answers because he did not see any questions. Like Machen, he was prepared for a geologically informed reading of the Genesis narrative, but his engagement with science was far less confident than the earlier Wesleyan contributions of Pope and Gamertsfelder.

THE GREAT DIVIDE

Within the incredibly short space of about two decades, the old cultured evangelicalism had given way to the bitter polemics of a ram-

---

37. Machen, *The Christian View of Man* (1937; rpt., London: Banner of Truth, 1965), p. 116.

38. Carnell, *An Introduction to Christian Apologetics: A Philosophic Defense of the Trinitarian-Theistic Faith* (Grand Rapids: Eerdmans, 1948), pp. 238-42.

39. Bassett, "The Fundamentalist Leavening of the Holiness Movement, 1914-1940: The Church of the Nazarene—A Case Study," *Wesleyan Theological Journal* 13 (1978): 65-91. See also William J. Abraham, *The Coming Great Revival* (San Francisco: Harper & Row, 1983).

40. Wiley, in *Introduction to Christian Theology*, by H. Orton Wiley and Paul T. Culbertson (Kansas City: Beacon Hill Press, 1947), pp. 132-33.

pant fundamentalism. It is quite a stretch from Warfield, who saw evolution as the expression of divine providence, to Price, who denounced it as a theory of Satanic origin. A number of the elements of this great divide—some theological, some cultural—stand out and are worthy of closer consideration.

Theologically, there was a clear shift in the perception of what Darwinism was actually challenging. For the older generation the issue centered on the problem of design; for the younger it was the authority of the Bible. Even Warfield, who gave the most formal expression to the doctrine of biblical inerrancy, found no contradiction here between his view of Scripture and his outlook on science. But by the first decades of the twentieth century, the argument from design had substantially diminished in intellectual significance. Currents of thought were moving too strongly in the opposite direction, and those who retained a predilection for teleological concerns tended to find satisfaction more in the "spiritual" temper of process thought championed by Hartshorne, Whitehead, Bergson, and Alexander than in the old evangelicalism of Princeton. In theological circles Darwin's theory was also suffering a loss of credibility among conservatives who associated it with higher biblical criticism, the quest for a demythologized historical Jesus, and an evolutionary account of human religious development from animism via polytheism to monotheism.

And, as I have noted, the scientific aspects of Darwinism were also coming under severe attack from different sources during the first decades of the new century. On the one hand, despite its lack of empirical corroboration, Neo-Lamarckism survived in a number of forms; it retained a number of defenders among those who prized its congruence with socialism, idealism, and progressivism—all of whom were unhappy with the exclusivist claims of natural selection. On the other hand, the rediscovery of Mendel's findings and the rise of genetics under such biologists as William Bateson at Cambridge cast Darwinism in the shade until the construction of the "synthetic theory" in the early 1930s. In the interregnum, there were abundant expressions of doubt concerning the sufficiency of Darwin's proposals to fuel the suspicions and bolster the cases of the antievolutionists.

On the cultural side, the post–Civil War crisis, particularly in America's southern states, led many evangelicals to sense a turning from Christian to secular civilization; to this many felt the best response would be a firm attitude of "No Compromise." Southerners had every reason to stick to the letter of the law rather than the spirit. As Marsden writes, "Committed to the letter of the Scriptures regarding slavery, such southerners were hardly in a position to play fast and loose with other passages that might be interpreted in the light of modern progress."[41] The further

---

41. Marsden, *Fundamentalism and American Culture*, p. 573.

radical questioning of progress that followed the First World War and the suspicion that the German "might is right" ideology was rooted in Social Darwinism only served to reinforce this stance. The concept of theistic evolution stood little chance in such an environment.

The ideological component of the emergence of evangelical anti-evolutionism remains evident among modern creationists in their continued denunciation of Darwinism's presumed social implications. Bryan rejected human evolution because he "regarded it as profoundly subversive of Christian morality and American civilization,"[42] but more recently Henry Morris has stated flatly that "those who were desirous of destroying Christianity and the general theistic world view, as well as the existing social order built upon it, realized that a general return to atheism or humanistic pantheism, which necessarily must be grounded on evolutionism, would have to be preceded by the popularization of some system which would make evolution appear scientific to the general public." Morris goes on to say that Lamarck "hated the Bible and Christianity, and his ideas became popular with communists and other radicals."[43] In such material, the validity of evolution as scientific theory is scarcely in question; the issues are solely ideological.

The period that marked the rise of antievolutionist sentiment among evangelicals was a time of fast and furious change generally. In art, conventions of harmony and decorum disintegrated in the shock waves of the modernist impulse. In philosophy, irrationalism and naturalism rode roughshod over any surviving Victorian sensibilities. In literature and drama, rebellion against conventional standards was the order of the day. In the cities, new clubs, theaters, magazines, movies, and jazz music rocked the American mind. A cultural transformation and a moral revolution were well underway. The death rattle of traditionalism was the birth pang of modernity. Against this background, it seems clear that opposition to evolution was significantly a cultural as well as a religious phenomenon: it was, as much as anything else, a protest against change and a part of a campaign to preserve America.[44] Did not Price accuse one of his erstwhile disciples of currying favor with "tobacco-smoking, Sabbath-breaking, God-defying" evolutionists?[45] A hard theological literalism and widespread social pessimism joined to spawn the antievolutionist movement.

As important as this episode was, however, we must not let it

---

42. Durant, "Darwinism and Divinity," p. 25.
43. Morris, *History of Modern Creationism* (San Diego: Master Book Publishers, 1984), pp. 32, 33.
44. On this, see William E. Leuchtenburg, *The Perils of Prosperity, 1914-32* (Chicago: University of Chicago Press, 1958).
45. See Numbers, "Creationism in 20th-Century America," p. 541.

obscure that fact that the later fundamentalists constitute a fundamental departure from the tradition of mainstream evangelicalism, whose greatest Victorian advocates had promoted a Christian evolutionism that was uncompromisingly scholarly, theologically sensitive, and scientifically informed.

CHAPTER 6

RETROSPECT
AND PROSPECT

The antievolutionist movement, as it crystallized in the mid-1920s, represented a more or less radical departure from the tradition of mainstream evangelicalism as it had developed throughout the previous century. This of course does not mean that the earlier evangelical tradition had achieved a complete consensus on the Darwin question. Hesitancies, uncertainties, and ambiguities characterized much of its literature. And yet those recognized evangelical leaders on whom we have concentrated displayed a quite remarkable openness to the new biology. Let us remember that evangelical scientists were among the first in America to adopt and later to promote an evolutionary outlook. I think it can be argued that this was just the latest expression of the longstanding Puritan assurance that God had revealed himself both in the book of Scripture and in the book of Nature. That theological tradition, moreover, was one in which the dynamic doctrine of divine providence was given full and rich expression.

On the whole, the evangelicals of the late nineteenth and early twentieth centuries resembled a fairly close-knit family, prone to squabbling perhaps but a family nonetheless. The fundamentalists who arrived in the 1920s more closely resembled stepchildren than children of this family. The characteristic scholarly cast of mind, rhetorical discipline, scientific tolerance, and ecclesiastical latitude of the evangelicals significantly distance them from the sectarian spirit, scientific suspicion, and social pessimism of later fundamentalism. And if the creationists have severed their links with the nineteenth-century giants of evangelicalism, a fortiori their attitudes have alienated them from other branches of the Christian community.[1] Nor is this analysis entirely unwelcome to present-day creationists themselves.[1]

---

1. See the following recent assessments: Roland M. Frye, "So-called 'Creation-science' and Mainstream Christian Responses," *Proceedings of the American Philo-*

CREATIONIST HISTORIOGRAPHY

The ambivalence of scientific creationists toward the approach of historical evangelicalism to the evolution issue is itself an important indicator of where they see themselves fitting into the general scheme of Christian culture. The way in which any group deals with the burden of its history—whether casually dismissing it, slavishly guarding it, or capriciously manipulating it—reveals much about the way it perceives itself. We can learn a good deal about the creationists by looking at some of the things they have written about the history of the Christian reaction to the theory of evolution—particularly the reaction of evangelicals.

Some creationists have dealt with evangelical proponents of the theory of evolution by calling into question the validity either of their evangelicalism or of their advocacy of evolutionism. The way in which Bolton Davidheiser, a zoologist, treats Asa Gray in his *Evolution and Christian Faith* is an instructive case. "It turns out that Asa Gray is a very questionable example of an evangelical Christian," he tells us, "but he is a good example of a person who has a Christian testimony and who is used by the evolutionists to influence other Christians to accept the theory of evolution." It looks suspiciously as though Davidheiser is assuming anti-evolutionism to be a touchstone of evangelical orthodoxy, especially when he claims that it "is characteristic of the position which Gray took that it leads in the direction of evolutionary belief and not in the direction of Christian faith." Davidheiser deals with James Orr in an equally rough-shod manner:

> Dr. Orr had the theory of evolution thrust upon him and he had to deal with it. He seems to have been convinced that the scientists had proved evolution to be true and that he had to do the best he could with it. He should not have capitulated so easily, and if he had not, he could easily have shown that the theory of evolution and the Bible are incompatible. Although the Bible gives a clear answer, we have something in addition which James Orr did not have, and that is a knowledge, based upon experience, that the espousal of the theory of evolution leads to compromises which in turn lead to liberalism, modernism, and a repudiation of the gospel.[2]

It is an even more common creationist strategy simply to ignore the whole tradition of evangelical evolutionism. Davidheiser's writings again

---

sophical Society* 127 (1983): 61-70; Richard P. Aulie, "Evolution and Special Creation: Historical Aspects of the Controversy," *Proceedings of the American Philosophical Society* 127 (1983): 418-62; and *Is God a Creationist? The Religious Case against Creation-Science*, ed. Roland M. Frye (New York: Charles Scribner's Sons, 1983).

2. Davidheiser, *Evolution and Christian Faith* (Nutley, N.J.: Presbyterian and Reformed Publishing Company, 1969), pp. 80, 78, 38-39.

illustrate this. The only evangelical proponents of evolution other than Gray and Orr that he mentions are McCosh and Strong, and he mentions these only in passing. This omission of substantial evangelical stalwarts from Wright to Warfield, from Dana to Van Dyke, plainly reveals a dilatory approach to historical research. And the other face of Davidheiser's questionable vision of the past is tellingly evident in a laudatory biographical piece he wrote on Louis Agassiz.[3] The significance of this essay must not be underestimated. Davidheiser accords so much importance to opposing evolutionism that he is willing to praise the "creationist" science of the conspicuously unevangelical Agassiz while denouncing evangelical evolutionists and avoiding any mention of Agassiz's use of the doctrine of special creation for racist ends. His commitment to creationist science clearly seems to outweigh his regard for other significant theological issues.

Malcolm Bowden goes even further than Davidheiser in downplaying the tradition of evangelical evolutionism. Ostensibly a history, Bowden's book *The Rise of the Evolution Fraud* mentions no evangelical supporters of Darwin other than Gray, and even then it offers no information at all about Gray's religious convictions; it merely notes his role as Darwin's American correspondent and chief protagonist in the New World. It is ironic that although Bowden complains at length about Darwin's "inadequacy of facts," "vague authorities," and "devious argumentation," he himself indulges in a surfeit of speculation, as in the account he gives of Darwin's illness:

> I would suggest that the root cause of Darwin's illness was the stress generated in him when he was writing about a theory *which he knew was basically false*. All his symptoms are those of a man who is under prolonged emotional stress—stress due to his continual mental acrobatics as he sought to "wriggle" (a word he used to describe his arguments) around a whole series of facts against his theory.
>
> What inner promptings could have driven him to continue along this course, regardless of its effect upon his mental and physical state? Not a desire to avoid God, but an inordinate hunger for fame and recognition—a factor which we will consider in some depth later.[4]

---

3. Davidheiser, "Louis Agassiz," in *A Symposium on Creation VI*, ed. Donald W. Patten (Seattle: Pacific Mendian Publishing, 1977), pp. 116-35.

4. Bowden, *The Rise of the Evolution Fraud* (Bromley, Kent: Sovereign Publications, 1982), p. 87; italics his. Bowden's subsequent discussion of this claim "in some depth" involved the following evidence: Darwin described natural selection as "my" theory; he remembered a compliment paid to him when he was eighteen years old for the rest of his life; he "made no suggestion that his autobiography was strictly for private use" even though he prefaced it by saying that it would interest his children; and as a child he "invented falsehoods."

Overall, Nigel M. de S. Cameron displays a distinctly more astute historical awareness. His *Evolution and the Authority of the Bible* contains an estimable review of nineteenth-century British evangelical commentators on the Genesis narratives. Their testimony, he acknowledges, essentially sought to harmonize the biblical record with the science of their day. But much as their scholarship is to be admired, says Cameron, they should be understood as "creatures of their age, desirous of making the biblical faith palatable, ever hopeful of achieving that aim and so showing all men the essential harmony of science and Scripture." He goes on to say that "they could not foresee . . . the gathering of forces that were to lead to the complete break-up of the Christian consensus which had hitherto allowed Scripture and the leading men of science to be in agreement. So their attempts at harmony left them high and dry."[5]

Cameron's rather abrupt dismissal of the British evangelical tradition of biblical exegesis is in itself rather surprising, but his treatment of the dogmatics formulated by its American counterpart is even more arresting. The heart of Cameron's objection to Darwinism is his belief that it is incompatible with biblical authority. And yet although he explicitly sustains his doctrine of Scripture by referring to Warfield's inerrancy thesis, he never acknowledges Warfield's substantive evolutionary outlook or explains how Warfield conceived of the relationship between science and Scripture. Moreover, while he insists that Hodge had "good grounds" for concluding that Darwinism is atheism,[6] he does not say what those grounds are. As we have seen, Hodge's rejection of Darwinism—not of "evolution"—rested on philosophical rather than philological considerations. It was the argument from design, not the infallibility of the Bible, that was the issue. In light of the fact that Cameron gives no evidence of a sensitive understanding of this Princeton tradition, his position would seem to be every bit as divorced from these systematic theologians he claims to follow as it is from the British evangelical exegetes he himself reviews.

The same sort of dislocation is evident in Henry Morris's *History of Modern Creationism* (1984). Morris is well aware of the evangelical tradition of theological reconciliation with evolutionary thought, but he chooses to characterize the strategies of such men as Orr, Warfield, and Strong as a "chronicle of . . . pervasive theological apostasy." Indeed, he presses the charge all the way back to Augustine, describing his interpretation of the Genesis record as one of "the old compromising types of exegesis used by early theologians."[7]

---

    5. Cameron, *Evolution and the Authority of the Bible* (Exeter: Paternoster Press, 1983), p. 83.
    6. Cameron, *Evolution and the Authority of the Bible*, p. 10.
    7. Morris, *History of Modern Creationism* (San Diego: Master Book Publishers, 1984), pp. 39, 37.

On the basis of this evidence, one might be inclined to conclude that the evangelical tradition matters little or nothing to the scientific creationists. But it is noteworthy that in a different context they seem quite eager to present themselves as the latest expression of the tradition. One example must suffice. Henry Morris's *Men of Science, Men of God* (1982), written with a self-confessedly "evangelistic thrust and motivation," is a compilation of biographical sketches of leading scientists who were professing Christians and who "believed that the universe, life, and man were directly and specially created by the transcendent God of the Bible." Right away, however, it is clear that Morris has had to allow, even by his own standards, some "unorthodox" figures into the story. He admits the theistic evolutionist James Dana, though Gray and Wright (not to mention Winchell and Macloskie) are conspicuous by their absence; he includes J. W. Dawson, a proponent of the day-age theory, but excludes Miller; he describes the uniformitarian Buckland as "a strong creationist," but he ignores John Fleming; he makes reference to Virchow but suppresses his commitment to neo-Lamarckism; and he includes Mendel and Agassiz, who of course come from nonevangelical wings of the Christian community.

In the end, then, Morris's history is inclusive rather than exclusive—but it is a *selectively* inclusive review for all of that. On the one hand, the fact that he includes individuals whose doctrines are denounced elsewhere in the creationist literature as everything from fraudulent to Satanic is puzzling at best. On the other hand, by excluding so many prominent evangelical evolutionists from the work, Morris is giving a distorted account of their historical significance within the conservative Christian tradition. And when he concludes his survey by listing various creationist agencies as representatives of latter-day twentieth-century Christian science, he creates the impression that these are the true heirs of post-Reformation evangelical scholarship.

Our reflections on these examples of creationist historiography are, I believe, doubly important—first because they reveal the real ambiguity that creationists face with regard to their position in the historical evangelical tradition, and second because they expose the degree to which history is being distorted, even rewritten, in the cause of the creationist crusade. Such an approach to the past is always a serious matter, because those who control the writing of a community's history control, in some measure at least, that community's future.

At least some creationists appear to have an appreciation of the power of history. E. H. Andrews, professor of materials science at the University of London and president of the Biblical Creation Society, has said that some people "accept both evolution and the existence of a God, but the *kind* of God who remains is no longer the Almighty Who called the worlds into being, and certainly not the God of creation and providence revealed in the Christian Scriptures. Instead He is a vague and somewhat redundant being, banished from involvement with the material world in which we live, hovering on the rim of human consciousness, a ghost of a God."[8] If Andrews's assessment is correct, an entire tradition of evangelical thought is, at a stroke, condemned as biblically heterodox and theologically deist. Only a free and open acknowledgment of history can prevent expectation masquerading as description, personal opinion as conventional wisdom, individual prejudice as the results of scholarly judgment.

UPDATING THE STORY

However tenuous the links between the early twentieth-century creationists and their evangelical predecessors may have been, the creationist influence on evangelicalism in the past half century has been far from inconsiderable. In the immediate aftermath of the Scopes trial, the creationists lost the international press coverage they had been enjoying and found that they were having little success in converting professional scientists to their way of thinking. In the mid-1930s, feeling the need to regroup, they established the Religion and Science Association in order to present "a unified front against the theory of evolution," but internal feuding about the precise creationist line on the age of the earth soon broke the fledgling body apart. Various other organizations were formed, but few withstood for any length of time; cracks widened into chasms as members failed to hew to the strictest creationist line.

It was not until the 1960s that a creationist renaissance really got under way again, largely through the efforts of Henry M. Morris and John C. Whitcomb, a theologian from the Grace Theological Seminary. Soon creationist organizations were beginning to proliferate almost, as it were, by spontaneous generation. In 1963 the Creation Research Society was formed. Its original constituency has been succinctly summarized by Ronald L. Numbers:

> The society began with a carefully selected, 18-man "inner-core steering committee." . . . The composition of this committee reflected, albeit imperfectly, the denominational, regional, and professional bases of the creationist revival. There were six Missouri-Synod Lutherans, five Baptists, two Seventh-day Adventists, and one each from the Reformed Presbyterian Church, the Reformed Christian Church, the Church of the Brethren, and an independent Bible church (information about one member is lacking). Eleven lived in the Midwest, three in the South, and two in the Far West. The committee included six biologists but only one geologist, an independent consultant with a master's degree. Seven members taught in church-related colleges, five in state

---

8. Andrews, *Is Evolution Scientific?* (Welwyn: Evangelical Press, 1977), p. 3.

institutions; the others worked for industry or were self-employed.[9]

For a more popular clientele, the Bible Science Association came into being in 1964, but its occasional flirtation with such fringe views as geocentricity and a static earth undermined its appeal for those creationists who aspired to scientific credibility. Then in 1970 the Creation-Science Research Center, associated with Christian Heritage School in San Diego, was set up to publicize creation science at the elementary school level and to produce literature relevant to their educational objectives. On the research side, the organization reported its finding that evolution had fostered "the moral decay of spiritual values which contributes to the destruction of mental health and . . . [the prevalence] of divorce, abortion, and rampant venereal disease."[10] But fractures soon began to appear in this group as well, in this case over aims and strategies, and Morris established the Institute for Creation Science for the pursuit of scientific rather than political objectives. Again and again the creationists' concern to purge their ranks of all liberalizers has led them to lay down such stringent criteria for membership that even such early creationists as Bryan and Riley would be unable to pass scrutiny.

The effects of these creationist maneuvers soon began to be registered in Great Britain also. By 1970 the membership of the Evolution Protest Movement had risen to about 850, but its focus on biblical rather than scientific issues seems to have prevented further expansion. The Newton Scientific Association, born in 1972, expressly stated that its objective was to conduct its affairs on scientific principles without explicit resort to the Bible, thereby to refute any charge that it is a "religious" organization.[11] This organization, too, is now "dormant." The Biblical Creation Society, with headquarters in Glasgow, is now the largest creationist institution in the United Kingdom.

The educational strategies, religious stance, scientific objectives, and promotional literature of the modern creationist movement have been so thoroughly explored elsewhere that I will not devote any more time to them here.[12] Rather I want briefly to note that while creationism

---

9. Numbers, "Creationism in 20th-Century America," *Science* 218 (1982): 541.

10. Numbers, "Creationism in 20th-Century America," p. 542.

11. See Eileen Barker, "In the Beginning: The Battle of Creationist Science against Evolutionism," in *On the Margins of Science: The Social Construction of Rejected Knowledge*, ed. Roy Wallis, Sociological Review Monograph 27 (Keele: University of Keele, 1979), pp. 179-200.

12. For those who are interested in more information, I recommend the studies by Numbers, Marsden, and Barker cited elsewhere in this volume as well as the following: Dorothy Nelkin, *The Creation Controversy: Science or Scripture in the Schools* (New York: W. W. Norton, 1982); John R. Cole, "Anti-evolutionism and the Effects of the Scopes Trial," *Proceedings of the Iowa Academy of Science* 89 (1982): 50-54; Laurie R. Godfrey, "The Flood of Anti-evolutionism," *Proceedings of the Iowa*

has enjoyed a considerable popularity among evangelicals, it is by no means universally accepted.

First, creationist sentiments have made substantial inroads into the evangelical community. The antievolution tracts of Richard Ackworth, H. Enoch, Sylvia Baker, and E. H. Andrews, for example, have been published by the Evangelical Press, certain American Calvinists have displayed their creationist colors in the publications of Rushdoony and the Chalcedon Ministry, and such international spokesmen for evangelicalism as Martin Lloyd-Jones and Francis Schaeffer have expressed substantially creationist sentiments.[13] And of course for everyone who has denounced evolution as publicly as these, many more harbor hidden doubts and fears that have been raised by the emotional pressures of those who persistently equate evolution with atheism.

Still, the stream of the nineteenth-century tradition has continued to flow in some tributaries of evangelical scholarship. In the United States, Bernard Ramm's 1954 work *The Christian View of Science and Scripture* did much to keep the strain of evangelical evolutionism alive. Then the American Scientific Affiliation finally broke away from its strictly creationist stance with the publication in 1959 of a collection of essays by some of its members entitled *Evolution and Christian Thought Today*. Contributors to this volume variously dismissed such ideas as a young earth, a universal flood, and the fixity of species; some promoted theistic evolution outright. Even more recently, Davis Young's *Christianity and the Age of the Earth* has helped redress the geological balance in the face of the creationist explosion.[14] In Britain, Douglas Spanner, Malcolm Jeeves, P. J. Wiseman, Donald MacKay, R. J. Berry, Derek Kidner, and John Stott as individuals, and the Research Scientists' Christian Fellowship of the Inter-Varsity Fellowship as an institution, have in different ways given their approval to the viability of reconciliation between evolutionary science and evangelical faith.[15] Central to their vision of the rela-

---

Academy of Science 89 (1982): 59-61; and Robert M. May, "Creation, Evolution and High School Texts," *Nature* 296 (1982): 109-10.

13. Richard Ackworth, *Creation, Evolution and the Christian Faith* (Welwyn: Evangelical Press, n.d.); H. Enoch, *Evolution or Creation* (London: Evangelical Press, 1967); Sylvia Baker, *Bone of Contention* (Welwyn: Evangelical Press, 1976); Andrews, *Is Evolution Scientific?*; Rousas J. Rushdoony, *The Mythology of Science* (Nutley, N.J.: Craig Press, 1967); Gary North, ed., "Symposium on Creation," in *The Journal of Christian Reconstruction* 1 (1974): 1-178. See also Philip Edgcumbe Hughes, *Christianity and the Problem of Origins* (Nutley, N.J.: Presbyterian and Reformed Publishing Company, 1974).

14. See Ronald L. Numbers, "The Dilemma of Evangelical Scientists," in *Evangelicalism and Modern America*, ed. George M. Marsden (Grand Rapids: Eerdmans, 1984), pp. 150-60.

15. I have particularly in mind Douglas Spanner's *Creation and Evolution* (London: Falcon, 1965); Malcolm Jeeves's *The Scientific Enterprise and the Christian Faith* (London: Tyndale Press, 1969); P. J. Wiseman's *Creation Revealed in Six Days*

tionship between science and Scripture is the idea of complementarity—an idea given its most rigorous philosophical defense by MacKay in the pages of the Aristotelian Society's journal. This principle, as applied to the question in hand, suggests that science answers the question How and Scripture provides the complementary answer to the question Why.

Obviously this list of individuals and institutions is not a complete inventory of evangelicals with a tolerant attitude to Darwin's theory. But these at least point to the inadequacy of those approaches to the relationship between science and religion that have recently polarized Christian creationists and secular evolutionists—not to say the folly of those participants in the debate itself who assume they know which side of the fence the angels are on.

UNFINISHED BUSINESS

That the latter-day creationist movement is largely cut off from its own theological roots in nineteenth-century evangelicalism does not mean that the creationists have failed to raise some important questions for modern scientific culture, as George Marsden and Eileen Barker have, from different perspectives, pointed out. Marsden, for example, notes that "William Allen White said of Bryan that he was never wrong in political diagnosis and never right in prescription. We might say the same of the creation science movement that has been heir to his work. They have correctly identified some important trends in twentieth-century American life and that these trends have profound cultural implications."[16] And Barker writes in the conclusion to her sociological analysis of creationist science that

> Just as Durkheim suggested the pathological or the deviant can serve a positive function by defining what is "right" and what "wrong," so, it could be argued, those whose work [is] outside an accepted paradigm can clarify boundaries of knowledge, highlighting the distinctions between fact and interpretation of fact, between beliefs, metaphors, heuristic organising principles, theories, laws and all the other paraphernalia of categories that man employs in his search for truth. What is unknown and what unknowable can be made clearer and the bases of what knowledge we have can be more scrupulously examined.[17]

(London: Marshall, Morgan & Scott, 1958); Donald MacKay's *The Clockwork Image* (London: Inter-Varsity Press, 1974); R. J. Berry's *Adam and the Ape: A Christian Approach to the Theory of Evolution* (London: Falcon, 1975); Derek Kidner's *Genesis: A Commentary* (London: Tyndale Press, 1967); and John Stott's *Understanding the Bible* (London: Scripture Union, 1978).

16. Marsden, "Creation versus Evolution: No Middle Way," *Nature* 305 (1983): 74.

17. Barker, "In the Beginning: The Battle of Creationist Science against Evolutionism," pp. 197-98.

Nor does the prevalence of evolutionary explanations in science itself mean that the evolutionary paradigm has furnished a viable foundation for an all-embracing view of the world. There are a number of areas—scientific, philosophical, and cultural—in which the consensus needed for such a *Weltanschauung* is quite lacking. The standard distinction between evolution as science and evolutionism as philosophy is, in my view, perfectly defensible at this point. Creationists and scientific evolutionists alike are surely within their rights to draw up an agenda of unfinished business for those who claim evolution as a comprehensive philosophy of life.

At the simplest level, creationists clearly provide more than self-justification for the fundamentalist view of the world. Their critique of substantive issues in evolutionary science shows, according to Barker, "that there is enough sloppy thinking by Evolutionists to allow the Creationists to point legitimately to difficulties which the former all too often smugly ignore. . . . Where the battle of Creationist science involves a challenge within the battlefield of science (as defined by the prevailing paradigm) it is Evolutionism which risks the consequences of complacency when it does not pick up the gauntlet."[18] The recent collection of essays edited by Laurie Godfrey entitled *Scientists Confront Creationism* (1983) represents just one attempt to take up the challenge. But the appearance of Francis Hitching's thoroughly popular *The Neck of the Giraffe; or, Where Darwin Went Wrong* in 1982 suggests that the neo-Darwinian theory is in sufficient disarray to warrant a more cautious, less doctrinaire response by at least some of evolution's most devoted disciples. Ted Steele's controversial Lamarckian experiments on adaptive immunological inheritance, the theory of punctuated equilibria advanced by Stephen Gould and Niles Eldredge, Rupert Sheldrake's postulation of the existence of morphogenetic fields, the British Museum's adoption of a new taxonomic model termed "transformed cladistics," and the possibility of chromosomal speciation in opposition to the traditional theory of point mutations are just a few of the more recent challenges to the standard evolution theory that surely call for greater humility within the community of scientific evolutionists.[19]

If evolutionists have unfinished business in the more purely scien-

---

18. Barker, "In the Beginning: The Battle of Creationist Science against Evolutionism," p. 198.

19. *Scientists Confront Creationism*, ed. Laurie Godfrey (New York: W. W. Norton, 1983). Other defenses include P. Kitcher's *Abusing Science: The Case against Creationism* (Cambridge, Mass.: MIT Press, 1982); Michael Ruse's *Darwinism Defended: A Guide to the Evolution Controversies* (Reading, Mass.: Addison-Wesley, 1982); N. Newell's *Creation and Evolution: Myth or Reality?* (New York: Columbia University Press, 1982); and Douglas J. Futuyma's *Science on Trial: The Case for Evolution* (New York: Pantheon Books, 1983). See also Francis Hitching's *The Neck of the Giraffe; or, Where Darwin Went Wrong* (London: Pan, 1982).

tific sphere, in the philosophical arena their case is even less clear cut. Allow me to mention briefly four areas in which the philosophical claims of evolutionists remain thoroughly contested. In each case my own feeling is that these "myths" arise out of the absolutizing of the evolutionary metaphors we have already discussed in detail.

The first is what is conventionally termed "evolutionary ethics." Some have pressed the concept of survival in the context of evolutionary theory beyond its metaphorical sense, maintaining that the theory might serve as a creed by identifying the "good" as whatever is useful for survival. Such schemes sometimes explain the qualities of altruism, cooperation, self-sacrifice, and the like by defining the group rather than the individual as the fundamental unit of selection, reasoning that gregarious animals who practice mutual aid have greater survival potential than more individualistic organisms. Sometimes the terms are redefined so as to make them measurable units of evolutionary fitness. Either way detractors object on a number of grounds to the suggestion that human ethics can be derived from the survival mechanism in natural selection. Some argue that evolutionary ethics involves a circular argument—that the good is whatever pertains to survival because whatever pertains to survival is good; the claim sounds suspiciously like the moral impasse of Pope's pungent couplet,

> And, spite of pride, in erring reason's spite,
> One truth is clear, "Whatever is, is RIGHT."

Other critics contend that evolutionary ethics commits the naturalistic fallacy, moving from "is" to "ought," from the descriptive to the prescriptive, from the indicative mood to the imperative mood. The fact that we may have developed by a process of mutation and natural selection does not in itself explain what it *means* to be an ethical animal. MacKay suggests that at the very most evolution can only be a "description of the mechanism by which species showing moral behaviour have come into being" rather than a code by which their moral choices can be governed. Ethics, it may be contended, has to do with the nature, authority, and expression of moral standards, not with the origin of the creatures who practice them. Clearly on this issue creationists and others are within their rights to press evolutionists to clarify their arguments.[20]

A similar propensity to mystify nature is evident in the humanistic celebration of what can be called evolutionary progressivism—the idea, now expanded into a comprehensive philosophy of history, that evolution

---

20. For various perspectives, see MacKay, *The Clockwork Image*; A. G. N. Flew, *Evolutionary Ethics* (London: Macmillan, 1967); and Colin McGinn, "Evolution, Animals, and the Basis of Morality," *Inquiry* 22 (1979): 81-99. In this section and in what follows I have drawn on my "Evolution as Metaphor and Myth," *Christian Scholar's Review* 12 (1983): 111-25.

theory somehow guarantees bio-social progress. Pierre Teilhard de Chardin and Julian Huxley, for example, have postulated an internal *telos* intrinsic to the evolutionary process that is moving irresistibly toward some cosmic goal. Perhaps this is most dramatically revealed in the speculations of the geneticist Theodosius Dobzhansky, who contends that "selection is a fully creative agency just like the composition of a poem or a symphony." The philosopher Marjorie Grene has not minced her words in dismissing such a conception as "nonsense." To compare the selective processes in nature, she says, with the composition of Milton's *Paradise Lost* or Beethoven's *Eroica* is to "get into a dreadful muddle." Selection, being thoroughly opportunistic on every occasion, may explain the survival of whatever survives, but, as Grene argues, it cannot at the same time be creative in the sense of contriving to move toward a goal in anything like the way an artist's creativity lies behind the creation of a great work of art.[21] Moreover, it is not always clear exactly what evolutionary progress might mean. It has been variously defined as greater environmental independence, increased information, higher specialization, and more egalitarianism. Again the onus is on the evolutionists to spell out the warrants for their proposals in other than metaphorical terms.

Some votaries of evolution have claimed that natural selection may serve as a paradigm for the growth of knowledge. Put simply, proponents of this evolutionary epistemology, as it is sometimes called, argue that claims to knowledge can be judged by survival—for example, that the better a scientific theory is, the more likely it will be to survive. This proposal, too, has its detractors, some of whom claim that it is simply false. Certain bad theories survive, they say, because they provide coherent accounts of reality for particular communities regardless of the fact that they have been *ultimately* falsified. The ability of scientific method to get at truth in the long run is clearly independent of natural selection as a short-term opportunistic mechanism. As Marjorie Grene has put it, "when we say we *know* something we are not saying it is true because it will survive but contrariwise, it will survive because it is true."[22] Survival, it would seem, is not the cause of truth but its condition.

Finally, there are those evolutionists who maintain that everything in this multifaceted world can be reduced to its material constituents or

---

21. See Dobzhansky, "Evolution as a Creative Process," *Proceedings of the Ninth International Congress of Genetics* (1954), pp. 435-38; and Marjorie Grene, "A Philosopher Looks at Evolution," radio lecture for the Open University course "Science and Belief from Copernicus to Darwin."

22. For more on this, see Peter Skagestad, "C. S. Pierce on Biological Evolution and Scientific Progress," *Synthese* 41 (1979): 85-114; Marjorie Grene, "Darwin and Philosophy," *Connaissance scientifique et philosophie colloque* (Brussels: Palais des Academies, 1975), pp. 133-45; and the special issue of *Theoria*, vol. 49, no. 1 (1983), on evolutionary epistemology.

genetic formula—to a fortuitous concourse of atoms, as John Draper put it at that infamous Oxford meeting of the British Association in 1860. When Julian Huxley tells us that in "the evolutionary pattern of thought there is no longer either need or room for the supernatural," when G. G. Simpson confirms that "man is the result of a purposeless and materialistic process that did not have him in mind," when Carl Sagan claims that the "cosmos is all there is or ever was or ever will be," we can be pretty sure that they are talking philosophy of religion, not science.[23] These surely are confessional claims that cannot be tested by the normal procedures of scientific analysis. Moreover, I do not think that one has to have any religious convictions to defend in order to question the adequacy of this line of reasoning. Gestalt psychologists, emergent evolutionists, and systems theorists, to name but a few, have expressed their dissatisfaction in various ways with reductionist explanations.[24] Again, the precise logic of the arguments need not concern us; the point is that the ontologically reductionist statements of some evolutionists are contentious, not to say tendentious, claims. Creationists have good grounds to challenge the adequacy of such proposals.

When the devotees of evolution begin to wax lyrical in their claims to have found in natural selection an axiom for ethics, a warranty for social progress, a scientific theory of knowledge, or a new metaphysics, they need to be reminded that their theory is assuming mythic proportions. This is not to say that any of these philosophical claims is necessarily indefensible but rather to recognize that they are thoroughly disputed and can be resolved only by philosophical scrutiny, not scientific analysis. No less mythic, I believe, is the cultural role played in contemporary society by science in general and evolution in particular.

The cult of science has attracted many worshipers. Various writers have pointed this out, but to my mind few have conducted a more telling critique of scientism of late than the Marxist historian of science Robert M. Young. Just as Social Darwinians and their Lamarckian counterparts in the Victorian era found grounds for cultural self-justification in the "biologizing" of society, so in more recent times polemicists including Desmond Morris, Konrad Lorenz, and Robert Ardrey, who dilate on the inevitability of human aggression, have produced what Young calls "ideologically prescriptive works in the guise of descriptive and generalized accounts based on genetics, ethology, archaeology and anthropology, and general biology." In the face of this sort of scientistic

---

23. Huxley, "The Evolutionary Vision," in vol. 3 of *Evolution after Darwin*, ed. Sol Tax and Charles Callender (Chicago: University of Chicago Press, 1961), pp. 249-61; Simpson, *The Meaning of Evolution* (New Haven: Yale University Press, 1949), p. 344; Sagan, *Cosmos* (New York: Random House, 1980), p. 4.

24. See the review essay by Eileen Barker, "Apes and Angels: Reductionism, Selection, and Emergence in the Study of Man," *Inquiry* 19 (1976): 367-99.

manipulation, Young calls for opening up the context of science "to public debate so that conflicting values can be discussed *as such*" and not subsumed beneath a veneer of scientific rhetoric.[25] As he has more recently written in concluding his discussion of the naturalization of values in the human sciences,

> It is a problem for the future to grant the place which legitimately belongs to biological and other scientific explanations of human evolution and of individual and social development, while at the same time retaining the integrity of moral and political discourse, the basis for transcendent values and hopes, and the husbanding of human decency.[26]

Given these sentiments on Young's part, it is perhaps not too surprising to find him expressing an ambivalence regarding the modern creationist movement on the grounds that some "of the enemies of fundamentalism are also enemies of the Left—sexploitation, the liberal consensus and, at the scientific level, sociobiology." Indeed it is precisely because the creationists are critics of the scientific establishment that Young can warn his Marxist colleagues that "it would be a mistake, be it one often made by the Left, to side uncritically with the scientific opposition in the Little Rock Trial in opposition to the creation scientists."[27] And yet for all of that, the creationists have gone about the job of creating their own scientific status quo. For if in its inception, to use Moore's words, "the New Creationism was at least in part a reaction against the triumphal positivism and overweening professionalism of established scientific authorities . . . now, under the banner of 'scientific creationism' or 'creation-science,' it apes what it once abhorred. In the end all that the New Creationism has to offer society is . . . a countervailing professionalism, with its accredited institutions, approved textbooks, official media, and scholarly publications."[28]

These latter observations plainly alert us to a danger too frequently ignored by students of the history of evolution theory and religion—namely, the tendency to make an ideological critique of only the religious side of the debate. In fact, evolutionists were and continue to be just as deeply involved in ideological play. In 1927, in the wake of the Scopes trial, for example, Maynard Shipley issued a bitter chronicle of the fundamentalists' war against modern science. He says in the introduction to the

25. See Young, "Evolutionary Biology and Ideology: Then and Now," *Science Studies* 1 (1971): 177-206.

26. Young, "The Naturalization of Value Systems in the Human Sciences," in *Science and Belief: From Darwin to Einstein*, Block 6: *Problems in the Biological and Human Sciences* (Milton Keynes: Open University Press, 1981), p. 102.

27. Young, "The Darwin Debate," *Marxism Today*, April 1982, pp. 21, 22.

28. Moore, "Interpreting the New Creationism," *Michigan Quarterly Review* 22 (1983): 332.

work, "The background of Fundamentalism has now been sketched. A brief survey of the sinister and reactionary forces now being organized in this country for the purpose of establishing a virtual union of Church and State (to the detriment of science) may serve to show that one need not be an alarmist to recognize that a turning-point in the history of the United States has been reached, and that the forces of progress are face to face with a grave period to our modern civilization." To nail home the point, he included an appendix drawing together supportive extracts from scientific luminaries. One of these, Luther Burbank, an advocate of eugenics as the key to a better humanity, stated that "There is no personal salvation, there is no national salvation, except through Science." Another, William E. Ritter, concurred, adding that to "forbid the teaching of evolution would mean taking away from our children the guarantee that man may go on using the means by which he has already attained something of the glory of life to the attainment of that glory in a much fuller measure."[29]

As Young's diagnosis reveals, such extravagantly ideological claims did not die out in the late 1920s. Far from it. Indeed, in the wake of his assessment, E. O. Wilson—founder of modern sociobiology—has claimed in a book entitled *On Human Nature* (which John Greene describes as a latter-day Bridgewater Treatise) that the scientific spirit is "superior to religion." He maintains that biology provides an ultimate explanation of human nature, culture, and moral worth. The attempt to naturalize human values in evolutionary biology and invest the results with the aura of transcendental authority has continued to attract a growing number of evolutionist partisans, notably the circle associated with the journal *Zygon*, contributors to which have gone about the job of constructing a new naturalized natural theology grounded in scientism and promising the American nation moral, political, and social regeneration.[30]

It goes without saying, of course, that these superadditions to the theory of evolution are logically independent of the central thesis that natural selection can serve as a calculus for quantifying differential reproductive success in terms of the relative frequencies of certain genes as opposed to their alternatives. Critics of Darwinism have all too frequently ignored this point, the result being that scientific and philosophical problems are confused, even conflated, when they should be carefully differ-

29. Shipley, *The War on Modern Science: A Short History of the Fundamentalist Attacks on Evolution and Modernism* (New York: Knopf, 1927), pp. 43, 389-90, 399.

30. In this analysis I have derived much help from two unpublished papers by John Durant, "The New Creationism and the World of Science," presented at the Teach-In on Creationism in American Culture and Theology, Lutheran School of Theology at Chicago, 9 October 1982; and "Evolution and Ethics: Ethology, Sociobiology, and the Naturalization of Religious Values," read at the Science and Religion Symposium at the 17th International Congress of History of Science, University of California at Berkeley, August 1985.

entiated and dealt with by the appropriate analytical tools. Of course it can be difficult to separate the scientific, political, philosophical, and social dimensions of this issue, but that is scarcely an excuse for abandoning the attempt. It might be easy to confuse, say, soda water and petroleum spirits too, but we would nonetheless do well to make the effort to keep them apart and to make good use of the relevant labels. Failure to do so can have disastrous results.

EPILOGUE

The encounter between evangelical theology and evolutionary thought in the wake of the Darwinian revolution is itself testimony to how complex the ongoing story of the relationship between science and religion really is—so much so that no single explanation, no blanket formula yet advanced seems to me to be sufficient to account for all the subtleties of the record. If the old warfare thesis of Draper, White, and others has turned out to be sterile, that in itself does not undermine the fact that many *thought* there was a struggle between science and religion. Charles Hodge perceived a direct clash between the claims of natural theology and those of natural selection; Alexander Winchell felt it necessary to publish the four-hundred-page *Reconciliation of Science and Religion* in 1877—a task evidently assuming mutual antagonism. And certainly the accommodationist strategies of the theological modernists only makes sense against the background of a perceived need to reconstruct the Christian faith along lines dictated by scientific overlords. In any event, the fact that the vocabulary of hostility fumes in the literature of both latter-day creationists and their opponents should caution against a too facile dismissal of the warfare analogy. Moreover, there is growing evidence that the warfare portrait was forced at least as much from the side of secularists who wanted to wield science in the service of secularism. This was undoubtedly so in the case of T. H. Huxley, whose "chief aim," Ruth Barton reminds us, was "the secularization of society through the cultural domination of science."[1] Ever sensitive to the polemical styles

---

1. Barton, "Evolution: The Whitworth Gun in Huxley's War for the Liberation of Science from Theology," in *The Wider Domain of Evolutionary Thought*, ed. David Oldroyd and Ian Langham (Dordrecht: D. Reidel, 1983), p. 262.

appropriate to particular audiences, Huxley did not hesitate to modify his stance on evolution to suit the occasion.[2]

If the *conflict* model exhibits both strengths and weaknesses, this is no less the case with the alternative that transmutes the conflict into a *competition.* This competition is applied not so much to science and faith per se, but to the "struggle" for cultural ascendancy in society contingent on the appearance of the new scientific professional. As Frank Miller Turner presents the case, there was a Victorian battle for social preeminence between the ecclesiastical hierarchy and the vigorous new scientific elite. The competition, then, focuses on the shift in intellectual authority from the preprofessional clerical sage to the middle-class professional intelligentsia. The amateur parson-naturalist who had hitherto played a noble role in the advance of science's discoveries was somehow by late Victorian days a quaint anachronism in the laboratorial world of the emerging specialists. Turner concludes that "If the movement from religion to science in western culture represented, as some would contend, the exchange of one form of faith for another, it also meant the transfer of cultural and intellectual leadership and prestige from the exponents of one faith to those of another. . . . It was a clash between established and emerging intellectual and social elites for popular cultural preeminence in a modern industrial society."[3]

This analysis has certainly much to commend it. It helps explain, for example, the rise of the Wilberforce-Huxley legend: the later passion to purge the British Association of the stain of clerical dilettantism would have favored a reconstruction of that debate in the baldest medieval-versus-modern terms. On the other side of the Atlantic, moreover, some of the early Princeton opposition to evolution ought to be seen in the context of attempts to dissolve links between the college and the seminary and therefore disengage science from theology.[4] And I think this "competitive reading" clarifies much of the otherwise ambiguous rhetoric produced by certain proponents of evolutionary theory. Galton's hankering after a "scientific priesthood," Huxley's craving for an evolutionary teleology, and Geddes's substitution of Darwin for Paley certainly invite

2. See Mario A. di Gregorio, *T. H. Huxley's Place in Natural Science* (New Haven: Yale University Press, 1984), especially pp. 188-89.

3. Turner, "Rainfall, Plagues, and the Prince of Wales: A Chapter in the Conflict of Religion and Science," *Journal of British Studies* 13 (1974): 65. See also Turner's essay "The Victorian Conflict between Science and Religion: A Professional Dimension," *Isis* 69 (1978): 356-76. This interpretation is further supported by T. W. Heyck, another student of Victorian intellectual life, who finds at least one locus of the "conflict between science and theology" in "the effort by scientists to improve the position of science. They wanted nothing less than to move science from the periphery to the centre of English life" (*The Transformation of Intellectual Life in Victorian England* [London: Croom Helm, 1982], pp. 87-88).

4. See J. David Hoeveler, Jr., *James McCosh and the Scottish Intellectual Tradition* (Princeton: Princeton University Press, 1979), p. 274.

such exegesis.[5] Indeed, if intellectual authority in modern society has not passed to the professional scientist, why is it that cries of "pseudo-science" are so often heard on the lips of both creationists and evolutionists? Still, for all that, this approach does not solve all the problems. Religious knowledge cannot be cut loose from religious knowers, to be sure, nor scientific theory from scientific practice. Both *are* rooted in society, and we do well to remember that they can be manipulated to serve particular group interests. But this in and of itself tells us very little about the nature of religious and scientific understanding. Both scientists and theologians make claims to truth, the adequacy of which surely cannot be determined solely by looking at the political strategies of either community. Focussing on the social struggles of scientists and theologians has without any doubt opened up important questions, but since the average Jesus freak knows just as much about theology as the average pop ecologist knows about environmental science, we may well be justified in asking what relation Victorian folk religion bears to biblical Christianity.

It would seem that neither the conflict nor competition approaches will provide a conclusive interpretation of the great nineteenth-century debates, and the same is apparently true of the approach that emphasizes the *cooperation* that science has received from the Christian community. Certainly the development of modern science owes much to Christian theology. Moore has argued that the evolutionary challenge was most easily absorbed by those of orthodox belief, and I believe the evidence I have offered in this volume substantially supports that contention. But having said that, I readily acknowledge the fact that there were also many orthodox Christians who perceived Darwinism as a dire threat and retaliated aggressively. As I indicate at the outset of this book, it is not my purpose here to offer a complete portrait but rather to depict *a* tradition of evangelical scholarship that found the resources to meet the evolutionary challenge. Determining how representative the figures I have chosen to illustrate the case really were is admittedly problematic, but I am confident in asserting that they were among the intellectual leaders of evangelical thought.

Perhaps the most coherent effort to transcend all these emphases is the argument for ideological *continuity* most forcefully articulated by the Marxist historian of science Robert Young. In a number of influential articles, Young has advanced the proposal that "conflict" readings of the great Victorian debate on "man's place in nature" have only obscured the

---

5. See Francis Galton, *English Men of Science: Their Nature and Nurture* (London: Macmillan, 1874), p. 193; Sheridan Gilley and Ann Loades, "Thomas Henry Huxley: The War between Science and Religion," *Journal of Religion* 61 (1981): 285-308; and Patrick Geddes's article on biology in vol. 2 of *Chambers's Encyclopaedia* (1882; rpt., London: W. & R. Chambers, 1925), pp. 157-64.

fact that both religion and science are socially sanctioned ideologies. Young suggests that the ideology or theodicy grounded in theology (justifying the ways of God to humanity) has been replaced by a scientific theodicy (justifying the ways of nature to society). In both cases the existing social order is ratified, and so science, no less than religion, continues to support the principles of adjustment and conformity. Darwin is Paley in reverse.

Whatever the inadequacies of Young's pointedly Marxist program, he has nonetheless compiled an imaginative travelogue to guide us through the maze of the Victorian intellectual landscape. The much-vaunted talk of a "church scientific," lay sermons, a scientific priesthood, and what not begin to make sense in the context of a transition to a new theodicy. It puts the ultimate imprimatur of establishment acclaim—burial in Westminster Abbey, which was accorded to Darwin thanks to the frenetic string-pulling of John Lubbock—in a whole new light. Moore, following the broad sweep of Young's portrait, finds much symbolic significance in the solemn bearing of Darwin's body "up the nave by Huxley, Wallace and other dignitaries . . . to its resting place a few feet from the monument of Sir Isaac Newton." It was, he suggests, "the trojan horse of naturalism entering the fortress of the Church."[6] Young's arguments also do full justice to the pre-Darwinian roots of secularization and to the inclination of the intellectuals of the new status quo to turn to the scientific creed as they cast about for some new consensus. The fact that religious believers shared precisely the same value system only seems to strengthen the case.

And yet Young's treatment is open to objections both historical and philosophical. Both Asa Gray and B. B. Warfield, to take random examples, used evolutionary doctrines to *challenge* the status quo on the question of racialism, even if Winchell saw it the other way. And in light of the fact that some historians have argued that natural theology in the pre-Darwinian period was actually relatively *in*coherent, perhaps Young's "common context" is not so clear after all.[7] Finally, there is the question of how much Young's own political framework has influenced his in-

---

6. Moore, "1859 and All That: Remaking the Story of Evolution-and-Religion," in *Charles Darwin, 1809-1882: A Centennial Commemorative*, ed. Roger G. Chapman and Cleveland T. Duval (Wellington, New Zealand: Nova Pacifica, 1982), p. 194. For more on Young's position, see the articles cited in chapter 2 herein and also "The Historiographic and Ideological Contexts of the Nineteenth-Century Debate on Man's Place in Nature," in *Changing Perspectives in the History of Science: Essays in Honour of Joseph Needham*, ed. Mikuláš Teich and Robert Young (London: Heinemann, 1973), pp. 344-438.

7. So, for example, John Hedley Brooke, "The Natural Theology of the Geologists: Some Theological Strata," in *Images of the Earth: Essays in the History of the Environmental Sciences*, ed. L. J. Jordanova and Roy Porter (Chalfont St. Giles: British Society for the History of Science, 1979), pp. 39-64.

terpretation. To say that science and society are closely related, or indeed that scientific theory is often socially conditioned, is one thing, but to claim that values and politics are *necessarily* constitutive of scientific explanation as Young does is quite another. Philosophy of science, surely, cannot be so easily transmuted into the sociology of knowledge, nor science into ideology. Various strategies remain open to those who view science as a method of finding out something about the way the world is rather than merely an expression of social relations.[8]

From what I have said, I think it is plain that in various ways all of these approaches to the historical question have aspects that commend them and that none of them provides the whole truth. I think I have also shown that beyond the world of historical scholarship, our investigation of the evangelical encounter with evolution has immediate implications both for those who are part of the evangelical tradition and for those outside it. For those who share the evangelical emphases of the Christian heritage, some awareness of the quite powerful tradition of evangelical evolutionism should help underscore the genuine plurality of opinion within its ranks and the arrogance of those who equate orthodoxy with one particular scientific perspective. The changing perception of the nature of the Darwinian challenge—from design in the world to biblical inerrancy—itself shows how dynamic that theological enterprise has been. For those outside this camp, whether hostile or indifferent, the realization that evangelicals have played an honorable role in the world of science should help undermine the image of a violent death-struggle between science and Christianity and at the same time expose as sheer myth the assumption that reactionary religion has always stood in the way of radical science.

If only to curtail the abuses of rhetoric, creationists and evolutionists alike need to be made more aware of Darwin's forgotten defenders. Neither needs to be protected from the facts of history. For after all, as someone has said, history is too important to be left to historians.

---

8. For just one such strategy, see Ernan McMullin's essays "History and Philosophy of Science: A Marriage of Convenience?" in *Boston Studies in the Philosophy of Science*, ed. R. S. Cohen et al. (Dordrecht: D. Reidel, 1976), pp. 585-600; and "A Case for Scientific Realism," in *Scientific Realism*, ed. Jarrett Leplin (Berkeley and Los Angeles: University of California Press, 1984), pp. 8-40.

BIBLIOGRAPHY

Abraham, William J. *The Coming Great Revival: Recovering the Full Evangelical Tradition*. San Francisco: Harper & Row, 1983.

Ackworth, Richard. *Creation, Evolution and the Christian Faith*. Welwyn: Evangelical Press, n.d.

Allen, Frank E. *Evolution in the Balances*. New York: Fleming H. Revell, 1926.

Andrews, E. H. *Is Evolution Scientific?* Welwyn: Evangelical Press, 1977.

Aulie, Richard P. "Evolution and Special Creation: Historical Aspects of the Controversy." *Proceedings of the American Philosophical Society* 127 (1983): 418-62.

Baker, Sylvia. *Bone of Contention*. Welwyn: Evangelical Press, 1976.

Bannister, R. C. *Social Darwinism: Science and Myth in Anglo-American Social Thought*. Philadelphia: Temple University Press, 1979.

Barker, Eileen. "Apes and Angels: Reductionism, Selection, and Emergence in the Study of Man." *Inquiry* 19 (1976): 367-99.

——. "In the Beginning: The Battle of Creationist Science against Evolutionism." In *On the Margins of Science: The Social Construction of Rejected Knowledge*, edited by Roy Wallis. Keele: University of Keele, 1979. Pp. 179-200.

Barton, Ruth. "Evolution: The Whitworth Gun in Huxley's War for the Liberation of Science from Theology." In *The Wider Domain of Evolutionary Thought*, edited by David Oldroyd and Ian Langham. Dordrecht: D. Reidel Publishing Company, 1983. Pp. 261-87.

Bassett, Paul. "The Fundamentalist Leavening of the Holiness Movement, 1914-1940— The Church of the Nazarene: A Case Study." *Wesleyan Theological Journal* 13 (1978): 65-91.

Beach, Henry H. "Decadence of Darwinism." In vol. 8 of *The Fundamentals*. Chicago: Testimony Publishing Company, 1910-1915. Pp. 36-58.

Berry, R. J. *Adam and the Ape: A Christian Approach to the Theory of Evolution*. London: Falcon, 1975.

——. "Happy Is the Man That Findeth Wisdom." *Biological Journal of the Linnean Society* 17 (1982): 1-8.

Black, Max. *Models and Metaphors: Studies in Language and Philosophy*. Ithaca, N.Y.: Cornell University Press, 1962.

Blaisdell, Muriel. "Natural Theology and Nature's Disguises." *Journal of the History of Biology* 15 (1982): 163-89.

Bowden, M. *The Rise of the Evolution Fraud*. Bromley, Kent: Sovereign Publications, 1982.

Bowler, Peter J. "Darwinism and the Argument from Design: Suggestions for a Reevaluation." *Journal of the History of Biology* 10 (1977): 29-43.

——. *The Eclipse of Darwinism: Anti-Darwinian Evolution Theories in the Decades around 1900*. Baltimore: The Johns Hopkins University Press, 1983.

——. *Evolution: The History of an Idea*. Berkeley and Los Angeles: University of California Press, 1984.

Brent, Peter. *Charles Darwin*. London: Heinemann, 1981.

Brooke, John Hedley. "Natural Theology in Britain from Boyle to Paley." In *Science and Belief from Copernicus to Darwin*. Units 9-10. *New Interactions between Theology and Natural Science*. Milton Keynes: The Open University, 1974.

————. "The Natural Theology of the Geologists: Some Theological Strata." In *Images of the Earth: Essays in the History of the Environmental Sciences*, edited by L. J. Jordanova and Roy Porter. Chalfont St. Giles: British Society for the History of Science, 1979. Pp. 39-140.

————. "The Relations between Darwin's Science and His Religion." In *Darwinism and Divinity*, edited by John Durant. Oxford: Blackwell, 1985. Pp. 40-75.

Bruce, Alexander Balmain. *The Providential Order of the World*. London: Hodder & Stoughton, 1897.

Bucke, Emory Stevens, editor. *The History of American Methodism*. 3 vols. New York: Abingdon Press, 1964.

Bystrom, Robert E. "The Earliest Methodist Response to Evolution." M.A. thesis, Northwestern University, 1966.

Cairns, David. "Thomas Chalmers's Astronomical Discourses: A Study in Natural Theology." *Scottish Journal of Theology* 9 (1956): 410-21.

Cameron, Nigel M. de S. *Evolution and the Authority of the Bible*. Exeter: Paternoster Press, 1983.

Cannon, Susan Faye. *Science in Culture: The Early Victorian Period*. New York: Dawson and Science History Publications, 1978.

Cannon, Walter F. "The Uniformitarian-Catastrophist Debate." *Isis* 51 (1960): 38-55.

————. "The Problem of Miracles in the 1830's." *Victorian Studies* 4 (1961): 5-32.

Carnell, Edward John. *An Introduction to Christian Apologetics: A Philosophic Defense of the Trinitarian-Theistic Faith*. Grand Rapids: Eerdmans, 1948.

Carozzi, Albert V. "Guyot, Arnold." In vol. 5 of the *Dictionary of Scientific Biography*. New York: Scribner's, 1971. Pp. 599-60.

Chadwick, Owen. *The Victorian Church*. London: Adam & Charles Black, 1970.

Chapman, Roger G. "Charles Darwin: The Scientist and His Science." In *Charles Darwin, 1809-1882: A Centennial Commemorative*, edited by Roger G. Chapman and Cleveland T. Duval. Wellington, N.Z.: Nova Pacifica, 1982. Pp. 101-30.

Chapman, Roger G., and Cleveland T. Duval, editors. *Charles Darwin, 1809-1882: A Centennial Commemorative*. Wellington, N.Z.: Nova Pacifica, 1982.

Churchill, F. B. "Rudolf Virchow and the Pathologist's Criteria for the Inheritance of Acquired Characteristics." *Journal of the History of Medicine and Allied Sciences* 31 (1976): 117-48.

Clark, David S. "Theology and Evolution." *Princeton Theological Review* 23 (1925): 193-212.

Clark, T. H. "Sir John William Dawson, 1820-1899." In *Pioneers of Canadian Science*, edited by G. F. G. Stanley. Toronto: University of Toronto Press, 1966. Pp. 101-13.

Cohen, I. Bernard. *Revolution in Science*. Cambridge: Harvard University Press, 1985.

Cole, John R. "Anti-Evolutionism and the Effects of the Scopes Trial." *Proceedings of the Iowa Academy of Science* 89 (1982): 50-54.

Cook, Joseph. *Biology, with Preludes on Current Events*. Boston: James R. Osgood, 1877.

Cornell, John F. "From Creation to Evolution: Sir William Dawson and the Idea of Design in the Nineteenth Century." *Journal of the History of Biology* 16 (1983): 137-70.

Dabney, Robert L. "Geology and the Bible." In vol. 3 of *Discussions*. Edinburgh: Banner of Truth, n.d. Pp. 127-51. Reprinted from *Southern Presbyterian Review*, July 1861.

————. *Lectures in Systematic Theology*. 1878. Reprint. Grand Rapids: Zondervan, 1980.

Dallinger, William Henry. *The Creator, and What We May Know of the Method of Creation*. London: T. Woolmer, 1888.

Dana, James D. "Biographical Memoir of Arnold Guyot." *Biographical Memoirs. National Academy of Sciences* 2 (1886): 309-47.

_____. "Biographical Memoir of Arnold Guyot." *Annual Report of the Board of Regents of the Smithsonian Institution for 1887.* Washington, D.C.: Government Printing Office, 1889. Pp. 693-722.

Darwin, Charles. *The Origin of Species by Means of Natural Selection; or, The Preservation of Favoured Races in the Struggle for Life.* 6th edition. London: John Murray, 1872.

_____. *The Descent of Man and Selection in Relation to Sex.* London: John Murray, 1871.

Darwin, Francis, ed. *The Life and Letters of Charles Darwin.* 2 vols. London: John Murray, 1887.

Davenport, F. Garvin. "Scientific Interests in Kentucky and Tennessee, 1870-1890." *The Journal of Southern History* 14 (1948): 500-21.

_____. "Alexander Winchell: Michigan Scientist and Educator." *Michigan History* 35 (1951): 185-201.

Davidheiser, Bolton. *Evolution and Christian Faith.* Nutley, N.J.: Presbyterian and Reformed Publishing Company, 1969.

_____. "Louis Agassiz." In *A Symposium on Creation VI,* edited by Donald W. Patten. Seattle: Pacific Mendian Publishing Co., 1977. Pp. 116-35.

Davis, W. M. "The Progress of Geography in the United States." *Annals of the Association of American Geographers* 14 (1924): 154-215.

Dawson, J. William. *The Story of the Earth and Man.* Montreal: Dawson Brothers, 1872.

_____. "Primitive Man and Revelation." In *History, Essays, Orations, and Other Documents of the Sixth General Conference of the Evangelical Alliance,* edited by Philip Schaff and S. Irenaeus Prime. New York: Harper & Brothers, 1874. Pp. 272-75.

_____. "Man in Nature." *Princeton Review* 4 (1885): 217-30.

_____. *Modern Ideas of Evolution.* Rpt., New York: Prodost, 1977.

De Beer, Gavin. "Darwin, Charles Robert." In vol. 3 of the *Dictionary of Scientific Biography.* New York: Scribner's, 1971. Pp. 565-77.

Dillenberger, John. *Protestant Thought and Natural Science: A Historical Interpretation.* London: Collins, 1961.

Dobzhansky, T. "Evolution as a Creative Process." *Proceedings of the Ninth International Congress of Genetics* (1954): 435-38.

Draper, John William. *History of the Conflict between Religion and Science.* London: Henry S. King, 1875.

Duffield, John T. "Evolutionism Respecting Man, and the Bible." *Princeton Review* 1 (1878): 150-77.

Dupree, A. Hunter. *Asa Gray.* Cambridge: Harvard University Press, 1959.

Durant, John. "The New Creationism and the World of Science." Paper presented at the Teach-In on Creationism in American Culture and Theology, Lutheran School of Theology at Chicago, 9 October 1982.

_____. "Darwinism and Divinity: A Century of Debate." In *Darwinism and Divinity,* edited by John Durant. Oxford: Blackwell, 1985. Pp. 9-39.

_____. "Evolution and Ethics: Ethology, Sociobiology, and the Naturalization of Religious Values." Paper read in the Science and Religion Symposium at the Seventeenth International Congress of History of Science, University of California at Berkeley, August 1985.

Eiseley, Loren. *Darwin's Century: Evolution and the Men Who Discovered It.* New York: Anchor Books, 1961.

Ellegård, Alvar. *Darwin and the General Reader: The Reception of Darwin's Theory of Evolution in the British Periodical Press, 1859-1872.* Göteborg: Acta Universitatis Gothenburgensis, 1958.

Enoch, H. *Evolution or Creation?* London: Evangelical Press, 1967.

"Evolutionary Epistemology." *Theoria,* vol. 49, no. 1 (1982).

"Evolutionism in the Pulpit." In vol. 8 of *The Fundamentals*. Chicago: Testimony Publishing Company, 1910-1915. Pp. 27-35.

Faunce, D. W. *A Young Man's Difficulties with His Bible*. London: Hodder & Stoughton, 1877.

Fitch, Robert E. "Charles Darwin: Science and the Saintly Sentiments." *Columbia University Forum*, Spring 1959, pp. 7-11.

Fleming, Ambrose. *Evolution or Creation?* London: Marshall, Morgan & Scott, n.d.
————. *Memories of a Scientific Life*. London: Marshall, Morgan & Scott, n.d.

Fleming, J. "The Geological Deluge, as Interpreted by Baron Cuvier and Professor Buckland, Inconsistent with the Testimony of Moses and the Phenomena of Nature." *Edinburgh Philosophical Journal* 14 (1826): 205-39.

Flew, A. G. N. *Evolutionary Ethics*. London: Macmillan, 1967.

Forsyth, P. T. "Some Christian Aspects of Evolution." *London Quarterly Review*, October 1905, pp. 209-39.

Freeman, R. B. "The Darwin Family." *Biological Journal of the Linnean Society* 17 (1982): 9-21.

Frye, Roland Mushat. "So-Called 'Creation-Science' and Mainstream Christian Responses." *Proceedings of the American Philosophical Society* 127 (1983): 61-70.

Frye, Roland Mushat, editor. *Is God a Creationist? The Religious Case against Creation-Science*. New York: Scribner's, 1983.

Fulton, John F., and Elizabeth H. Thomson. *Benjamin Silliman, 1779-1864: Pathfinder in American Science*. New York: Henry Schuman, 1949.

Futuyma, Douglas J. *Science on Trial: The Case for Evolution*. New York: Pantheon Books, 1983.

Galton, Francis. *English Men of Science: Their Nature and Nurture*. London: Macmillan, 1874.

Gamertsfelder, S. J. *Systematic Theology*. 1921. Reprint. Harrisburg, Pa.: Evangelical Publishing House, 1938.

Geddes, Patrick. "Biology." In vol. 2 of *Chambers' Encyclopaedia*. London: W. & R. Chambers, 1925.

George, Wilma. *Darwin*. London: Fontana, 1982.

Ghiselin, Michael. *The Triumph of the Darwinian Method*. Berkeley and Los Angeles: University of California Press, 1969.

Gilley, Sheridan. "The Huxley-Wilberforce Debate: A Reconsideration." In *Religion and Humanism*, edited by Keith Robbins. Oxford: Basil Blackwell, 1981. Pp. 325-40.

Gilley, Sheridan, and Ann Loades. "Thomas Henry Huxley: The War between Science and Religion." *Journal of Religion* 61 (1981): 285-308.

Gillispie, Charles Coulston. *Genesis and Geology: A Study in the Relations of Scientific Thought, Natural Theology, and Social Opinion in Great Britain, 1790-1850*. New York: Harper & Row, 1959.

Gilman, Daniel C. *The Life of James Dwight Dana*. New York: Dodd, Mead, 1910.

Glacken, Clarence J. *Traces on the Rhodian Shore: Nature and Culture in Western Thought from Ancient Times to the End of the Eighteenth Century*. Berkeley and Los Angeles: University of California Press, 1967.

Godfrey, Laurie R. "The Flood of Anti-Evolutionism." *Proceedings of the Iowa Academy of Science* 89 (1982): 59-61.

Godfrey, Laurie R., editor. *Scientists Confront Creationism*. New York: W. W. Norton, 1983.

Gossett, Thomas F. *Race: The History of an Idea in America*. Dallas: Southern Methodist University Press, 1963.

Gould, Stephen Jay. "Is Uniformitarianism Necessary?" *American Journal of Science* 263 (1965): 223-28.
————. "Flaws in a Victorian Veil." *New Scientist*, 31 August 1978, pp. 632-33.
————. *Ever since Darwin: Reflections in Natural History*. Harmondsworth: Penguin Books, 1980.

Gray, Asa. Review of *Manual of Geology*, by James Dana. *North American Review* 96 (1863): 375.

_____. *Darwiniana*. Reprint. Cambridge: Harvard University Press, 1963.

Greene, John C. "Silliman, Benjamin." In vol. 12 of the *Dictionary of Scientific Biography*. New York: Scribner's, 1975. Pp. 432-34.

Greene, William Brenton, Jr. Review of *Christian Faith in an Age of Science*, by William North Rice. *Princeton Theological Review* 2 (1904): 504-7.

_____. Review of *The Religion of Evolution*, by Carma. *Princeton Theological Review* 6 (1908): 118-21.

_____. "Yet Another Criticism of the Theory of Evolution." *Princeton Theological Review* 20 (1922): 537-61.

Gregorio, Mario A. di. *T. H. Huxley's Place in Natural Science*. New Haven: Yale University Press, 1984.

Grene, Marjorie. "Darwin and Philosophy." In *Connaissance scientifique et philosophie collogue*. Brussels: Palais des Academies, 1975. Pp. 133-45.

Guralnick, Stanley M. "Geology and Religion before Darwin: The Case of Edward Hitchcock, Theologian and Geologist (1793–1864)." *Isis* 63 (1972): 529–43.

Guyot, Arnold Henry. "Cosmogony and the Bible; or, The Biblical Account of Creation in the Light of Modern Science." In *History, Essays, Orations, and Other Documents of the Sixth General Conference of the Evangelical Alliance*, edited by Philip Schaff and S. Irenaeus Prime. New York: Harper & Brothers, 1874. Pp. 276-87.

_____. *Creation; or, The Biblical Cosmogony in the Light of Modern Science*. New York: Charles Scribner's Sons, 1884.

_____. *The Earth and Man: Lectures on Comparative Physical Geography in Its Relation to the History of Mankind*. 1849. Reprint. New York: Charles Scribner's Sons, 1897.

Haller, John S., Jr. *Outcasts from Evolution: Scientific Attitudes of Racial Inferiority, 1859-1900*. Chicago: University of Illinois Press, 1971.

Haller, Mark. *Eugenics: Hereditarian Attitudes in American Thought*. New Brunswick, N.J.: Rutgers University Press, 1963.

Hamilton, Floyd E. "Modern Aspects of the Theory of Evolution." *Princeton Theological Review* 24 (1926): 396-448.

_____. *The Basis of Evolutionary Faith*. London: James Clark, [1931].

_____. *The Basis of Christian Faith*. London: Marshall, Morgan & Scott, n.d.

Haven, E. O. "Darwinism and Christianity." *Northwestern Christian Advocate*, 27 March 1872.

Hesse, Mary P. *Models and Analogies in Science*. Notre Dame, Ind.: University of Notre Dame Press, 1966.

Heyck, T. W. *The Transformation of Intellectual Life in Victorian England*. London: Croom Helm, 1982.

Hill, Christopher. *Intellectual Origins of the English Revolution*. Oxford: Oxford University Press, 1965.

Hitchcock, Edward. *Report of the Geology, Mineralogy, Botany and Zoology of Massachusetts*. Amherst: J. S. & C. Adams, 1833.

_____. *Elementary Geology*. Amherst: J. S. & C. Adams, 1840.

_____. *The Religion of Geology*. 2d edition. Boston: Phillips Samson, 1859.

Hitching, Francis. *The Neck of the Giraffe; or, Where Darwin Went Wrong*. London: Pan, 1982.

Hodge, Archibald Alexander. Review of *Natural Science and Religion*, by Asa Gray. *Presbyterian Review* 1 (1880): 586-89.

_____. *Outlines of Theology*. Revised edition. New York: A. C. Armstrong and Son, 1891.

Hodge, Charles. "Unity of Mankind." *Biblical Repertory and Princeton Review* 31 (1859): 103-49.

_____. *Systematic Theology*. 3 vols. 1872-73. Reprint. London: James Clark, 1960.

————. *What Is Darwinism?* New York: Scribner's, 1874.

Hoeveler, J. David, Jr. *James McCosh and the Scottish Intellectual Tradition.* Princeton: Princeton University Press, 1981.

Hooykaas, R. "The Parallel between the History of the Earth and the History of the Animal World." *Archives Internationales d'Histoire des Sciences* 10 (1957): 1-18.

————. *Natural Law and Divine Miracle: The Principle of Uniformity in Geology, Biology and Theology.* Leiden: E. J. Brill, 1959.

————. "Geological Uniformitarianism and Evolution." *Archives Internationales d'Histoire des Sciences* 19 (1966): 3-19.

————. *Religion and the Rise of Modern Science.* Edinburgh: Scottish Academic Press, 1972.

Howard, Jonathan. *Darwin.* Oxford: Oxford University Press, 1982.

Hughes, Philip Edgcumbe. *Christianity and the Problem of Origins.* Nutley, N.J.: Presbyterian and Reformed Publishing Company, 1974.

Hunter, Michael. *Science and Society in Restoration England.* Cambridge: Cambridge University Press, 1981.

Huxley, Julian. "The Evolutionary Vision." In vol. 3 of *Evolution after Darwin,* edited by Sol Tax and Charles Callender. Chicago: University of Chicago Press, 1961. Pp. 246-61.

Illick, Joseph E. III. "The Reception of Darwinism at the Princeton Theological Seminary and the College at Princeton, New Jersey." *Journal of the Presbyterian Historical Society* 38 (1960): 152-65; 234-43.

Irvine, William. *Apes, Angels and Victorians: A Joint Biography of Darwin and Huxley.* London: Weidenfeld & Nicolson, 1956.

Iverach, James. *Is God Knowable?* London: Hodder & Stoughton, 1884.

————. *Evolution and Christianity.* London: Hodder & Stoughton, 1894.

————. *Theism in the Light of Present Science and Philosophy.* London: Hodder & Stoughton, 1899.

James, Preston E. *All Possible Worlds: A History of Geographical Ideas.* Indianapolis: Bobbs-Merrill, 1972.

Jeeves, Malcolm. *The Scientific Enterprise and the Christian Faith.* London: Tyndale Press, 1969.

Johnson, Deryl Freeman. "The Attitude of the Princeton Theologians toward Darwinism and Evolution from 1859-1929." Ph.D. diss., University of Iowa, 1968.

Johnson, William Hallock. "Evolution and Theology Today." *Princeton Theological Review* 1 (1903): 403-22.

Jones, Greta. *Social Darwinism in English Thought: The Interaction between Biological and Social Theory.* Sussex: Harvester Press, 1980.

Jordan, William Leighton. *The Ocean: Its Tides and Currents and Their Causes.* London: Longmans, 1873.

Keith, Arthur. *Darwinism and Its Critics.* London: Watts, 1935.

Kidner, Derek. *Genesis.* Tyndale Old Testament Commentary. London: Tyndale Press, 1967.

Kitcher, P. *Abusing Science: The Case against Creationism.* Cambridge: MIT Press, 1982.

Klaaren, Eugene M. *Religious Origins of Modern Science: Belief in Creation in Seventeenth-Century Thought.* Grand Rapids: Eerdmans, 1977.

Laidlaw, John. *The Biblical Doctrine of Man.* Edinburgh: T. & T. Clark, 1895.

Lawrence, Philip J. "Edward Hitchcock: The Christian Geologist." *Proceedings of the American Philosophical Society* 116 (1972): 21-34.

Leatherdale, W. H. *The Role of Analogy, Model and Metaphor in Science.* Amsterdam: North Holland Publishing Company, 1973.

Leuchtenburg, William E. *The Perils of Prosperity 1914-32.* Chicago: University of Chicago Press, 1958.

Lewis, Tayler. *The Six Days of Creation; or, The Scriptural Cosmology with the Ancient*

Idea of Time-Worlds in Distinction from Worlds in Space. Schenectady: G. Y. Debogert, 1855.

Lisle, James. "Evolution." *Northwestern Christian Advocate,* 12 November 1879.

Livingstone, David N. "Evolution as Metaphor and Myth." *Christian Scholar's Review* 12 (1983): 111-25.

————. "The Idea of Design: The Vicissitudes of a Key Concept in the Princeton Response to Darwin." *Scottish Journal of Theology* 37 (1984): 329-57.

————. "B. B. Warfield, the Theory of Evolution and Early Fundamentalism." *Evangelical Quarterly* 58 (1986): 69-83.

————. *Nathaniel Southgate Shaler and the Culture of American Science.* University, Ala.: University of Alabama Press, 1987.

————. "Preadamites: The History of an Idea from Heresy to Orthodoxy." *Scottish Journal of Theology* 40 (1987): 41-66.

Lowenberg, Bert James. "The Reaction of American Scientists to Darwinism." *American Historical Review* 38 (1932-33): 687-701.

Lucas, J. R. "Wilberforce and Huxley: A Legendary Encounter." *Historical Journal* 22 (1979): 313-30.

Lurie, Edward. *Louis Agassiz: A Life in Science.* Chicago: University of Chicago Press, 1960.

Lyell, K. M. *Life, Letters and Journals of Sir Charles Lyell, Bart.* 2 vols. London: John Murray, 1881.

Lyon, George M. "Supreme Indifference of Christianity." *Northwestern Christian Advocate,* 24 April 1872.

McCosh, James. *The Method of the Divine Government, Physical and Moral.* 3d edition. Edinburgh: Sutherland & Knox, 1852.

————. *Christianity and Positivism: A Series of Lectures to the Times on Natural Theology and Christian Apologetics.* London: Macmillan, 1871.

————. "Religious Aspects of the Doctrine of Development." In *History, Essays, Orations, and Other Documents of the Sixth General Conference of the Evangelical Alliance,* edited by Philip Schaff and S. Irenaeus Prime. New York: Harper & Brothers, 1874. Pp. 264-71.

————. *Energy: Efficient and Final Cause.* Philosophic Series, no. 2. Edinburgh: T. & T. Clark, 1884.

————. *Development: What It Can and Cannot Do.* Philosophic Series, no. 3. Edinburgh: T. & T. Clark, 1885.

————. *The Religious Aspect of Evolution.* New York: Charles Scribner's Sons, 1890.

McCosh, James, and George Dickie. *Typical Forms and Special Ends in Creation.* Edinburgh: Thomas Constable, 1856.

McGiffert, Michael. "Christian Darwinism: The Partnership of Asa Gray and George Frederick Wright, 1874-1881." Ph.D. diss., Yale University, 1958.

McGinn, Colin. "Evolution, Animals and the Basis of Morality." *Inquiry* 22 (1979): 81-99.

Machen, J. Gresham. *The Christian View of Man.* 1937. Reprint. London: Banner of Truth, 1965.

MacKay, Donald M. *The Clockwork Image.* London: Inter-Varsity Press, 1974.

Macloskie, George. "Scientific Explanation." *Presbyterian Review* 8 (1887): 617-25.

————. "Concessions to Science." *Presbyterian Review* 10 (1889): 220-28.

————. "Theistic Evolution." *Presbyterian and Reformed Review* 9 (1898): 1-22.

————. "The Origin of Species and of Man." *Bibliotheca Sacra* 60 (1903): 261-75.

————. "The Outlook of Science and Faith." *Princeton Theological Review* 1 (1903): 597-615.

————. "Mosaism and Darwinism." *Princeton Theological Review* 2 (1904): 425-51.

McMullin, Ernan. "History and Philosophy of Science: A Marriage of Convenience?" In *Boston Studies in the Philosophy of Science,* edited by R. S. Cohen. Dordrecht: D. Reidel Publishing Company, 1976. Pp. 585-600.

————. "A Case for Scientific Realism." In *Scientific Realism*, edited by Jarrett Leplin. Berkeley and Los Angeles: University of California Press, 1984. Pp. 8-40.

Mahan, Asa. "The Self Glorification of Modern Evolutionists." *Northwestern Christian Advocate*, 10 December 1873.

————. "Evolution and Theology." *Northwestern Christian Advocate*, 4 March 1874.

Marsden, George M. *Fundamentalism and American Culture: The Shaping of Twentieth Century Evangelicalism, 1870-1925*. New York: Oxford University Press, 1980.

————. "Creation versus Evolution: No Middle Way." *Nature* 305 (1983): 571-74.

————. "A Case of the Excluded Middle: Creation versus Evolution in America." Forthcoming.

Martin, S. A. Review of *Creative Evolution*, by Henri Bergson. *Princeton Theological Review* 10 (1912): 116-18.

Matheson, George. "Modern Science and the Religious Instinct." *Presbyterian Review* 5 (1884): 608-21.

————. "The Religious Bearings of the Doctrine of Evolution." In *Alliance of the Reformed Churches Holding the Presbyterian System: Minutes and Proceedings of the Third General Council, Belfast 1884*. Belfast: Assembly's Offices, 1884. Pp. 82-88.

————. *Can the Old Faith Live with the New? or, The Problem of Evolution and Revelation*. Edinburgh: William Blackwood & Sons, 1885.

Maury, M. F. "On the General Circulation of the Atmosphere." *Proceedings of the American Association for the Advancement of Science* 3 (1850): 126-47.

————. *The Physical Geography of the Sea*. New York: Harper & Brothers, 1855.

May, Robert M. "Creation, Evolution and High School Texts." *Nature*, March 1902, pp. 109-10.

Merrill, George P. *The First One Hundred Years of American Geology*. New Haven: Yale University Press, 1924.

Meyer, John R. "The Life and Philosophy of Matthew Fontaine Maury, Pathfinder of the Sea." *Creation Research Society Quarterly* 19 (1982): 91-100.

Miller, Hugh. *Footprints of the Creator; or The Asterolepis of Stromness*. Edinburgh: W. P. Nimmo, Hay & Mitchell, 1849.

————. *The Old Red Sandstone; or, New Walks in an Old Field*. Edinburgh: William P. Nimmo, 1877.

Miller, William. *God, . . . or Natural Selection?* Glasgow: Leader Publishing Company, n.d.

Moore, James R. *The Post-Darwinian Controversies: A Study of the Protestant Struggle to Come to Terms with Darwin in Great Britain and America, 1870-1900*. Cambridge: Cambridge University Press, 1979.

————. "Charles Darwin Lies in Westminster Abbey." *Biological Journal of the Linnean Society* 17 (1982): 97-113.

————. "1859 and All That: Remaking the Story of Evolution-and-Religion." In *Charles Darwin, 1809-1882: A Centennial Commemorative*, edited by Roger G. Chapman and Cleveland T. Duval. Wellington, N.Z.: Nova Pacifica, 1982. Pp. 167-94.

————. "Interpreting the New Creationism." *Michigan Quarterly Review* 22 (1983): 321-34.

————. "Evangelicals and Evolution: Henry Drummond, Herbert Spencer, and the Naturalisation of the Spiritual World." *Scottish Journal of Theology* 38 (1985): 383-417.

Morison, William James. "George Frederick Wright: In Defense of Darwinism and Fundamentalism." Ph.D. diss., Vanderbilt University, 1971.

Morrell, Jack, and Arnold Thackray. *Gentlemen of Science: Early Years of the British Association for the Advancement of Science*. Oxford: Clarendon Press, 1981.

Morris, Henry M. *Men of Science, Men of God: Great Scientists Who Believed the Bible*. San Diego: Creation-Life Publishers, 1982.

————. *History of Modern Creationism*. San Diego: Master Book Publishers, 1984.
Nelkin, Dorothy. *The Creation Controversy: Science or Scripture in the Schools*. New York: W. W. Norton, 1982.
Newell, N. *Creation and Evolution: Myth or Reality?* New York: Columbia University Press, 1982.
Noll, Mark A., editor. *The Princeton Theology, 1812-1921: Scripture, Science, and Theological Method from Archibald Alexander to Benjamin Warfield*. Grand Rapids: Baker Book House, 1983.
North, Gary, editor. "Symposium on Creation." In *Journal of Christian Reconstruction* 1 (1974).
Numbers, Ronald L. *Creation by Natural Law: Laplace's Nebular Hypothesis in American Thought*. Seattle: University of Washington Press, 1977.
————. "Creationism in 20th-Century America." *Science* 218 (1982): 538-44.
————. "The Dilemma of Evangelical Scientists." In *Evangelicalism and Modern America*, edited by George M. Marsden. Grand Rapids: Eerdmans, 1984. Pp. 150-60.
————. "From Christian Darwinist to Fundamentalist: The Strange Career of George Frederick Wright." Forthcoming.
O'Brien, Charles F. *Sir William Dawson: A Life in Science and Religion*. Philadelphia: American Philosophical Society, 1971.
Ormond, Alexander T. "James McCosh as Thinker and Educator." *Princeton Theological Review* 1 (1903): 337-61.
Orr, James. *The Christian View of God and the World as Centering in the Incarnation*. Edinburgh: Andrew Elliott, 1893.
————. *The Progress of Dogma*. 4th edition. London: Hodder & Stoughton, 1901.
————. *God's Image in Man and Its Defacement in the Light of Modern Denials*. London: Hodder & Stoughton, 1905.
————. *The Faith of a Modern Christian*. London: Hodder & Stoughton, 1910.
————. *The Bible under Trial: Apologetic Papers in View of Present-Day Assaults on Holy Scripture*. London: Marshall Brothers, n.d.
————. "Science and Christian Faith." In vol. 4 of *The Fundamentals*. Chicago: Testimony Publishing Company, 1910-1915. Pp. 91-104.
————. "The Early Narratives of Genesis." In vol. 6 of *The Fundamentals*. Chicago: Testimony Publishing Company, 1910-1915. Pp. 85-97.
Ospovat, Dov. "Perfect Adaptation and Teleological Explanation: Approaches to the Problem of the History of Life in the Mid-Nineteenth Century." *Studies in the History of Biology* 2 (1978): 33-56.
Paley, William. *The Works of William Paley*. London: T. Nelson & Sons, 1853.
Patton, Francis Landey. "Evolution and Apologetics." *Presbyterian Review* 6 (1885): 138-44.
Pearce, E. K. V. *Who Was Adam?* Exeter: Paternoster Press, 1969.
Peckham, Morse, editor. *The Origin of Species by Charles Darwin: A Variorum Text*. Philadelphia: University of Pennsylvania Press, 1959.
Pfeifer, Edward J. "United States." In *The Comparative Reception of Darwinism*, edited by Thomas F. Glick. Austin: University of Texas Press, 1972. Pp. 168-206.
Playfair, John. *Illustrations of the Huttonian Theory of the Earth*. Edinburgh: Cadell & Davies, 1802.
Pointer, Steven R. "The Perils of History: The Meteoric Career of Joseph Cook (1838-1901)." Ph.D. diss., Duke University, 1981.
————. "Apologetics and Science in the Career of Joseph Cook." Paper presented at the American Society of Church History Conference, Denver, Colorado, March 1984.
Pope, William Burt. *A Compendium of Christian Theology: Being Analytical Outlines of a Course of Theological Study, Biblical, Dogmatic, Historical*. 2d edition. 3 vols. London: Wesleyan Conference Office, 1880.
————. *A Higher Catechism of Theology*. London: T. Woolmer, 1883.

Price, George McCready. "Modern Botany and the Theory of Organic Evolution." *Princeton Theological Review* 23 (1925): 51-65.

Reist, Irwin. "Augustus Hopkins Strong and William Newton Clarke: A Study in Nineteenth Century Evolutionary and Eschatological Thought." *Foundations* 13 (1970): 26-43.

Rice, Daniel F. "Natural Theology and the Scottish Philosophy in the Thought of Thomas Chalmers." *Scottish Journal of Theology* 24 (1971): 23-46.

Rosie, George. *Hugh Miller: Outrage and Order*. Edinburgh: Mainstream Publishing Co., 1981.

Rossiter, Margaret. "Benjamin Silliman and the Lowell Institute: The Popularization of Science in Nineteenth-Century America." *New England Quarterly* 44 (1971): 602-26.

Ruse, Michael. *Darwinism Defended: A Guide to the Evolution Controversies*. Reading, Mass.: Addison-Wesley, 1982.

Rushdoony, Rousas J. *The Mythology of Science*. Nutley, N.J.: Craig Press, 1967.

Russell, Colin A. "Some Approaches to the History of Science." In *Science and Belief from Copernicus to Darwin*. Unit 1. *The "Conflict Thesis" and Cosmology*. Milton Keynes: The Open University, 1974.

————. *Cross-Currents: Interactions between Science and Faith*. Grand Rapids: Eerdmans, 1985.

Sagan, Carl. *Cosmos*. New York: Random House, 1980.

Sandeen, Ernest. *The Roots of Fundamentalism: British and American Millenarianism, 1800-1930*. Chicago: Chicago University Press, 1970.

Sanford, William F., Jr. "Dana and Darwinism." *Journal of the History of Ideas* 26 (1965): 531-46.

Schuchert, Charles. "A Century of Geology—The Progress of Historical Geology in North America." *American Journal of Science* 46 (1918): 45-103.

Scott, Hugh M. "Has Scientific Investigation Disturbed the Basis of Rational Faith?" *Princeton Theological Review* 4 (1906): 433-53.

Secord, James A. "Nature's Fancy: Charles Darwin and the Breeding of Pigeons." *Isis* 72 (1981): 163-86.

Shea, William R. Introduction in *Modern Ideas of Evolution*, by Sir J. William Dawson. New York: Prodost, 1977.

Shedd, William G. T. "The Idea of Evolution Defined, and Applied to History." In *Theological Essays*. New York: Scribner, Armstrong & Co., 1877. Pp. 121-210.

Sherwood, Morgan B. "Genesis, Evolution, and Geology in America before Darwin: The Dana-Lewis Controversy, 1856-1857." In *Toward a History of Geology*, edited by Cecil J. Schneer. Cambridge: MIT Press, 1969. Pp. 305-16.

"Shields, Charles Woodruff." In vol. 5 of *Appleton's Cyclopaedia of American Biography*, edited by James Grant Wilson and John Fiske. New York: D. Appleton, 1888. Pp. 509-10.

Shields, Charles Woodruff. *Philosophia Ultima, or Science of the Sciences*. 2 vols. London: Sampson Low, Marston, Searle & Rivington, 1889.

Shipley, Maynard. *The War on Modern Science: A Short History of the Fundamentalist Attacks on Evolution and Modernism*. New York: Knopf, 1927.

Short, A. Rendle. *Modern Discovery and the Bible*. 4th edition. London: Inter-Varsity Fellowship, 1954.

————. *The Bible and Modern Research*. London: Marshall, Morgan & Scott, n.d.

Simpson, George Gaylord. *The Meaning of Evolution*. New Haven: Yale University Press, 1949.

————. "Uniformitarianism: An Inquiry into Principle, Theory and Method in Geohistory and Biohistory." In *Philosophy of Geohistory*, edited by Claude C. Albritton. Stroudbury, Pa.: Dowden, Hutchinson & Ross, 1975. Pp. 256-309.

Skagestad, Peter. "C. S. Pierce on Biological Evolution and Scientific Progress." *Synthese* 41 (1979): 85-114.

Sloane, William Milligan, editor. *The Life of James McCosh: A Record Chiefly Autobiographical.* Edinburgh: T. &. T. Clark, 1896.

Smith, Gary S. "Calvinists and Evolution, 1870-1920." *Journal of Presbyterian History* 61 (1983): 335-52.

Smith, George Adam. *The Life of Henry Drummond.* London: Hodder & Stoughton, 1899.

Spanner, Douglas. *Creation and Evolution.* London: Falcon, 1965.

Stanton, William. "Dana, James Dwight." In vol. 3 of the *Dictionary of Scientific Biography.* New York: Scribner's, 1971. Pp. 549-54.

Stokes, G. G. *Natural Theology: The Gifford Lectures Delivered before the University of Edinburgh in 1891.* London: Adam & Charles Black, 1891.

_____. *Natural Theology: The Gifford Lectures Delivered before the University of Edinburgh in 1893.* London: Adam & Charles Black, 1893.

Stott, John. *Understanding the Bible.* London: Scripture Union, 1978.

Stout, Cushing. "Faith and History: The Mind of W. G. T. Shedd." *Journal of the History of Ideas* 15 (1954): 153-62.

Strawson, William. "Methodist Theology, 1850-1950." In vol. 3 of *A History of the Methodist Church in Great Britain,* edited by Rupert Davies, A. Raymond George, and Gordon Rupp. London: Epworth Press, 1983. Pp. 181-231.

Strong, Augustus Hopkins. *A Systematic Theology: A Compendium.* 1907. Reprint. London: Pickering & Inglis, 1956.

Szasz, Ferenc Morton. *The Divided Mind of Protestant America.* University, Ala.: University of Alabama Press, 1982.

Thomson, Keith Stewart, and Stan P. Rachootin. "Turning Points in Darwin's Life." *Biological Journal of the Linnean Society* 17 (1982): 23-37.

Torrey, R. A. *What the Bible Teaches: A Thorough and Comprehensive Study of What the Bible Has to Say Concerning the Great Doctrines of Which It Treats.* Chicago: Fleming H. Revell Company, 1898.

_____. *Difficulties and Alleged Errors in the Bible.* London: James Nisbet, 1907.

Tristram, H. B. "Recent Geographical and Historical Progress in Zoology." *Contemporary Review* 2 (1886): 103-25.

Turbayne, C. M. *The Myth of Metaphor.* New Haven: Yale University Press, 1970.

Turner, Frank Miller. "Rainfall, Plagues, and the Prince of Wales: A Chapter in the Conflict of Religion and Science." *Journal of British Studies* 13 (1974): 46-65.

_____. "The Victorian Conflict between Science and Religion: A Professional Dimension." *Isis* 69 (1978): 356-76.

Vorzimmer, Peter J. *Charles Darwin: The Years of Controversy.* London: University of London Press, 1972.

Warfield, Benjamin B. Review of *Christianity and Evolution,* by George Matheson. *Presbyterian Review* 9 (1888): 355.

_____. Review of *The Religious Aspect of Evolution,* by Joseph Le Conte. *Presbyterian Review* 9 (1888): 510-11.

_____. Review of *Christianity and Evolution,* by James Iverach. *Presbyterian and Reformed Review* 6 (1895): 366.

_____. "Editorial Note." *The Bible Student* 8 (1904): 241-51.

_____. Review of *God's Image in Man,* by James Orr. *Princeton Theological Review* 4 (1906): 555-58.

_____. Review of *Darwinism Today,* by Vernon L. Kellogg. *Princeton Theological Review* 6 (1908): 640-50.

_____. Review of *Naturalism and Religion,* by Rudolf Otto. *Princeton Theological Review* 7 (1909): 106-12.

_____. "On the Antiquity and the Unity of the Human Race." *Princeton Theological Review* 9 (1911): 1-25.

_____. "Calvin's Doctrine of the Creation." *Princeton Theological Review* 13 (1915): 190-255.

_____. Review of *The Natural Theology of Evolution*, by J. N. Shearman. *Princeton Theological Review* 14 (1916): 323-27.

_____. "Personal Reflections of Princeton Undergraduate Life." *The Princeton Alumni Weekly*, 6 April 1916, pp. 650-53.

_____. "Charles Darwin's Religious Life: A Sketch in Spiritual Biography." In *Studies in Theology*. New York: Oxford University Press, 1932. Pp. 541-82.

_____. *The Present-Day Conception of Evolution*. Emporia, Kans.: College Printing Office, n.d.

Webster, Charles, editor. *The Intellectual Revolution of the Seventeenth Century*. London: Routledge & Kegan Paul, 1972.

Wertenbaker, Thomas Jefferson. *Princeton, 1746-1896*. Princeton: Princeton University Press, 1946.

Westfall, Richard. *Science and Religion in Seventeenth Century England*. New Haven: Yale University Press, 1958.

Why be an Ape—? Observations on Evolution. London: Marshall, Morgan & Scott, n.d.

Wiley, H. Orton, and Paul T. Culbertson. *Introduction to Christian Theology*. Kansas City: Beacon Hill Press, 1947.

"William Henry Dallinger." *Journal of the Royal Microscopical Society* 32 (1909): 699-702.

"William Henry Dallinger." *Nature* 82 (1909): 71-72.

"William Henry Dallinger." *Proceedings of the Royal Society* 82 (1910): B, iv-vi.

Williams, Frances Leigh. *Matthew Fontaine Maury, Scientist of the Sea*. New Brunswick, N.J.: Rutgers University Press, 1963.

Wilson, Ambrose J. "What Charles Darwin Really Found." *Princeton Theological Review* 26 (1928): 515-30.

Wilson, David B. "A Physicist's Alternative to Materialism: The Religious Thought of George Gabriel Stokes." *Victorian Studies* 28 (1984): 69-96.

Winchell, Alexander. *Creation: The Work of One Intelligence and Not the Product of Physical Forces*. Ann Arbor: Young Men's Literary Association, 1858.

_____. *Sketches of Creation: A Popular View of Some of the Grand Conclusions of the Sciences in Reference to the History of Matter and Life*. London: Sampson Low, Son & Marston, 1870.

_____. *The Doctrine of Evolution: Its Data, Its Principles, Its Speculations, and Its Theistic Bearings*. New York: Harper & Brothers, 1874.

_____. *Reconciliation of Science and Religion*. New York: Harper & Brothers, 1877.

_____. *Preadamites; or, A Demonstration of the Existence of Men before Adam, together with a Study of Their Conditions, Antiquity, Racial Affinities, and Progressive Dispersion over the Earth*. Chicago: S. C. Griggs & Company, 1880.

Winship, Win. "Oren Root, Darwinism and Biblical Criticism." *Journal of Presbyterian History* 62 (1984): 111-23.

Wiseman, D. J. *Creation Revealed in Six Days*. London: Marshall, Morgan & Scott, 1958.

Wright, George Frederick. *Studies in Science and Religion*. Andover: W. F. Draper, 1882.

_____. "The Affinity of Science for Christianity." *Bibliotheca Sacra* 46 (1889): 701-20.

_____. *Man and the Glacial Period*. New York: D. Appleton & Co., 1892.

_____. "The Passing of Evolution." In vol. 7 of *The Fundamentals*. Chicago: Testimony Publishing Company, 1910-1915. Pp. 5-20.

Yoder, H. S., Jr. "Winchell, Alexander." In vol. 14 of the *Dictionary of Scientific Biography*. New York: Scribner's, 1971. Pp. 439-40.

Young, Davis A. "Nineteenth Century Christian Geologists and the Doctrine of Scripture." *Christian Scholar's Review* 11 (1982): 212-28.

Young, Robert M. "The Impact of Darwin on Conventional Thought." In *The Victorian Crisis of Faith*, edited by A. Symondson. London: S.P.C.K., 1970. Pp. 13-35.

_____. "Darwin's Metaphor: Does Nature Select?" *The Monist* 55 (1971): 442-503.

_____. "Evolutionary Biology and Ideology: Then and Now." *Science Studies* 1 (1971): 177-206.

_____. "The Historiographic and Ideological Contexts of the Nineteenth-Century Debate on Man's Place in Nature." In *Changing Perspectives in the History of Science: Essays in Honour of Joseph Needham*, edited by Mikulás Teich and Robert Young. London: Heineman, 1973. Pp. 344-438.

_____. "Natural Theology, Victorian Periodicals and the Fragmentation of a Common Context." In *Darwin to Einstein: Historical Studies on Science and Belief*, edited by Colin Chant and John Fauvel. Harlow: Longman, 1980. Pp. 69-107.

_____. "The Naturalization of Value Systems in the Human Sciences." In *Science and Belief: From Darwin to Einstein*. Block VI. *Problems in the Biological and Human Sciences*. Milton Keynes: The Open University Press, 1981. Pp. 63-110.

_____. "The Darwin Debate." *Marxism Today*, April 1982, pp. 20-22.

INDEX

Ackworth, Richard, 176
Adams, Henry, 126
Adams, Herbert Baxter, 126
Agassiz, Alexander, 68
Agassiz, Louis, xi, 9, 11, 21, 23, 44, 54, 72, 74, 79, 93, 103, 113, 121, 149, 171, 173; and Darwinism, 59; early life of, 57–58; and Gray, 63; and glacial theory, 58; and race, 59–60; and Rogers in debate, 35
Age of earth, 12, 13, 52, 159, 160
Alexander, Archibald, 100
Allen, Frank, 161–62
American Scientific Affiliation, 176
Andrews, E. H., 173–74, 176
Anthropology, 90–91. *See also* Evolution, human; Human origins; Monogenism; Polygenism
Ardrey, Robert, 181
Argument from design. *See* Natural theology
Augustine, Saint, 76, 172

Baconianism, 93, 126, 153
Baker, Sylvia, 176
Bangs, Nathan, 90
Barker, Eileen, 177, 178
Barton, Ruth, 185
Bassett, Paul, 165
Bateson, William, 166
Beach, Henry, 152–53
Beagle, voyage of, 30–31, 71
Beaumont, Elie de, 43, 44
Beecher, Henry Ward, 129

Bergson, Henri, 122
Berry, R. J., 92, 176
Biblical Creation Society, 175
Bibliotheca Sacra, 66, 96
Birks, T. H., 132
Blending inheritance, 52
Boston Society of Natural History, 35, 68
Bowden, Malcolm, 171
Boyle, Robert, 4
Braun, Alexander, 57, 58
Brent, Peter, 36
Brewster, David, 27
Bridgewater Treatises, 4, 8, 62, 108
Briggs, Charles A., 92
British Association for the Advancement of Science, 1, 6, 12, 33
Bruce, Alexander Balmain, 138
Bryan, William Jennings, 158, 160, 175
Buckland, William, 11, 12, 14, 16, 44, 173
Burbank, Luther, 163
Burnet, Thomas, 4
Burr, E. F., 133

Calderwood, Henry, 144
Calvin, John, 119, 120
Calvinism, 61, 65, 126, 132; and Darwinism, 67, 119–20
Cameron, Nigel M. deS., 172
Candolle, Alphonse de, 62
Cannon, Susan Faye, 26
Cape Verde Islands, 37
Carlyle, Thomas, 9
Carnell, Edward John, 165